BELIEVE

Elaine Henderson

Published in 2018 by Elaine Henderson

Publishing services provided by Lumphanan Press
www.lumphananpress.co.uk

ISBN: 978-1-9993010-0-2

For

Jill

my Lifeline, my Rock,
my Social Worker

Chapter One

When I was fifteen years old, I made up my mind that I was ready to ask the question, 'Who am I?'

It had taken me a full two years from making this decision to mustering enough courage to approach the person I called Mum, to ask her what she knew of my natural background. Up until that moment of my life, I had known nothing about my true identity. That is to say, no one who had held any knowledge about it had ever sat me down and spoken to me about what I considered to be a glaring fact: I was not a blood relative of the family with whom I was growing up. I had never been told anything of my origins.

One of my very earliest and extremely tenuous memories, however, is when I would have been aged about seven or eight. The whole family were sitting around the large kitchen table. We were having our evening meal, during which a discussion was going on about what everyone's middle names were. I, upon realising that it seemed that everyone had a middle name except for me, asked what mine was.

I was told that my middle name is Mann.

'Man!' I said. 'Girls can't be called man!'

Feeling very confused, I thought to myself that they could not be telling me the truth because I had neither heard nor ever known it as being my name.

'That's not even a proper name,' I feebly protested.

'It's the name you were given.'

This was the only perplexing response proffered.

I then distinctly remember that there was a lot of laughter around the table and, feeling embarrassed, I lowered my head and tried, very probably unsuccessfully, to block my tears. Looking back at that memory now, from an adult's perspective, I have to say that it positively reeked of ridicule. They were enjoying making a mockery of me. At the time, all I knew was that it made me feel very unhappy. I did not ask any more questions like that one.

At least not until I was fifteen.

I was made to feel that I was different from the others. I recall with great clarity this Mum putting a plate beside a fruit loaf during tea time and shaving off an extremely thin slice. After it had crumbled onto the plate, she put it in front of me and told me, 'That's yours.'

She then continued to slice up the loaf into proper-sized slices for the rest of the family. I was told that I was not allowed to eat the same food from the cupboards, tins or fridge because I was, 'Not part of the business.'

By the time I hit puberty this person I called Mum told me that I 'smelled', and she made me hand-wash my under-wear in the kitchen sink, which eventually led on to all my washing being separated out and me having to wash my own while she did everyone else's. These are just two examples of the ways in which they demonstrated that I was not one of them.

All this and much more meant that I grew up believing and very much feeling that I was not a part of the family. However, at that time, not being in possession of the facts, naively the only conclusion that I could think of was that I must have been adopted by them. I had never heard of the word fostered, but I had heard the word adopted.

Where I was brought up was very rural and quiet. When I was around eleven years old an old lady moved into the house next to where we lived. I began helping her out by fetching in her coal and she would make me cups of tea. We became extremely close; our relationship grew similar to grandmother and granddaughter. Things progressed to my going round to her house every day and I would be the one to make the cups of tea. I suppose I can look back now and see her as my rescuer and her home as my refuge. She would tell me all about her life and she helped me with my grammar and with my homework. There were times when I would turn up at her house distressed about unpleasant situations going on at home. One day I ran round to her house after a particularly nasty incident. I could not talk for crying. Instead I just told her I was not any company for her that day and returned home to be in my room. My neighbour was so worried about me that she telephoned over at nine in the evening to ask me if I was alright. I ran straight back round to her house and I hugged her. I felt very thankful to have someone who showed me how much they cared. When I grew older and had my own car, we would go out together every weekend to coffee shops and garden centres. She showed me the places up north where she once lived. Things morphed from her helping me to my helping her.

One evening, as I cleared away the dinner-time dishes, I asked the question.

'You know how I'm adopted? Well…'

'Fostered!'

This person, who had me calling her 'Mum', cut in with a short, snatched glance, followed by a flaccid expression betraying her futile attempts to mask her surprise at the audaciousness of my unexpected question.

'You can't say you were treated any differently from the others. You got exactly the same as they did.'

Her answer was completely unexpected. I did not believe her right away and even corrected her by repeating the word 'adopted', as if I knew better. I had no idea about what being fostered meant. Deep down, I think I desperately needed to know that I was adopted, as it would have meant that in so being, I would be reassured that I was also wanted. She explained that it meant that I was in their care but also in the care of Social Services, and that they were being paid to raise me. At that moment a very familiar, intangible but inescapably recurring feeling of rejection stirred inside me and settled over my heart.

My foster mother was not able to say anything of any substance about my real background, stating that she knew little about it. She did say, however, that I was placed with them on a voluntary basis. Her version of events amounted to her having the belief that my natural mother was an alcoholic. Her rather draconian statement culminated in words to the effect of, 'They could have come and taken you back at any time, but they never did.'

Now, as I reflect on her words, delivered in her cold, casual way, it occurs to me that she was perhaps somehow defending herself, as if she felt she was being attacked. Whatever her reason for saying them to me, they felt sharp and calculated.

What happened next was incredible, in my small fearful world. A social worker materialised out of nowhere.

Unbeknown to me, I had an appointed social worker, who had been in place for the whole duration of my time in foster care. This person had never been introduced as such to me and in my innocence I had thought that she was a friend of the person I called Mum. She looked around the same age as my foster mother and had a very cavalier way about her. My only recollection of having any involvement with this person was on a random, handful of occasions, on my return home from school, finding her sitting in the kitchen with my foster mother, enjoying a cup of tea and homemade shortbread biscuits. The only words I remember her uttering to me were simply to pass comment on trivial matters.

'Gosh, look how tall you have become. Are you one of the tallest in your class?' This was the common theme she endorsed.

'You have such good, thick hair and it is so long now.'

'Your mum tells me you're doing well at school.'

This social worker never gave me any opportunity to speak about my origins, nor did she ever ask if I would like to know anything of my natural background. She never asked me whether I was happy. She certainly never sat me down to explain that I was fostered.

My foster mother carried herself with confidence during these visits, being sure to smile while keeping a firm hold of the reigns. All the while looking at me with a certain false fondness, which was reserved only for when there was someone there to fool. We were all playing out our individual roles in a game of let's pretend, as if we were in some kind of charade. The thing was that I had been already acutely aware of my part in my foster mother's pantomime. My heart, my mind, my very core knew it was a lie, every single time. My foster mother's actions towards me were not always subtle.

This social worker had never given me any time alone with her, except I recall on one occasion she unexpectedly came into the living room while I practised on the piano. At the time I felt very aware that this was so that she could feign her delight at how well I was doing. She did not say anything beyond this but left rather sharply.

This social worker mysteriously disappeared. A new social worker, Lynne then came to the fore. She materialised as I walked into the house after school one day, right at the most crucial point in my school life, with impending exams just around the corner. However, I have to say in all earnestness that questions about my true identity were far more important to me than doing well in my exams.

Lynne was in direct contrast to the original social worker. She was much younger, vivacious and positively oozed confidence. As soon I entered the room, Lynne stepped forward enthusiastically with her hand extended, introducing herself as someone whose job it was to supply me with the answers to any questions I had regarding my natural background.

My foster mother was standing right behind her at the time and this total stranger's unveiling of what for me had always felt like a secret – given that it was never ever mentioned – was extremely disconcerting. I do not think I had the nerve to say anything in response to her statement while my foster mother was within such proximity. I do not remember if I dared to even speak.

As a youngster, I had wanted to run away so many times. I had even gone as far as concealing a packed bag down the side of a cabinet in our dining room in readiness to execute my plan of escape the next day. However, when the morning came I had been too afraid to go through with it. Moreover, my foster mother had threatened me more than once.

'Go ahead, but just you wait and see what you get when you come back.'

I was to very quickly see this new social worker as a potential means of escape and I duly expressed my desire to leave, on numerous occasions. However, her response was always the same.

'I think you are confused.'

Nevertheless, unlike the original social worker, Lynne seemed to want me to talk about my fostering experience and encouraged this by asking me lots of questions.

I tried to be brave enough to communicate my unhappiness. However, as I look back I have seen quite clearly that she did not believe how terrible I really felt and actually that she was choosing to ignore it. At the time, I wondered if her casual dismissal of my feelings was a direct consequence of the fact that, by that time, I had lived in foster care for twelve years and because a social worker had been in place for all of these years. There would have been no previous reports on file to endorse what I was so desperate to reveal. I have come to the conclusion that there are people who work in the so-called caring profession who do not in actual fact care.

One of the questions Lynne asked me was about how much pocket money I was getting. When I told her I was receiving one pound each week she told me, 'That's not enough.'

My foster mother then told me she would be giving me five pounds each week and that I was to start buying all my own toiletries, tights and socks.

Looking back, I can now see that Lynne was an exceptionally enthusiastic social worker but also that she was potentially an irresponsible fledgling to her career. I believe she failed to see what was going on and tried to lure me into a false sense of security with her by being extremely amiable with me. However, my guard was always high, in case she turned out to be someone who was going to be just as untrustworthy as the previous social worker had been.

I was right.

Lynne sent me a letter stating that she intended to take me out with her so that we could talk about things and to give me an opportunity to ask any questions that I had. Her letter was addressed to me personally and this very much confused me as I was so used to things going through my foster parents. I wondered whether I needed their permission to go with her. It was a very new and alien experience for me to have someone offer me this kind of one-to-one attention. I felt awkward. It was impossible for me to relax enough to really be myself.

On that very first occasion when she turned up at the house to take me out we went, rather bizarrely, on a trip to the ski slope. While we were driving along the road, for some inexplicable reason she chose that most inappropriate moment to enquire if I wanted to ask her any questions about my past. So I asked the only question I had, which was about my mother.

'I would like to know about my real mum,' I tentatively said.

'Your mum's dead,' she bluntly informed me. 'But your dad's still alive.'

I was to learn that my mother had died ten years ago, in 1977, when I was five.

To hear her flippantly brush aside news of my mother's

death was crushing. The minute I heard those words I instantaneously shut down. My real mother was the only person I had ever wanted and all I had desperately wished for, my whole life. Suddenly all my dreams of ever having my mum were obliterated. There was nothing I had yearned for more than having my mother in my life. I had no other questions in my head to ask at that time and I was unaware of anything else that Lynne said to me on that very first outing with her.

When I was delivered home I went straight to my bedroom in a state of utter shock. I could not cry. No one spoke to me about my time out with Lynne or enquired how I was, which was normal and actually suited me fine. Some time later I asked my foster mother whether she knew that my natural mother had died so long ago. She answered my question with a terse reply.

'You were told at the time.'

In response to my protests that surely it was inconceivable for a child to forget being told that her own mother had died, all she could muster was, 'Well, you were definitely told, but it obviously wasn't important enough for you to remember.'

In truth, had this person who I was calling Mum actually told me that my mum was dead, surely this would have confused my five-year-old self. My mum is standing in from of me, telling me my mum is dead! I did not even know I was fostered.

My heart iced over at her blatant callousness. Her words

were not unfamiliar to me. Throughout my childhood I had been frequently told that I did not listen, so much so that it made me doubt myself; perhaps they were right and that I was indeed a poor listener. There were countless events and occasions occurring without my knowledge and whenever I would ask why I was never told, my foster mother would always say, 'You were told, same as everyone else was.' Or, 'It was discussed when you were in the room but you obviously weren't listening.'

The emotional neglect even stretched to the point where my foster parents would go off on a holiday, with me returning home to find them already gone, having had no previous idea about their plans to go. Every time it happened I was left feeling extremely hurt and humiliated because everyone seemed to know about it except for me. However, their slip-up came one day when they had, once again, gone on holiday without my knowing. When I walked into the house and noticed that they were not around, I nonchalantly asked, 'Where's Mum and Dad?'

'They're away on holiday,' my eldest foster brother replied. It was routine for him to be left in charge while my foster parents were absent.

I overheard a conversation he had afterwards with his girlfriend in which he said, Mum told me Elaine doesn't know.'

I knew, in that moment, that it was a deliberate act of concealment, and that I was being ostracised.

So now, as 'Mum' stood looking me square in the eyes,

her cold statement that I had not heard or retained the news of my mother's death chilling my heart, I knew the truth.

As a mother, I can now clearly see that all their secrecy seriously intensified my confusion, anxiety and low self-worth. However, at the time it stocked the hatred and anger building inside me. I knew I was helpless to do anything to change things.

All I could do was wait, like a tabloid journalist, poised for the killer revelation.

Chapter Two

I had spent my whole childhood fantasising. I had been waiting for the genuine, realistic love and compassion that could only come from my own mother. There was an ache inside me, like a fundamental, immature want that was so basic and literal it had quite blatantly ruled my life. And now this had been replaced by something entirely different, a thing dark and impossibly bleak. I felt a new level of fear and completely on my own. I had no means to deal with it, so I did the only thing I could. I repressed it.

As the months passed and I continued to be taken out with Lynne, she informed me that my mother had given birth to eight children and that I was the youngest of them all. Lynne gave me a piece of paper which listed each of their names and the year of their births. We were all born in Glasgow. I have four half-sisters and one half-brother. Firstly, there is Rhona who was born in 1958, when my mother was twenty-four years old. Three years later came the arrival of her first set of twins, Sandra and Avril. They were followed four years on by her second set of twins, Bruce and Hazel.

My mother then separated from her husband and went on to meet my biological father. Four years later came the arrival of my mother's third set of twins, Joanna and Edith, my full blood sisters. I was her last-born child, almost three years later, in 1972. My mother was, by then, thirty-seven years old. Five years after my birth she was dead.

My mother had put all eight of her children into care.

I learned many years later that Avril was the only one out of us all who was adopted, being separated from her twin Sandra when they were just babies.

Lynne went on to tell me that my father's name is Gordon. She told me that he had subsequently married but that he did not go on to have any more children. Lynne then gave me something which she said Gordon had written for his children. It consisted of four typewritten pages that he had entitled, 'My Story'. Lynne said that he had compiled it some years ago and had left it in the hands of Social Services to be passed on to us whenever they deemed appropriate. I was told he had written it because he wanted us to have some understanding of why we were where we were and not living with our mother and him. The date written in the top right-hand corner read 18 October 1983. I worked out, from his date of birth which was also written at the top of the page, that he was thirty-nine when he wrote it. I would have been eleven years old. Lynne said that Gordon would have had support from Social Services with the writing of it. Gordon had made the decision to put his story down on paper for his children at the point in his life when he had realised a need to turn things around for himself. This also happened to be at a time when he had chosen to receive the help he required to tackle two decades of alcohol abuse.

It was very hard to read about the man who regarded himself as being my father but who I had thought nothing of until then.

Whenever I spent time with Lynne hearing facts about my natural family it was like being snatched out of all that I knew as normal and swept into some other person's surreal and dramatic life, then being placed back into my own life. I was becoming increasingly aware that my world in foster care was full of lies, secrecy and deceit.

In Gordon's Story I read phrases such as:

after being tied to my mother's apron strings for so long, I was now free and was determined to have a fling to myself so, understandably, an awful lot of money went down the drain through my drinking and elaborate spending, eventually developing into a drink problem

from the day I left the house (at 21) till the day I met Irene at 24 years old (the children's mother), I had a hell of a good time to myself

looking back in hindsight, we were two irresponsible adults

rather than let this state of affairs carry on, I called in the social workers

…decided that the twins would go into care…

Elaine would be taken straight into care from the hospital.

I have left a lot of blanks in my relaying of Gordon's story. It was when I actually met him that I heard his full version of the events which took place between my mother and himself, and which eventually lead to my sisters and me being taken into care. I will go on to tell about this meeting later.

Reading Gordon's story gave me an outlet to be angry, I think because he was still alive and she was dead. Although I was curious about him, on reading his story my natural instincts were instantly alerted against being hurt.

Right up to that point in my life it had only ever been my mother who I had thought of. All my thoughts were of how much I longed for her to come for me. I do not believe a single day went by without my dreaming of the moment I would meet her. When I was very little, in my dreams I saw her as being very young and beautiful with long blond hair and blues eyes, dressed like a princess. In my mind she was perfect. As I grew I held onto the idea that the exact instant my mother saw me she would know that she loved me and would never be able to let go of me ever again. There was even a time in my life when I had imagined that she was everywhere. Watching me from a distance, in the shadows, in the trees or around a corner, keeping a constant and protective vigil. She was my one constant, my rock to cling to. She followed me around, forever concealed just out of sight, hiding herself away whenever I turned around, lying in wait until the time was right for her to come for me. This notion sometimes even made me curtail my behaviour, because I believed that she could see me and I wanted her to be proud of me. The better I behaved the easier it would be for her to love me and therefore she would naturally want to take me back. Whenever I was upset, I would sit on my bed looking out of the window to the woods beyond the garden. There was a particular tree that drew my attention. It sat squarely in my line of vision both from the kitchen and my bedroom window. On a branch I could distinctly make out the image of a person, casually standing, strong, with an arm stretched out and their head firmly fixed in the direction of the house. I truly believed it was my mum. I was completely convinced that she was everywhere. I so often willed her to read the words in my head. 'Come now. Look at me, I am crying for you. Please see me. Come now.'

And yet, in all that time, she had been dead.

The truth came slamming down on me: I was suddenly a different person. I was now someone whose mother had died when I was still just an infant. To somehow turn away from my dream of having her in my life was like wrenching a vital organ from my body and leaving behind a cavernous dead space of eternal emptiness.

This rather bewildering idea of having a father had never entered my brain. Now I was forced to face the reality that I had no mother, but that Gordon was very much still around. The situation was completely alien to me. Just as Lynne had told me on that very first outing with her, there on the page were the words, confirmed by Gordon in his story, that Irene had died in 1977 when I would have been a mere five years old. The fact that she had gone without us ever having known each other was to prove impossibly difficult for me to come to terms with or to accept.

Naturally, it was not long before I began to be curious about Gordon. I wondered what he looked like and where he lived. Perhaps not surprisingly, I pondered the idea of meeting him. I had questions I needed answers to, the most salient of which was: why had he never come back for me?

I was to find out from him, much later when I had for many years been out of the care of Social Services that Lynne, unbeknown to me, had travelled up to Fort William, to where he lived at that time, to talk to him about me. When I eventually met Gordon, he informed me that at the time when the social worker had visited him all those years ago she had told him that she sensed I was unhappy where I was and that she considered I might be feeling confused. He went on to say to me that he believed that the social worker had put this to him as a suggestion that perhaps it might be possible for me to come up to Fort William to live with him, but that it was not directly asked so he did not consider it. I was speechless! Enraged. He was an insular person. His words completely incensed me and my impression of Gordon was cemented. This fixed judgement of Gordon was to stay unshifted for many years into my adulthood until, with age and experience, it did eventually soften. But it was never completely erased.

At that time in my life, I could not help but question his callousness because, by then, I had hoped to become a mother myself. How could someone who had pulled himself out from the grip of alcoholism and managed to create a stable life for himself, not then surely felt a degree of desperation to have his children back with him? This man, who has the audacity to call himself my father, sat before me and boasted about the fact that he had for many years held down a decent trade as a painter and decorator and yet as he relayed this to me, I could not fathom why he had never even considered the notion of returning to his children. Gordon now had a wife and a house, but his new situation was not enough for him to use the opportunity to share his new life with his own daughters.

When Gordon furnished me with this knowledge, hearing him tell it in his cavalier manner simply served to further stoke the coals of rage which already burned inside me.

However, thinking back to when I was a teenager, this monumental time of devastating revelations, coming while I was running with the punches which teenage years naturally throw, was provoking a within me which at that time was understated and very much disregarded.

Everything I was learning, rather inevitably, intensified my feelings of isolation, abandonment, rejection and compounded my already low self-esteem. This was coupled with an ever-increasing sense of paranoia, but I was unaware that I was sinking fast and completely helpless to do anything about it. By then I was full throttle into my journey of self-discovery and all my energy was channelled in that one direction.

My social worker Lynne, after informing me of my

mother's death, then of Gordon's life, had immediately proceeded to ask me, 'Would you like to meet your sisters?'

I did not need any thinking time.

Whether it was the right time and whether I was properly prepared or not, I was going to meet my twin sisters Joanna and Edith.

We met when I had turned sixteen. My sisters were three years older.

Although my heart was positively pounding, I more than gladly went along with whatever Lynne's plans were for me that day; I was floating on her magic carpet with promise of the joy which our sisterly union would surely exude. I did not allow even the tiniest slip of my true emotions of trepidation to show. There was a voice in my head pleading, please, please don't let them be pretty. I know this sounds shallow, but what I was really thinking was, please don't let them think I am ugly. Please let them like me.

Lynne arrived to collect me early in the morning on a warm day in early summer in 1988. I was feeling full of anticipation, anxiously unsure what to expect. The night before, I said a prayer for good weather and for everything to reflect my dreams of blissful happiness. To be honest, I was never someone who believed in the idea of a paragon of virtue keeping vigil from an invisible heaven, standing by ever-ready to make things perfect. Now, thinking back, it is obvious that the weather was just one of the many things which I had absolutely zero control over. I pondered over what to wear, not that my wardrobe held much of a variety of choice, and settled on what I can only describe as my old faithful, sticking to my comfort zone of black trousers, black and purple striped shirt, a black cardigan which belonged to my old neighbour, black shoes and white socks. Who knows what I was thinking! At the time, I was content that it was the appropriate attire for the day. It is strange how, at such a pivotal time in my life, I wasted energy on futile worries.

Before we set off to meet my sisters, Lynne firstly took me to visit Blairvadach Children's Home. This is where I had spent my first years of my life until the age of three, when I had then left to go and live with my foster family. I had no recollection of having any previous discussions with Lynne about planning a visit to Blairvadach. It was something which I had not foreseen and I confess that the fact that I had lived in a Children's Home felt more than a little mystifying to me. This was especially so, given that it had only very recently been brought to my knowledge. It was impossible to imagine what it would have been like. I suppose this revelation had not really had time to truly sink in yet. I felt a little like being a participant in a dramatisation of someone else's life and not the actual, true events of my own. Nevertheless, after around an hour and a half's drive, we had arrived.

The house was still serving as a children's home at that time. We were introduced to a lady who very kindly showed us around. As we took the wide staircase, I caught a glimpse of two young girls who looked like they might be around my own age. They were standing looking inquisitively at me from just across the landing and I felt intimidated by the confident, self-assured air which they had. I did not want to meet their gaze so I kept my eyes averted from their direction and pretended not to see them. I felt very strange, as if this was all a fantasy world which could not possibly exist in my world. Things like this just did not feel real to me and the fact that I was too young to remember anything of my time as a resident there made it seem all the more surreal. However, I could not help but wonder whether I had been happy living there.

The whole time, it was obvious to me that no one was noticing the fact that I was not at ease. My surroundings were on the one hand very intimidating but on the other hand immensely intriguing for me. The lady who took us round, whose name I have forgotten, told us that the layout of the bedrooms would look very different now from how it would have done when I was there. Although she had a lot to say, I found it very hard to absorb anything of substance. I tried to hear what Lynne and she were saying but my eyes were darting from room to room. I was desperate for something to trigger a memory or even the smallest hint of something which would alleviate my feelings of yearning, of needing to know that I had belonged here, that I had been well looked after and cared for. I was eager to ask the trivial, immature questions that were piling up in my head, such as which room I would have slept in? How many beds would there have been in each room? My mind was battling with a kaleidoscope of conflicting emotions.

For many years when I lived with my foster family I had a recurring dream of being in a dormitory consisting of rows of bunk beds. I and some children had sneaked out to steal some biscuits, when suddenly our carers had caught us, sending us hastily jumping back into bed, telling us to go to sleep. I had not ever known if my dream was a memory or just a fantasy but being in that place highlighted to me that there may be some tenuous threads of memory lying dormant in my subconscious mind.

I wanted to know if there was anyone still working there who would have known me way back then and if so I wanted to meet them so that I could ask them if I had been a good baby or a difficult one. Was I held? Did they love me? Are there any photographs? Yet somehow I could not open my mouth to speak the words.

I imagined myself on the day when my foster family came for me. I had been told nothing of this but I played it out in my imagination. I pictured myself standing in a row of many children of differing ages, all presented in our best clothes, hair shiny and faces smiling, expectant, terrified. My foster parents pacing up and down the line, studying each child, scrutinising us individually, surveying the group as a whole, seeing who among us stood out enough to warrant the privilege of being plucked from obscurity and whisked off to live a life shielded from the threat of eternal insecurity.

Now, being in that children's home where my mind could only fabricate the events of a time which I could not recall, I was not feeling at all comfortable and really just felt terribly shy. I was reticent and so was unable to ask any of the questions I longed to say. Instead I politely followed the lady round, keeping Lynne in front of me, almost hiding in her shadow, so as to conceal how increasingly confused about my past I was feeling.

When we were saying our goodbyes, I breathed a sigh of relief to be leaving. Before we drove away, Lynne took a photograph of me standing in the doorway to Blairvadach Children's Home. A few weeks later when she gave me the picture, I cried, although it was many years later before I understood what I was crying for.

At last we could get on our way to meet Joanna and Edith. By now, the anticipation of the moment when I would finally see my actual sisters was becoming all-consuming.

The arrangement was that we would all meet inside an office of Social Services in Glasgow, with their own social worker, Cathie, also being present. I was so nervous. Our two social workers were to act as a kind of mediator; however, as it turned out, it was not really necessary for them to do so. I very quickly discovered that my sisters were very talkative and seemed extremely vivacious and inquisitive about me.

My twin sisters were smaller than me both in height and frame. I decided I looked slightly more like Joanna, who had the same facial features and was a touch nearer my height. Edith, on the other hand, was very small and extremely petite, with sharper features and they both had short hair that was fairer than my own mousy brown and styled almost identically to one another. I think I might have come across as being very quiet, but this was only because they were doing much of the talking, asking me lots of questions and commenting on my Edinburgh accent saying I sounded 'English and posh'. Their own accents were equally as alien to me, with their Glaswegian sing song lilt in the way they raised the tone of the last word of each sentence. I do not think I said very much. I was very conscious that I did not want to say anything which would make me come across as silly or immature, but their bubbly confidence did project onto us all and lifted the atmosphere. Also, I was exceptionally aware of the fact that although they were my family, they were also complete strangers to me but that they had never been strangers to each other. This made me feel somewhat inferior because they were kept together and I was raised separately. I do not think I was being the real me: I feel I was putting on a kind of facade so as to create an impression of being a strong, independent person. Inside, my feelings of paranoia would not allow me to lower my guard enough to allow myself to fully relax and when I looked at my sisters I wondered how much of the same emotions they were feeling.

The room we were in was very small, with five armchairs and a coffee table crammed inside it. The walls were covered in a floral-patterned wallpaper with a carpet matching the same blend of monotonous worn-out creamy colours. I do not remember whether the room had a window, but I do remember feeling some level of claustrophobia when we all initially sat down in such proximity to one another. I managed to relax enough to smile while Lynne took a few photographs of us, which was actually rather fun as my sisters playfully pushed their two chairs together and instructed me to sit on the arms of the chairs between them, then told me to put my arms on their shoulders while they put their arms on my lap. We looked so happy and natural, laughing into the camera. I hold these pictures dearly to this day as a precious reminder of the day I first met my sisters. I keep them inside a special folder where I store every item of my journey of discovery and which now serves as a commemorative correlation of my story.

My sisters and I made a good attempt at forming a relationship but, because of my intense insecurities, for me it was shaky. The fact that they already had what I perceived as a strong family history together was very hard to take in. They would have had no memories of ever being apart and because of this, their talk was predominantly centred around reminisces of their life with each other. Their stories were full of the energy of their childhood and on that day when we met for the very first time they spoke with great enthusiasm about happy times. I was jealous. I am profoundly aware that this is an ugly emotion, but it was very real and at that time it was exceptionally painful.

There was a particular story my sisters told me which took me by surprise and still sticks out in my memory. They spoke of a day when they were children. Gordon had turned up unannounced at their door.

'Dad came to our house one time, totally drunk, demanding to get us back.' When they told me this, their voices were a low shrill and they were very animated, as though attempting to recreate the drama of that day. I, on the other hand, was completely missing the point, which was that it must surely have been quite a dramatic time in their young lives and one that would have caused them a great deal of confusion. Instead, in that moment all I could think about was how lucky they were to know so much about our parents and the circumstances surrounding why we had been placed in care and to have learned the truth at such an early age. It reinforced how much every part of my past had been kept hidden from me.

A few years later, when I was invited by my sisters to travel through to Glasgow with a friend to join them at a party to celebrate their twenty-first birthdays, I found it incredibly difficult to reign in my feelings of envy. I took along with me my oldest friend so that I did not have to feel like I was completely alone but nevertheless found the experience exceptionally demanding. My sisters' foster family very kindly asked us to stay with them in their home and meeting with their foster parents and extended family was somewhat awkward. They were so open and outwardly demonstrative with their affection for each other. This was something which was totally alien to me. I did what I always did in situations like this: I sat in silence and watched in complete wonder with an all too familiar sense of sadness like a brick in my stomach.

At the party, it was immediately obvious that all their friends had already been prepared for the arrival of their long-lost sister and they were curious about me. I found I was being stared at a lot throughout the evening. It was very disconcerting to find eyes fixed on me and to see people whispering and pointing. With the attention which was being forced onto me, it felt like the celebration was being diverted from my sisters and it might well have been easy to forget who the party was really for. Their foster father asked me up to dance with him, which was absolute agony. The dance floor was too empty; it was like we had centre-stage. He held me too closely, and I felt painfully embarrassed. All I wanted was to get out of there.

I was unable to show my true colours and be myself with my new sisters, choosing instead to push them away. I was unable to stop my ever-present mistrust from distorting my judgement.

At that point in my life, my being fostered was still being treated like a closely guarded secret. The subject was taboo and no one, least of all me, ever dared to mention it. I had only just told my best friend, whom I had known since first year at high school, and we were by then eighteen. She was utterly astounded and almost seemed angry with me. She could not believe that she had known me for five years and in all that time I had never let it slip. When she said this to me it made me realise just how much it had been entrenched in me not to tell anyone; especially given that I had by then already gone through the emotions of finding out about my mother, Gordon and my sisters. Through it all, I had simply continued going to school, then onto work each day without giving away even a hint that anything about me was different.

On the day when my friend had found out, we had been sitting chatting in my bedroom which, at that time, I still shared with my foster sister. My friend looked around the room and said, 'Who's that in that picture over there?'

'That's my sister,' I replied.

'Wow, you two look nothing like each other.'

'Yeah, that's because I'm fostered. Remember?'

'What! You're fostered? You've never told me that. I can't believe you've kept that from me all these years.' Her expression was questioning and full of bewilderment. 'How come you've never told me this before now? I can't believe you're fostered and have never said anything to me about it.'

I was equally as stunned by her retort.

It was becoming all too clear that talking about being fostered had never been an option for me. It was as though I had been conditioned to keep it secret, like I was not entitled to discuss it. For just a micro-second, I had believed that my best friend must surely have known. I was unsure if this was because, up to that moment, I may have falsely believed that everyone who knew me must somehow already know, without my having ever said it and yet in truth, the subject had never actually been aired. I suppose growing up believing I was adopted and never having been told I was fostered played its part in keeping me silent.

The warped reality was apparent. Not being related to the family I was growing up with had always been an unspoken subject and I had grown up firmly aware that I had a real fear of broaching it. Despite this fear, it had always been my right to be furnished with the facts of my background. This holding back of the facts of my origins was, in essence, covering over my own person reality. It set me apart from my peers in the most emotionally secretive way. I was unseen. An unheard, invisible entity was standing squarely in my face telling me with forthright unqualified conviction that I did not fit in. It meant that I needed to put in a greater effort than perhaps was normal in order to feel that I was accepted and at this I was inexorably failing. I increasingly found myself fighting against an internal, deep-rooted feeling of being unwanted.

Taking into account all of the aforementioned complex, integral feelings and then throwing in the revelation of suddenly discovering that I had actual, full-blood-related sisters it surely is not surprising that my expectations were hugely based on fantasy. I wanted the perfect scenario. Looking back, I think I was very naive and perhaps a little immature. I yearned for the fairy tale ending.

In truth, however, the fact that I had been fostered would remain forever a subject which was never brought up or spoken of at home. I was never offered any support whatsoever by my foster parents, even while being furnished with this new identity. Neither they nor anyone else ever asked me a single question about anything I was finding out or about how I was coping with it all. I thought the reason for their disinterest must be because no one remotely cared about any of it. I coped the only way I knew how: I cocooned this new, true self tightly away into a secret world where I could view my newly discovered identity without the chaos of my normal daily life imposing even the smallest blemish onto it. It was mine and I needed it desperately and no one would ever take it away from me.

I know now that I was feeling an almost fundamental, primal jealousy of my twin sisters who had literally been thrust into my life in the most frivolous fashion. I also know that I was expected to behave in a certain way. However, I had been unprepared and was without the emotional tools to manage what my social worker appeared to assume was a new life together, for us all to freely and happily embrace. The truth for me was precisely the reverse.

Learning that their social worker had, very rightly, enabled my sisters to spend their entire lives knowing of their natural background truly hurt. My sisters presented themselves in such a cool, self-contented manner that I questioned why they would possibly want to have me in their lives. Their togetherness made me recoil. It reminded me of how utterly alone I was. Moreover, their fantastically good social worker had been around for them all their lives and had been a permanent person who they were able to fully rely on while growing up. They unequivocally told me that they could turn to her at any time throughout their lives.

'So you could literally walk into her office any time you wanted?' I asked, incredulous.

'Yep. We would walk home from school and just decide we needed to pop in to see her for a chat.'

These words will sit with me forever. Our lives were worlds apart.

However, unbeknown to me, this was but a tiny speck in the enormity of the information on my background which I was still to unearth.

The social worker assigned to me before Lynne turned up had never given me any of her time and had never been someone who, I was taught, I could rely on or trust. Moreover, this second social worker actually only went on to spend a little over one year working with me and then simply bustled out of my life when I was seventeen, at a point when I very much needed her. Her departure at such a crucial juncture reinforced my feelings of isolation.

When I made the decision not to keep in touch with my sisters, I was having great difficulty managing life and their presence made things all the more complicated. It makes me terribly sad now to remember how I walked away from a potentially good and positive influence in my life, oblivious to the consequences. Joanna and Edith were lovely people. Edith was exceptionally easy-going, very confident and comfortable in her own skin. Joanna, on the other hand, was bubbly and zealous and they both oozed care and warmth. They had been brought up together in permanent foster care with what appeared to be a loving family.

My sisters were just trying to introduce me into their lives.

Looking back, it is now apparent to me that Lynne was trying to create something impossible, the perfect ending. She perhaps hoped that I would go on to unite with Gordon, keeping in touch with my own full blood sisters and that we would all get along, with the past forgotten, forever. Lynne was in my life as my social worker for just over one year and it was very difficult to say goodbye. She had been the catalyst for such hugely important discoveries for me. I was then briefly placed in the so-called care of a third social worker who was simply a gap filler until I reached eighteen years of age.

Chapter Three

When I turned eighteen years old, I was deemed to be no longer in the care of Social Services. Though I remained living with my foster family I was no longer officially a fostered person.

Going through teenage years, as we all know, can be troublesome. For me it was fraught with confusion and extreme emotions. On top of raging hormones and sitting fourth-year exams at school, I was finding out some immense truths about my natural family and origins. While my friends were becoming who they wanted to be, I was immersed in discovering who I really was. What I had missed out on. Trying hard to put the pieces together in my mind. All this while still living with my foster family and trying to cope with the daily abuse that entailed. For what I have, up to now, failed to mention is that the other fostered child in the family was verbally and physically abusive towards me at every moment he possibly could. This was not confined within the house but spilled out into other areas of our lives such as school and church. This grew worse as we grew older and my foster parents did little to intervene. I believe now that at the time they were turning a blind eye to his, and to their own children's, behaviour towards me.

My emotional highs and lows by my late teens were at times too intense. For my friendships to endure through-out this testing time was not easy as I think my behaviour became increasingly erratic. My energy was incredibly fraught with the challenge of keeping my thoughts on an even keel. The pressure of this quite literally brought me to the brink, insomuch that I even considered suicide. Thoughts of suicide began during my primary school years when I would consider the idea of throwing myself in front of the speeding cars on my long walk to school. By the time I was in my teens I decided I would prepare myself for the day when I could no longer cope. My elderly neighbour kept bottles containing one hundred paracetamol tablets in her cupboard. I stole a bottle one day and at home I put the pills into an envelope and crushed them into powder. I placed the envelope into a bedside drawer for when the time came.

Another low point came after a particularly acrimonious episode during a night out. While I drove my friend and one other home there ensued the most hurtful confronta-tion which was centred around the petty trivia of whether I had stuck up for her boyfriend when I knew that what he had done was wrong. When it was over and my friends had been dropped home, I was left alone in my car. I was utterly distraught and bereft. My mind was racing with the idea that I had just lost every friend I had and that the whole episode was entirely my fault even though in my heart I knew this was false. I was caught up in a blinding panic so severe that I actually considered the idea of deliberately crashing my car.

Although this may seem extreme to some, looking back, I realise that I was acting on my suppressed emotions connected to all the discoveries about my past and my very difficult, present and my expectations that anyone who happened to be remotely close to me should fully understand this. Of course, this was far from the truth, for without talking directly to them about it, how could they possibly comprehend? When I did start to lower my guard and reveal to my friends what was going on in my head, I expected some level of understanding and forgiveness. Instead I was told, 'You don't know how bad you have been.'

I was not aware that my behaviour had been bad enough to affect my friend. However, talking it through with her did not work either as she told me, 'I know it sounds selfish, but can you not tell me any more.'

In my head I was begging to be told that I was normal. I wanted to know that what I was feeling would go away. I needed so badly just to feel like an ordinary human being.

I was silently struggling, especially after learning the agonising news that my mother was dead. I was finding everything that I was hearing quite overwhelming and, being a teenager and ill-equipped to deal with the magnitude of it all, I just wanted, so much, to deny my emotions. I was not just afraid of them but I also did not feel entitled to talk about them. There was no one asking me how I was feeling about any part of what was being said to me and so I literally built up an inner mechanism of emotional independence which rendered me incapable of articulating my feelings. If I am honest with myself I would confess that actually, I fully believed that I was not entitled to outwardly express any emotional response to anything going on in my life.

It was not until much later when I was well into my thirties that I was to meet a person who invited me to freely open up and talk about my feelings, with the reassurance that it was alright to do so and that my world was not going to fall apart. I was also told that there would be no judgements held over me. I will introduce this person into my story later.

I had turned eighteen and had been dropped by Social Services. At this point I decided that I was ready to trace my natural father. I did not tell anyone, except one friend. I did it surreptitiously because I was afraid of how my foster parents would respond; I knew they would never approve and I might get myself into trouble with them. Despite this, I felt quite strongly about my right to make this decision without their permission. I practically made up my mind that I was unstoppable. I suppose I was off once again chasing that proverbial castle in the sky.

I telephoned the Social Work office in Glasgow where Lynne had worked and requested to speak to her manager, who I had met when he had accompanied Lynne to a review meeting at our home.

'I would like to know Gordon's address and telephone

number.' I said with as much confidence and air of authority in my tone as I could muster.

The response was an inane remark: 'I wonder if you are ready to be in direct contact with your father. Do you think this is the right time for you?'

However, I was in no mood to be fobbed off as I considered it to be my natural given right to hold this information and, moreover, that it was completely nothing to do with them, now that they had severed ties with me.

'I am not prepared to put down the phone until you have given me what I want.'

I have to confess that I even surprised myself by my unaccustomed forthright assertiveness and it evidently worked, as I was duly supplied with the details I requested.

The next tricky part was actually picking up the telephone to call Gordon, which required a fresh amount of courage. At this juncture I would point out that Gordon is always referred to as Gordon but my mum continues to be Mum or Mother. As my story unfolds I believe the reason for this will become evident.

I held onto the piece of paper with his details written on it for a number of weeks while I attempted to work up some measure of bravado. One day I absentmindedly left it sitting on top of the piano in the living room overnight and the next day when I returned home from my work I found it placed in plain sight, on the kitchen table. I was gripped with fear and panic. I grabbed it from the table and hid it away in my room.

Although I waited for my foster parents to confront me about it, no one ever approached me. Not a single word was ever said to me regarding the fact that I was evidently preparing myself to contact Gordon for the very first time in my life. I was dumbfounded. I was confused about what their silence meant. Were they angry at me for concealing something with such huge potential consequence or did they just not care? I never did find out their reasons for not mentioning it to me at the time when they had discovered it.

When I did eventually find the courage to dial Gordon's number, it took me several attempts to follow through with the call. However, after a time, I was brave enough to speak and to my relief, Gordon reacted with apparent extreme happiness to hear from me.

'You have made my day.'

These are the words which I remember most from that very first conversation. I felt that things went well on the telephone, that it was positive and boded well for a potential future relationship to develop. We also wrote back and forth for some time, allowing us to get to know each other a little. Gordon made the mistake of sending me birthday and Christmas cards and gifts that were more suited for a small child than for the young adult I had become. I put this down to the fact that he simply had no experience of dealing with teenagers, not to mention the glaring fact that he did not know me. Gordon's so-called generosity was a short-lived thing as the gifts and cards stopped coming rather abruptly.

I met Gordon on a Saturday in a hotel bar close to where I lived. He was small and stocky with dark receding hair and a goatee beard. He was dressed in a shirt, a black leather jacket and dark jeans. I immediately thought he had a rather hard look about him which was not helped by the fact that he was a heavy smoker. When he hugged me tightly and tried unsuccessfully to hold back his emotions on that first introduction, the musty smell of his cigarettes stifled the air. I noticed he had nicotine-stained fingers. We had an awkward first meeting, exchanging a little detail about ourselves.

By then I had left school and gained a job as a legal secretary. I had also passed my driving test and had recently bought a car with the aid of some money left in a will for me by my foster mother's stepfather who had shown a particular fondness for me during my early years in foster care. I was sadly to learn much later into my adult life exactly what this man's fondness for me meant.

In his conversations with me, Gordon would pass on advice on cars and safe driving. I think he was trying, unsuccessfully, to play the father figure but he merely succeeded in irking me for the futility of it.

Gordon vocalised his apparent eagerness for us to get along and said a few times on that first occasion that he would like us to get to know one another. He told me to come and visit him and to bring my toothbrush. It surprised me that my initial intuition when seeing Gordon was a negative one. I think it was because I did not want him to hug me or to cry, as it was me who had been abandoned by him and not the other way around. There were no feelings inside me for him. I had not, at that time, quite realised that I was holding a great well of anger and resentment towards him. Gordon had his wife, Jean, with him and I did not take well to her either, finding her very staid and straight-faced. I feigned happiness at meeting them.

Despite the nine years he had spent with my mother, Gordon told me that he did not have a single photograph of her, nor any item of sentiment to remember her by.

I met with Gordon a further two times. On these occasions he filled me in on the reasons as to why I was put into care. He described how, when he and my mother had met, they had a, 'merry old time to themselves' and that, if he was honest with himself, they were both very much 'two irresponsible adults'.

Gordon had been in the grip of alcoholism. He said his addiction often made him behave violently towards my mother. He told me that often, when he came home after a drinking spree, having stayed away for a few days or sometimes weeks, he would look at my mother and admit to himself: 'I did that to her.'

Then he said to me, 'It is something which I will have to live with for the rest of my life.' Gordon repeated these words to me a few times.

Gordon told me that my mother was not an alcoholic, as had been suggested to me by my foster mother when I was fifteen, but that she had suffered with severe clinical depression and had acute mental health problems. Over time, she left the house less and less, some days she did not even dress. Gordon told me that my mother was addicted to anti-depressants and when one doctor would refuse to continue to prescribe the tablets, she would simply go off and find another doctor who would. He continued by saying that she was completely incapable of looking after herself, never mind taking care of her children. He was, he said, 'single handedly holding down a full time job as well as trying to look after the twins' and 'was very much feeling the strain of this, especially since, in those days, there was no real support in the same way there is today'.

Then Gordon told me that he 'called in the social workers.'

Joanna and Edith went into care as toddlers and I was taken from birth, straight from the hospital into a children's home. Gordon by then placated himself with: 'Which is something else I am just having to live with. To continue beating myself up because of it would not be healthy for me so I have tried to get on with my own life the best way I can.'

Gordon told me my mother lived for another five years, during which time she sunk ever deeper into the depth of depression and was not dressing herself or leaving the house at all. She had become completely agoraphobic. Gordon was close to hitting rock bottom with his alcohol dependency.

Gordon's brutally honest recounting of his story ended with him dealing me the real knock-out strike.

He told me that my mother had taken her own life, after several failed attempts. The year was 1977 and she was just forty-two years old. Gordon had stormed off on another one of his drinking binges after beating her and threatening, for the umpteenth time, that this time he was leaving her for good. However, as was usually the case, he had eventually come back.

When he walked into the house, he found her sprawled on the floor partly lying up against the fire place. She was marked and bruised from when he had hit her. When the police arrived, they had immediately assumed that Gordon had murdered her because of the state he had left her in. He was arrested and taken to the police station, overnight, to be questioned. It was in actual fact an overdose of anti-depressants that had killed her.

At the time of my writing this, Gordon has achieved three decades of sobriety. He stressed that this was an achievement which he feels very proud of and projected this by describing alcohol addiction as a disease and going over the lengths to which he has had to strive to overcome it. He said he attends weekly meetings at Alcoholics Anonymous to keep him off the booze. As I was eighteen at the time of hearing this, I did not understand about the illness of alcoholism. What I would have liked to ask him was why he chose alcohol over his wife and children and why he waited until I was thirteen years old before wanting to address his addiction. Were we not enough of a jolt for him to want to change things and face up to his responsibilities? And why, once he was sober, did he not come for us or at least contact us?

At that point everything was too disturbing to deal with

and my life began spiralling into a parallel world whereby my mind seemed to slip into another dimension, a dark space suspended above reality where I floated unnoticed for a full year. I spent this time going through the motions of daily life without feeling anything of its passing. There was no one I could turn to and I grew incessantly paranoid. I was scared. I cried going to sleep and I cried waking up. Nobody saw it, or if they did, no one cared enough to help.

I had been craving for my mother to hold my hand, to keep me safe when things were precarious and to steady me through the utter chaos and sheer turmoil that just was. And now that I knew the truth, everything changed. No longer did I believe that I had a mother who would protect me from harm. My mother had taken her own life one month after my fifth birthday and I had wasted every day of my childhood believing that she was alive.

I felt incredibly alone and isolated.

Then one day when I was alone in my bedroom, I began to cry, but it was a crying of a different kind: I literally collapsed as my heart shattered over my mother's death. In my messed up, confused mind I was blaming myself for her demise. I thought that, because I was the last of her children, it was me who had pushed her over the edge. I was convinced that if she had not gone through yet another pregnancy and birth, then she might have had a chance to live. I was breaking inside and experiencing a kind of physical and terribly debilitating pain.

Suddenly, while I was on my knees sobbing, my bedroom

door opened and my foster mother stood there looking at me. She did not enter the room or make any attempt to come near me. She just stayed leaning against the door frame, showing no emotion or concern at the obvious distress I was in.

'My mum took her own life. If she hadn't have had me then she could still be alive,' I said through my tears, but despite witnessing my distress, all that my foster mother could say to me was, 'Suicide, the ultimate selfish act.'

When I asked her if she would please just this one time bring herself to at least put her arm around me, she told me that it was wrong for me to expect her to change the way she was, purely for my own selfish needs. Afterwards, when I had reached emotional exhaustion, I lay on my bed feeling regret at bringing down my internal wall of protection I had built so high against her. I sternly promised myself that no matter how much I ached for even the smallest touch of affection, I would never make the mistake of looking to her for it ever again.

In time, I began to see cracks of light through the thick veil of blackness. By then I felt I was ready to tell my friend. I desperately tried to articulate how I was feeling, saying it was like I had a brick in my stomach weighing everything inside me down, how impossibly heavy it was and my total inability to lift it. I said how I now, thankfully, could feel it getting lighter. I told her how I was now terrified of it happening again and of the awful feeling I had that I was completely alone and had no one. My friend turned to me, irritated, and scolded me by saying that I had been completely unbearable to be around.

'You don't know how bad you've been,' she said for the second time.

It was strange how I had not been aware of being hard on my friends. Her reaction to my opening up to her only served to pile on more layers of paranoia and intensified my belief that I really was all by myself. I wondered if perhaps that was the reason why I did not see so much of my friends during that spell in my life. My oldest friends had pulled away from me, or was it me who was pulling away from them? The one certainty I had was that it deepened my perpetual issues of mistrust and fed my insecurity.

The few years which followed that difficult time in my life were a kind of settling down and readjustment period for me. I was now in my twenties and had met my husband-to-be. We met when I was twenty-two and he was thirty. I was introduced to him on a night out through a mutual friend and, like lightening, I fell for his easy-going, forthright, head-firmly-screwed-on manner. He knew where he was going in life and I happily jumped into his secure, comfortable world. It was not long into our relationship when he asked me if I would like to move into his flat with him. I, however, wanted to wait. Even though I was sure that I had found the person I wanted to marry, that I loved him and could see that he loved me, in my heart I knew that I needed him to be really sure that I was the right person for him. Once I had moved out of the place I had called home for the past twenty-one years, I knew I had absolutely no intentions of ever returning there to live again.

It was to be another two years before I actually did go to live with him. On the day I was due to move out and into his flat, now aged twenty-four, something strange happened. I found that a teddy bear, which I distinctly remembered my foster brother having during the whole time I had lived there, had mysteriously appeared on the top of one of my boxes of belongings. When I questioned my foster mother about why it was there, she said, 'Oh, that came with you when you came to live with us.'

I could not understand it. I clearly remembered, perhaps a few days after going to live with them, or perhaps it was on the actual day, my memory is vague, walking into my room to find a box lying on my bed with a small brown teddy bear inside. As nobody had mentioned anything about it to me, I had presumed it was a gift to me from my foster parents. This much larger white teddy bear lying on the box was never something which I had any memory of owning. It was the one which my foster brother had always had. It was a mystery. Could it have possibly been that my mother gave it to me when she abandoned me to the children's home? Or perhaps one of my carers in the home had given it to me? Had my foster parents taken it away from me? I felt that I would never know the real truth about that white teddy bear. However, the answers to this mystery will come, further into my story. I finished up deciding to leave it with my foster family. It did not feel like mine.

My husband and I have two children, a girl and boy, born two years five months apart. I was twenty-two when we met, twenty-four when I moved in with him, twenty-six when we were married, twenty-eight when my daughter was born and thirty when my son was born. Such impeccable planning! For as long as I can remember I had wished for a loving husband and two beautiful children. I wanted to be a mother more than anything else in my life and my wish had been granted. Our wedding was the happiest day of my life, up to that point. My foster parents had refused any financial involvement of any sort from my husband's parents towards paying for our wedding. They insisted on paying for everything. What this meant was my husband and I had no say in some important aspects of our day such as the venue, the numbers and who they would invite. That day was all about their own need to be seen, to parade their wealth, their big hearts. Other than our best man and bridesmaid, my husband and I had no friends watching us get married. Our friends were invited only for the evening party!

Although my husband's family welcomed me, I could not detach from my fierce sense of emotional independence and found it impossible to see myself as part of their family. I remember the very first time I had dinner with his family. I was extremely jealous at the easy way they all talked and laughed around the table and I cried in bed that night because of the pain of it. Unfortunately, in my mind I deliberately kept myself on the periphery of my husband's family. I think this was a way of protecting myself, of feeling safe.

On the day when my husband and I announced our engagement, after we had dinner, I was standing at his mother's kitchen sink helping out with some dishes when she turned to me and said, 'Now that you two are engaged, you know you're just as important to me as my own two are.'

Instead of allowing her beautiful words into my heart where they surely belonged, I just let them pass right over my head without them even touching the sides because I could not lower my guard enough to trust them to be true.

There then began a time of immense wellbeing and extreme pride. I left my job as a legal secretary for good and became a full-time wife and mother. I had told my husband that I would happily live on the breadline to bring up my children if this was what it took. I did not want to rely on anyone to look after my children, very much seeing this as my role, my responsibility. My mind was full of the challenges and joys of motherhood, good housekeeping and presenting myself to my neighbours and new friends as a regular, well-adjusted person. These people in this new life knew nothing of my past and I was glad to feel free of any potential judgements linked to it. I had made a conscious decision to reinvent myself, unburdened from the person I was.

Having children of my own had a significant and positive effect on my self-esteem as it provided me with a purpose far beyond that of my own insular needs. Seeing my stomach swell with new life growing inside me was momentous.

This little person was all mine and no one else's. No one gave her to me, she was all my own creation and my husband's too. Of course, I must remember that I would have to share her with my husband, as she was also his!

Having my own children brought with it the realisation that I had, for the very first time, people in my life who were not only blood related to me but were unrelated to my foster family. That feeling was like no other I had ever experienced. I knew that I would not allow anyone to take care of them, that I would do everything for them myself and they would go everywhere with me.

I was determined I was going to do everything in my power to protect and guard my own children. I did not ever want them to feel anything like how I did as a child. I stuck religiously to routines and trusted my instincts which positively yelled at me to never let these two small, precious people out of my sight. I tended to rely on babysitters only when it was absolutely necessary and did not go back to work for seven years, once they were both in school. Even then, I managed to gain a job within a school so that I would always be there for my children when they came home. I would never need any child care. My parents-in-law fell head over heels in love with them and often offered to look after them while I was out but at first I hardly ever accepted. I much preferred to have them with me whenever I went out. I had learned many lessons when growing up in foster care, lessons on what not to do. The most salient of these was that I was unquestionably going to provide the kind of love, nurture and affection which I knew was absolutely essential for my children and which had been unavailable to me. This last part came very naturally to me. I poured all the love which had forever laid dormant inside me into my children. I still tell my children every day how loved they are and how proud I am of them.

In spite of this new sense of fulfilment from having created my own little family, it was difficult, not always easy to cope, particularly when my children were very small and proceeding through nursery and on to early primary school. I was becoming aware once more of my rather fragile self-esteem and low self-worth. Making friends presented new challenges. For example, when meeting potentially good friends, my instinct was to be wary. I did a lot of scrutinising. I would wait for rejection, constantly looking for it. Expecting it. I would see it in the form of a slight look, a subtle gesture or sometimes it was simply a trivial comment which I would take out of context. And I would tell myself, 'Ah ha! See, there it is. I knew it would come.' Even when it was not remotely there, I would somehow see it. It was torture.

Other times, it would be that I failed to be assertive or to stand up for myself. I would allow myself to be used. I would feel completely unable to step forward and be firm enough to say no. I knew what was happening but my need to fit in, to believe I had true friendships, was overpowering. Often, I foolishly laid myself wide open to be taken for granted because I needed to be needed. I was a chronic people-pleaser. It was an ingrained pattern which I had been used to for my whole life. I had a never-ending negative mechanism locked inside my brain, fuelled by a warped past which had been completely out with my control and which I now felt powerless to stop.

Nevertheless, I did manage to make some firm, true friends. The kind of people who were warm and thoughtful, who I felt at ease with and could share great times with. People who although hearing bits of my past were accepting of this new confident person I was working so hard to be. I was still trying hard to hide my real emotions and was happy that they could not see the real me and had no idea of the sad place from where I had emerged. They must have ignored or perhaps had looked past my flaws for I am now extremely privileged to have such genuinely good people as my friends.

Little did I know back then that this new life I had found was going to be pivotal in allowing me to feel able to open up to those closest to me and by letting them in, so I created real, absolute, concrete friendships. I now have a small circle of extremely special friends who I consider to be like having my own family separate from my husband and children. It is an incredible thing to have and I am utterly aware of how lucky I am.

When my daughter was a baby, I bathed her and changed her and adoringly rubbed cream into the little dry patches on her plump, pink skin. Once, as I lovingly went about this evening routine, a voice in my head asked the question, I wonder who did this for me? I looked at her, so vulnerable and tiny, lying there and thought of myself, once this small, this helpless and I could feel no sense for myself of the kind of nurture I was lavishing on my baby.

Then, when she reached three years old, I crouched down until my eyes were at the same level as her eyes and I looked around me, seeing how huge the world was for such a little girl of just three years old and I thought, gosh, I would have been this small when I was taken away from the children's home. Taken from the one and only place I had ever known as home and from the only people whom I would have looked upon as my family and dumped into a large house full of strangers. I must surely have been petrified.

Reminders were all around me of just how different a life I had experienced when compared to the one my own children were having. I did not have any of my true relatives in my world when I was a child and as I thought about this a very familiar sense of envy rippled through me.

I do hold something of a memory of the day when I left the children's home to live with my foster family, although I cannot say for certain whether what I am recalling is a memory or a dream. It plays out in my mind as this. We are all in the car driving away from the home. I am sitting in the front passenger seat on my foster mother's knee feeling painfully shy. My foster mother is saying in a jovial voice, 'These are your brothers and sister.' As she pointed, one at a time, to all four children, announcing their names.

Although this was supposed to be an introduction, to me

it felt more like a statement. Their names were told to me in the order in which they sat, along the back seat of the car. All four of them were staring at me. At the mention of each of their names I dared the smallest glance at their faces. There was an inescapable collective air of solidarity among them, which I was especially fearful of. Now, when I think of that formidable day, whether what I am seeing in my mind's eye is fact or not, the extremely negative emotions it conjures inside me are very much a reality.

Chapter Four

When I reached my mid-thirties, there was a shift inside me. My unquenchable thirst for knowledge of my origins was resurfacing. It was as though it had never actually left me but had simply been buried, or rather it had been resting a while, allowing me to manage my life with all its changes, without disruption or confusion. The secrets of my past were patiently waiting to be nudged into life.

At around the age of thirteen I had been given a brown cassette case for Christmas. On the outside it looked just like an ordinary case but on the inside it was fitted with a detachable plastic holder for storing cassettes. I cannot remember who gave me this gift but have to marvel at their idea, especially given that I had only ever owned a mere three cassettes as a child.

Anyway, I came up with the idea of throwing out the obsolete plastic holder and instead used the case to keep my personal mail inside. It had little locks with a tiny key and so I knew I could keep them private. I began filling it with letters from pen pals I had met during camping trips with the Guides or on school excursions and, later, I kept all the letters I received from Gordon and from Joanna and Edith locked inside my case. I happily squirrelled them away safe and secure, from any unwanted eyes.

Now, some twenty years later, I took the case from where it had been carefully placed right in the far corner of the wardrobe. It had a thick layer of dust along the edge, indicative of the fact that it had been hidden away and left unopened for so many years. I looked through the different piles of letters, each individual pile carefully held together with an elastic band, stored in specific groups pertaining to who the letters were from.

Taking out the piles of letters I had received from my sisters, I carefully re-read all of them. It cast my mind back to those teenage years and to what had turned into a mind-boggling, whirlwind of discovery at that time. The exact feelings I felt all those years ago were transported into that moment. I could hear their voices pulsing through the words on the pages. I once again felt the energy they had and their eagerness to get to know me. I was filled with a mixture of trepidation and anticipation of a reunion between my sisters and me. I was certain that the earliest letters I had received from them would have their address and telephone number written on them.

Charged with confidence and an innate assurance that I was going to find my sisters and that they would surely have remained exactly as I remembered them, I dialled the number. A recorded female voice came onto the line telling me that this number was no longer in use. It was the first but not the only time that my proverbial floating bubble burst, thrusting me back to earth. Considering it had been such a long time since we had written to each other, it should not have been a surprise that their contact details would have changed. Despite this, I could not stop myself from feeling just the slightest pang of despair that I was not going to find them.

I had no idea whether they had moved house or perhaps simply had a new telephone number. It was directory enquiries, nonetheless, who confirmed for me that there was no longer anyone by their name living at the address written in the letters. This was extremely frustrating. I had no experience of tracking people down as previously any information I had received had been passed to me by a social worker. I was clueless.

It took me a further two years from that first realisation that I had an extremely strong need to know so much more about my past and to have my unanswered questions resolved, before I finally begin to research in earnest. I had to get into action. During those two years I would periodically announce to my husband, 'Today's the day! I'm going to walk into Social Services and ask to see my file.' However, my resolve would ebb away and I would put it off.

When at last I managed to summon all my courage and steady my nerves, I tentatively stepped onto the first rung of the ladder.

On entering my local Social Work offices I gathered up some rare gumption, pressed myself forward and asked that crucial, burning question, 'Who am I?'

Once I was over that first hurdle, the next obstacle in my way was trying to get access to a social worker who was willing to take me seriously enough to help me. This was to prove very hard indeed.

Firstly, I was introduced to a lady who was of no help whatsoever and who asked me such fatuous questions as, 'Why do you want to know this information now?' I felt like answering, what's it to you?

She would then proceed to try to coax me into talking about my feelings by asking leading questions. She actually said to me, 'If I told you your mother was in the next room, what would you do?'

It was one of the most idiotic questions anyone could ever ask me and all I could do was answer, 'Well, of course, I would run to her.'

The very last thing on my mind right then was the idea of opening up to a perfect stranger. All I was there for was to gain access to Social Service's file on me and my natural family, which I was certain would hold everything I needed to know about my past.

However, I would then hear nothing from this person for many months and whenever I tried to telephone her the receptionist would tell me that she was either in a meeting or called out to an emergency. Although I always left a message for her to return my call, she would very annoyingly fail to do so. Things continued in this vein for a few months more until one day, feeling exceptionally irritated, I telephoned again but this time I was assertive and said I did not wish to be told of any more fake meetings and that I refused to put down the telephone until I had spoken to someone who could help me.

A female voice then came onto the telephone with the reassurance that I was entitled to have someone assist me and agreeing that the delays I had experienced within their offices was inexcusable.

True to her word, I was then contacted by another social worker, a man this time. After spending another two fruitless meetings with him over yet more wasted months it seemed clear that his intention, like the previous social worker, was not to provide me with my file but to entice me to tell him about my feelings. It was all so infuriatingly obstructive to my basic reason for being there.

Nevertheless, a full year after I had stepped inside the Social Work office, I received a call from this male social worker, announcing that he would be introducing me to a lady called Jill who, he said, 'Could provide me with the kind of time I deserved.'

On meeting Jill I felt instinctively that there was something right about her. She did not ask any inane questions and when she spoke she exuded an air of reassurance. I think I instantly connected with her. She seemed to say all the right things to me and it felt as if she understood what I was feeling even before I had expressed it. I felt positive that this lady was going to help me.

At the introductory meeting, the man informed me that he had succeeded in tracking down my file and that

unfortunately he had found that it held very little information on me but that most of the information pertained to
my siblings and my mother. He explained that the reason
there was so little about me in the file might be due to the
fact that the authorities had changed several times over the
years and perhaps bits of information had gone missing. I
asked if I could see what they held about my mother and he
said that it was not possible to pass on any details regarding
my mother or any other member of my family held in the
file, for confidentiality reasons. I protested that surely the
fact that my mother had been deceased for so many years
meant the confidential status would no longer apply. But
the law was against me. The social worker was emphatic in
his assurance that my mother's information could not be
read by me. Tears of frustration ran down my cheeks. Jill
turned to me and with sympathy in her eyes she said, 'This
must be very disappointing news for you but I promise to
go through the file with a fine tooth comb and rake out any
information I can share with you.'

Jill turned out to be an exceptional social worker and I
quickly saw how privileged I was to have her help and support. She was enthusiastic and thorough and my inhibitions
gradually dissipated as Jill's gentle coaxing helped me to feel
at ease enough to allow me to slowly let down my seemingly impenetrable guard. Jill was about the same average
height and build as me with short dark hair and glasses. She
was very professional, but also very caring and seemed to
get to know and understand me extremely quickly, which

felt strangely comforting. She had genuine warmth, patience and an intense self-assurance which I drew on immediately. Jill has continued to stand by me and support me throughout my arduous journey and her unyielding belief in me has been invaluable. I have immense respect for Jill and should there ever come a day when I must say goodbye to her, although my heart will hurt, she will remain there, for life.

When I met up with her on a one-to-one basis for the first time, she had brought along with her the meagre amount of detail which was held about me from the file. I felt like snatching it out of her hands in my eagerness to read it. Instead I listened while she read out what was written before passing it over for me to have. What was there would scarcely fill a standard A4 piece of paper.

It was presented as a list of dates in the margin with notes logged beside each one. The first date written was the 28 April 1972. The day after I was born.

It read that there seemed to be a debate going on between my parents on whether I should be taken home from the hospital and a warning from the authorities on the couple's *'general situation in this case'*. A meeting was set up for the beginning of May between Gordon and Social Services but it then went on to say that he could not attend due to having *'too much to do'*.

The penultimate date listed is 24 May 1972:

Baby admitted under Section 15. Taken from Rottenrow Maternity Unit to Blairvadach, Rhu.

Phrases are used in the Social Work file pertaining to my natural parents such as *'no trace of any favourable change in their attitude'* and *'still living in a world of make believe'*. It seemed that a warning was put to my parents regarding my future welfare and a question put to them, asking *'where their priorities were'*.

The notes end on a date in November 1973 when I would have been nearly eighteen months old. It said that my parents had been re-housed and detailed a little more on my mother's ill health. It ends with some optimistic wording about there appearing to be a *'favourable change in attitudes'* and that, although my mother was still very unstable, that with the correct support, she may still be able to *'care for me'*.

Jill asked me how it felt to read this but I was unable to properly articulate what I was feeling. I wanted to cry, however, releasing my pent-up emotion and allowing my tears to fall in front of Jill was something I was physically unable to do, frustrating though that was for both her and for me.

In actual fact, it took around three years of knowing Jill before I was able to cry in her presence. I think this was because ultimately, I was afraid to reveal my vulnerability for fear of losing her. Instinct fought hard against core belief and I held tightly to my emotional independence. This is how my life in foster care had taught me, so well, to be. My foster parents taught me how not to be true to myself.

I took the pages home and put them into the folder where I was placing the information I gathered on my past, a place where I could carefully store and catalogue everything I found.

Jill then advised me that the next step to finding out my origins was to visit Register House in Edinburgh. So with hope and anticipation coursing through my brain I took the train into Edinburgh, completely unsure of what to expect.

The building was huge and imposing and I very quickly realised that my resolve was going to be challenged at every possible turn as I steeled myself to step inside. I had no idea what to do and felt immediately intimidated by its grand and lavish interior. I was completely out of my comfort zone.

Moreover, I was unprepared and unexpectedly taken off guard when my deepest emotions were surprisingly quick to surface. I approached the woman behind the desk and announced my request regarding gaining my mother's details. After a brief couple of questions to me, the lady produced the actual Adoption Certificate for my mother on her computer screen. Within just a few seconds and with a few innocuous taps on her keyboard, the lady turned the screen towards me and there it was in black and white. I went from having nothing, to looking at my mother's name written right there in front of me.

'So there's her name, date and place of birth, and adoptive parents' names.'

I almost passed out. I could hardly read the words through the tears welling in my eyes. My hands were shaking and her voice seemed to resonate in my ears. My head began to spin.

I could hardly believe it. For the first time in my life, my natural mother had come closer to being a real person and not just an invisible fragment of air. The lady at the desk was kind and must have noticed my shaky response. She led me to a circular room lined with computers where there were people silently beavering away at their own research and with large desks in the centre. She gently explained how to work the computers to retrieve the relevant records and told me that there would be someone there to help me with my work at any time, should I need assistance.

It was staggering to learn how easy it was to obtain copies of certificates held at Register House. My mind was buzzing with possibilities and my imagination was off on a tangent. I looked up Gordon's birth record and then my own birth record, printing out a copy of my own to take home with me for my folder. I then saw the eldest twins' birth record, which gave me their father's name together with the date and place he and my mother were married.

Everything was coming along so well and I was feeling so confident that I was going to piece together such a large part of my family tree all in that one day, when I was abruptly faced with disappointment. I was told that I was not entitled to see a copy of my own mother's birth certificate, for confidentiality reasons, due to the fact that she had been adopted. I stated that I was her daughter and that she was deceased but the lady was emphatic and refused to budge. That beautiful elation I had felt at seeing her name was gone, replaced with a dejected acceptance of defeat. How could I gain information about my past without knowing my mother's birth name? 'It's not fair' was a cliché I was to find myself saying many times throughout my journey. It was exceptionally infuriating to know that the information I so badly needed was held right there in the same building where I was sitting and yet I could not get my hands on it.

When I returned home my mind meandered back down a familiar route of feeling very alone, disconnected and there being no one I could tell. Having a total stranger, someone with no connection to me whatsoever, tell me that the law dictates that I am not entitled to view my natural mother's birth record brought back old feelings of being worth nothing and very unimportant. What it actually confirmed was that being in care meant being stripped of everything that resembles family. It is like being ostracised from the one most basic, fundamental entity, which is as natural as taking in air, and here I was choking on it.

These feelings may well have been amplified by the fact that my eldest child was passing through ages that had been so intrinsically harder for me when I was her age. I could not help myself from marvelling at her exquisite innocence and casual attitude to her young life. She was now nearly eleven and was changing, growing, and her blissful complacency and contentment was sort of mystifying to me. The normality of our lives, though fitting and apt, I think would always be, to a certain degree, somewhat bewildering for me. For despite the fact that I truly adored my little family and loved the happiness which reverberated round my own home, the sadness I felt for the mountain of missing moments I had as a child was always there just below the surface.

The not knowing, the hoping, the yearning for my mother seemed to intensify and the dagger of determination twisted my defeated heart back to life. I was spurred back into action. So began a new and what ultimately turned out to be, a very long and agonising search for my own identity.

After the disappointment and deflation of my visit to Register House, I decided I would see if it would be possible to find my mother's grave. When I told my husband this, I confessed that I really had no idea where to even begin looking and that all I knew from her death record was the address in Glasgow where she had died. My husband told me that I should telephone the Bereavement and Cemeteries section of Glasgow City Council, giving them the details I had from her death certificate. This I did the very next day and was grateful to speak to a lady who was very good at her job and sympathetic towards my story.

'I am looking for my mother's grave. I realise it must sound strange that I don't know where my own mum is buried.' I said.

Nevertheless, this lady was immediately understanding and asked me, 'Were you adopted?'

Even though it was not strictly correct, I did not see it necessary to go into details about my being in permanent foster care and instead I simply relied, 'Yes.'

I was very lucky because this wonderfully attentive lady knew exactly what was required. She asked me to telephone again the next day at about three o'clock and to be sure to ask for her. She continued by saying that really, my request should be put into a queue and that she was not actually supposed to do this, but that she would see what she could find out for me. On calling the next day at three o'clock on the dot, the news I received was incredible.

'I've found your mum,' she wasted no time in saying. 'She is in Lambhill Cemetery in Maryhill.'

The lady then provided me with the lair and plot numbers. She then gave me the cemetery groundsman's name and telephone number, explaining that she had already spoken with him and that he had agreed that he would meet me there and show me directly to the grave. She also told me that my mother was buried in the same plot as her own adoptive parents. I could barely express my gratitude and decided that I would send her a card with my message of thanks and stating that at last due to her efficient care and attention to my request, I was going to be as close to my mother as I ever dared myself to believe.

It was with a sense of urgency, on a cold, bleak, wet and windy day in early December when I travelled through to Glasgow, to the cemetery, with an optimistic expectation of seeing my mother's name on her headstone and romanticising about the comfort that surely would bring. My husband had offered to come with me but I was definite that I wanted to go alone because at least that way I would have the freedom to let out whatever emotions I needed to without feeling inhibited. As promised, there was a man waiting to meet me to guide me through the large cemetery to where my mother's grave was. I followed his van in my car. The cemetery rose steeply and then sloped away as we continued down to the furthest edge where the neat rows of headstones stopped and the patchwork of fields began. When his van came to a halt, the man climbed out, pointed to the correct spot and stated, 'There's no headstone there.'

He did not wait for any response to this, but simply got back into his van and drove back up over the hill and out of sight.

Once again I was consumed with bitter disillusionment: the scene was harsh and brutal. There was, as the man declared, no headstone, only a solitary piece of wood sticking out of the muddy ground displaying the plot number. The cold air bit my ears, my lips, my nose, but it scarcely registered as I was engulfed with a sadness that felt so depressing it enveloped my heart and made me cry hot, heavy tears. I cried out loud, bent over with a genuine physical pain that felt crippling. I crouched down and laid my hands in the cold wet grass, desperate to feel a connection. There was nothing. By now the rain was driving down and the light was fading but this did not force me to leave. It felt like I was the only person in the world and could have stayed there unseen forever. The only noise came from the constant, howling wind which itself seemed to be the sound of God, crying at the dispirited spectacle which I must have looked, in a place where so many souls were laid. I looked around at all the varying headstone designs with their poignant words of loved ones missed and cried all the more that there had been no one who valued my mother enough to leave their permanent mark of love for her.

'I'm sorry. I'm so sorry, Mum,' I said loudly through my tears.

It was right in that moment when the idea struck me. I would put a stone in place myself.

'I promise I'll put this right,' I cried.

This was something I would do for my mother.

The next day I had an arrangement set for a meeting with Jill. I had previously told her that I would be taking a trip to visit my mother's grave and she, like my husband, had concerns that I was going by myself. However, Jill knew me well enough by then to be aware of my somewhat stubborn strength of will to go it alone. Despite this, I was grateful to be able to describe the situation I found myself in at the grave site and although I wanted to pour out all my emotions of that day, all I found myself saying was, 'It was quite hard.'

Feeble!

I was still having enormous difficulty with outwardly expressing the feelings which were most overwhelming for me, even though I was in the company of the one person with whom I felt safest.

I wasted no time in going ahead with organising the headstone and with my determined frame of mind driving me forward, I valiantly stepped into the local stonemason outlet. I donned my most authoritative voice and stated that I would like to put a headstone at the grave of my mother.

Admittedly this, in itself, proved to be a messy business as I needed to do a little explaining about why it had taken thirty years since the time of my mother's death for someone to get around to requesting that a stone be placed and the reasons why I, her youngest child, wanted to do it now.

Nonetheless, after putting myself through this awkwardness, I was yet again faced with more bad news. The lady had taken me into a tiny cramped office which was set up with a computer and brochures and was all ready to guide me through the various options when she stopped, turned to me, and said, 'I'm sorry, but you can't put a stone in place because you are not the owner of the lair. It is only the person who is in possession of the title deeds to the lair who can do this.'

When I said that I could not possibly know who that person could be, she stated that it would be my mother's first-born child. She continued by explaining that in order for me to place the stone, I would need to have my sibling sign a form of indemnity which would state that the permission had been passed on to me.

'Who is your mother's first-born?' she asked me.

A direct question which, if put to the average person, would have a direct answer but to me could only heap more unanswered questions on top of the ones I already had piling up inside my brain.

'All I know is that her name is Rhona. Apart from that I have no information about her and I've absolutely no idea where she is now. I have never even met her.' I sighed. 'I probably couldn't even find her. I wouldn't know where to begin.'

When I began on this exceedingly rocky journey, I never imagined that I would come up against so many obstacles. The only information I possessed on the children my mother had before she met my own father was the sheet of paper which the social worker had given me when I was fifteen, with their names, the year of their births and the city where they were born written down on it. There was nothing else to go on and before now, I had not imagined that I would ever have a reason to look for my eldest, half-sister. Yet here I was standing in front of the proverbial brick wall knowing that if I was going to be able to honour my promise of giving my mother the memorial she deserved, I would need to find a way to trace Rhona.

Around this time, while driving along in my car with my little boy sitting in the back seat chatting away to me, out of nowhere he said to me, 'Mummy, we all had to stand up in class one by one and tell the teacher who our heroes were and everyone was saying their football hero or some pop star. But I told the teacher that my Mummy is my hero because she loves me and does so much for me.'

A lesson I have been taught while on this journey is that at times when I find I am drowning in doubt, a lifeline is often thrown, strong enough to pluck me out of despair and back to a place where all is well and right and just as it should be. From the smallest ounce of unconditional love can come just the right amount of courage I needed to keep on going and to hold firm to my resolve.

Chapter Five

O
n every step of my journey, I have had consistent guidance and support from Jill, who has been like a rock to me, a permanent fixture who I could rely on and who has provided a kind of stability whenever things seemed impossibly hard to bear. She had a way of rationalising things so that I could better manage them and instinctively always knew what to say no matter what the situation. Moreover, whenever she felt that I needed it, when my head was disappearing into the clouds and she could see that my own rationale was running away with the fairies, she would not be afraid to say the things I did not want to hear. Reigning me back in. Keeping me grounded. And I almost always listened to Jill! Although there were times when I heard her advice but did not follow it because my heart was fixed on whatever it was that I needed to do. However, she never sat in judgement and she never failed to be there when I needed her most.

During one of my earliest meetings with Jill she asked me a particularly difficult question.

'What does it feel like to have been in permanent foster care?'

At that time I could not answer her. I was unable find the right words that would properly convey my true feelings. All I could reply was, 'It hurts.'

A few years on, when I put my mind to answering that question, I decided it was time to be brave and to speak openly and honestly about what it was actually like for me. Jill had always told me that whenever I needed to do something significant I would instinctively know when it was the right time, and at that time I felt ready to write down exactly what was genuinely inside me. This is what I wrote:

Being in permanent foster care was like having a murky shadow following me around everywhere I went. It was my one constant. A threat left hanging, waiting to be carried out. It was tenuous, never absolute. It was like living in a permanent state of limbo. I could not live with my birth parents, nor would I ever be adopted. I felt worthless and very much unwanted. It is strange now in a way because I am an adult, a wife and a mother yet somehow it has never gone away because I still 'feel' fostered.

Being that rejected new born baby in the hospital, never having even been held by my own mother and knowing that she could not even look at me, I can tell now that a part of me died. Then when I was relinquished over to the children's home, another part of me was broken. Then going from that situation, to my foster family, literally annihilated any hopes of gaining a sense of belonging.

Jealousy is a very salient and prevalent feeling. It stings my eyes and burns my throat. Listening to anyone talk of their own parents or siblings, especially at Christmas or birthdays, is so hard and makes me want to cry for myself. The pain of this reaches deep down to the very core of me, stirring up feelings of vulnerability and of being isolated and alone.

Another prominent feeling throughout my life has been the deep, deep sorrow of not being connected to anyone, because not only was I severed from my mother, but also cut off from my roots, my origins and my true self and I was helpless to do anything about it. As a child I very sadly searched for some kind of connection from people outwith my foster family. It is only now that I can identify why I craved it, because I so desperately needed to reconnect with my own mother, but I intuitively already knew that it would never happen. Now, armed with knowledge of the truth, I feel phlegmatic because it is like hearing something which I unconsciously already knew. The affirmation seemed almost as pivotal for me as the very act itself.

For too long I believed that I was the cause of it all, that I was to blame. I thought that I was being punished for being born because there was no room for me, so I was discarded, thrown in with a foster family and forgotten about. As if I had never existed.

The confirmation validated why I always seek reassurance. Why I am constantly hypervigilant against any kind of rejection and why I am extremely fearful of abandonment. It had already happened to me and it was thereafter consistently reinforced and exacerbated. I positively ached to be good *enough for love, affection, brains, but God said no, you cannot have that. So when bad things happened to me, I thought they were supposed to happen to me. I thought that was what I was born for. It is crippling to remember this.*

Any kind of touch felt painfully confusing. It was either completely denied, rejected or it hurt. So even the mere offer of a hand was extremely uncomfortable, because although I wanted it so much I could not believe the intentions were safe. Doubt overwhelms me, rendering even an ounce of trust almost impossible. As a child, watching my peers happily receive affection was excruciating. I so badly wanted to feel special like them. I would stand and stare, transfixed in a dream-like place where I was that child and their mum was my mum, wrapping her love around me. I have had to teach myself how to give affection and about how much feels alright to receive.

With my own children I am perhaps a little more over-protective and affectionate. My praise is a bit more emphasised and my need for honesty and to be open is more profound than may be usual. I never want them to have any of the negative emotions which I experienced. I just want to flood them with all my repressed love and care and warmth.

I think these feelings I have described are ambivalent because they vacillate between the initial separation and the events which followed. It seems difficult to separately define both.

I was glad to have written this. It was cathartic to at last find the nerve to do so. It brought a real sense of a shedding of secrecy. I had grown up hardly mentioning it to anyone and living with an entrenched, unspoken rule that being fostered was not allowed to be spoken about. Now, not only had I put down onto paper my honest genuine thoughts and emotions, but I had passed it onto Jill to read. Even though I could not help feeling just a little anxious, it was truly liberating.

Since then, I have used an analysis to describe what it feels like to have been in care. It goes along the lines of being like a kite without a string. Whenever you see a kite flying in the sky you know that there is a string attached to it and that if you track the string you will always find that someone has a hold of it. The kite belongs to that person and they are guiding it, holding tightly, careful not to let it fly away from them. I am someone who is freely float-ing through the air with no one holding onto to me. I am attached to nothing and no one.

During one of my meetings with Jill, I had taken my folder in with me and we were busy looking through it at all the information I had collected to date. Jill marvelled at all the hard work I had done. On studying my mother's adop-tion certificate, she suddenly suggested the idea of applying to Glasgow Sheriff Court where it was noted my mother's adoption had taken place, for access to her adoption papers. I would never have known that this was even an option and understandably, I was filled with a renewed excitement of finding out more about her. Jill warned me that there may be very little information contained in the papers but that it would be worth it in order to, at the very least, find out her birth name.

Jill asked me if I would like her to write to the Sheriff Clerk on my behalf and I absolutely did not hesitate in my agreement for her to go ahead. In just a few weeks, their return letter was received by Jill. It requested that I write a letter stating my own personal reasons for seeking to view the papers. So I duly wrote my letter with honesty, putting down the facts, including my deep longing for the truth. Then I tried to be patient.

After what seemed like an eternity but was actually only a couple of months, I received their response. It stated that on receipt of my letter they had applied for and received my mother's adoption papers from Edinburgh's Register Office.

I was asked to attend an interview with the Sheriff in order to explain to her in person my reasons and ask that she grant me permission to view my mother's adoption papers. The meeting was set for a Friday in early April. With my spirits soaring, I telephoned Jill who said that she would change her days for work that week, so that she would be available to come along with me for support.

Jill and I arranged to meet at the train station in Glasgow and travel to the Sheriff Court by taxi. The Court was an unusual, contemporary building which from the outside looked nothing like a Court, more like an ordinary office building and even less so when first entering the large spacious reception area with its massive central desk. We were directed to an escalator and up to the first floor where we were met by a lady who would introduce me to the Sheriff. Jill remained at the desk while I was shown in to the office.

The Sheriff had an impressive office with a desk at one side of the room and a conference table and chairs at the other. She was a small officious-looking lady who was petite and smartly dressed with shoulder-length blond hair. In my mind's eye, I had foreseen a no-nonsense, broad shouldered person fully regaled in traditional court robes and wig with me standing before them prepared to fight my corner!

The Sheriff stood behind her desk when we entered, which was strewn with official looking Court documents, and while she politely shook my hand, she glared at the lady who had brought me in. I got the impression that we had abruptly interrupted her, distracting her attention away from something of a much higher prominence. She slowly re-read my original letter of enquiry and as I patiently waited I must say I could not help feeling just a slight degree of insignificance. Then, when she had finished reading, she looked at me and said,

'Of course you may see the papers and I wish you the very best of luck with your search.'

I did not have to say a single word except, of course, to say thank you. It really was that simple!

I was then led back down the corridor to where Jill was and we were both shown to a much smaller, very narrow room which was quite the reverse from the office I had just been in. It contained merely a desk with two chairs and nothing else. The lady then retrieved the papers and brought them to us in the small room. They were held inside an archaic-looking rectangular brown envelope sealed with the official Court stamp. The lady broke the wax seal for the very first time in over seventy years, stating that it was not permitted for me to break the seal myself. It was evident that even though I was the youngest of eight children, no one before me had ever requested to see the papers. It felt like a tremendous privilege.

When the lady placed the papers down in front of us, the initial thing that struck me was my mother's birth name. It was completely different to the one on her adoption certificate, the name she had apparently used all her life, the one which Gordon had known her by. For the briefest of moments, I thought they had brought me the wrong papers until Jill explained that not so long ago, it was fairly common practice for adoptive parents to change the name of their adopted child.

It was a beautiful name: Elizabeth Hay. I could not believe they had changed it. I felt bewildered that they would rob her of her identity in this way.

Before I read the adoption certificate I first read the affidavit which gave an over view of the information on the original adoption certificate and the terms put down allowing for permission for me to view it. A warm sense of pride washed over me at reading the word 'daughter', as I had never before heard or seen that word written, pertaining to myself and my mother. I was indeed her daughter. What a new feeling that was. I turned to Jill.

'Look Jill, I actually was her daughter. They've written that I was her daughter. I've never actually thought of myself being referred to as anyone's daughter before.'

My foster mother had only ever referred to me as being her 'youngest'.

On my mother's adoption certificate, her own birth mother's name was, of course, written there: Muriel Ritchie Hay.

Some years on when I had reached deeper into my research, I was heartened to learn that Muriel's mother was also called Elizabeth and that Muriel had given her baby daughter her own mother's name. However, I also felt sad knowing that her baby would be forever lost to her and that this special name was taken away from her baby when she was adopted.

The moment I learned of my mother's birth name I fell in love with it. I considered it to be a much softer name than Irene, which was her adoptive name. Had I known about it at the right time, I would have given it to my own daughter so that it could have been kept within the family. This would have been something I could have done for my mother. It was just another missed opportunity. Nevertheless, when I told my daughter this story she turned to me and said, 'Mum, I promise that if I ever have a baby girl, I will give her the name Elizabeth.'

Some time later, she confessed that now she knew her grandmother's birth name, this was the one she held in her mind whenever she thought of her. This was also true for me.

On further reading the certificate, I learned that my grandmother had fallen pregnant when she was just fifteen years old and was sixteen at the time of my mother's birth. I guessed that this was very likely to be the reason why my mother was put up for adoption. It made me wonder about how much support my grandmother had received from her own parents and how terribly heart-breaking it must have been for her to hand her baby over. Jill told me that it looked as if it may have been a private adoption, which meant that the adoptive parents were already known to the family and the arrangement was put in place during Muriel's pregnancy. My mother was three weeks old when she went to live with her adoptive parents, William and Edith. The adoption became official about one year later. I then read a small and very heartening sentence: 'Muriel provided £5 towards an outfit for baby Elizabeth.'

On reading those words, I felt a tugging on my heart. I knew there was a connection in me to that tiny newborn baby being taken away from her mother, just as I had been taken away from her.

Then out of the blue, Jill asked, 'Do you have a camera on your mobile phone?'

To which I replied, 'Yes.'

'How about taking a photograph of the papers, since it is not permitted to take any photocopies?' she said in a low voice.

'Okay.' I whispered back, unaccustomed to this mischievous side to her normally serious character.

What a palaver we had! Jill laid the papers neatly on the desk and then said, 'There you are, I'll keep a look out.'

As I surreptitiously took my photos, I initially struggled with the video/camera icons on my mobile telephone. Back then I was not used to using my mobile for taking photographs and I mistakenly found myself taking a video of them while wondering why I was not hearing the clicking sound of the camera. For anyone watching us, we could have been acting a sketch right out of a comedy!

The photographs turned out much better than I had predicted under the circumstances and they are now kept inside my folder and form an important part of my story. Before handing my mother's precious adoption papers back to the lady, to be returned to storage, I had an impulse to kiss them and although Jill saw this, she just kindly smiled and said nothing.

Back at the train station, Jill and I said our goodbyes. She gave me a hug and said, 'Thank you for the privilege of allowing me to share this experience with you. It would never have been the same if you had simply described it to me.'

What I neglected to say to her at the time was that the experience would not have been the same without her and I was so very glad that she was with me.

With the information I had gained from my visit to the Sheriff Court, I eagerly took myself back to Register House in Edinburgh to see what more I could find out about my mother's natural family. My grandmother, as I said, was only sixteen when she gave birth to my mother in 1934, which coincidently is the same year in which my father-in-law was born. Once I had a hold of my mother's birth certificate I was then provided with my grandmother's occupation, which was stated as being an underclothing saleswoman. It also gave my mother's place of birth and the address in Glasgow where Muriel was living at that time. There was nothing written in the space where my mother's father's name should be.

Next I searched for and retrieved my grandmother's birth certificate and from that I discovered that her own father's name was William Scott Hay and he had married her mother Elizabeth Ritchie McEwen in Glasgow in 1917. William's occupation at the time that Muriel was born was stated as Marine Engineer and Lieutenant in the Royal Air Force. It also stated the address in Glasgow where Muriel was born.

When I told my husband of my great grandfather's occupation, he was very interested in the information regarding the Royal Air Force and urged me to track down his military service records. He told me I needed to apply to the National Archives in England by letter, requesting that they be kind enough to post on the records to me. He even stated that he would be prepared for us to travel down to London to retrieve them, should this turn out to be necessary.

I have to admit that learning that my great-grandfather had been a Lieutenant did instil just the smallest optimism that despite all the negativity associated with so much of what I was learning of my mother's life, that her own birth mother had perhaps originally come from an exceedingly respectable and very comfortable background. I surmised that very sadly things might have only begun to go terribly wrong when she became pregnant at such a young age.

The service records arrived by registered post only a few weeks after I sent off my request. They came in an exceptionally large, white cardboard envelope with the words National Archive in large letters across the top. There was a small note attached by paperclip, written by the officials at the Archives which read, 'Please note that these documents contain information which may cause distress.'

The records read that my great-grandfather was active predominantly in wireless communications, deciphering code and training up recruits in this, but that he did not actually fly due to a heart condition. In explanation to the note attached to the papers, there was also a line in the records which mentioned evidence of a sexually transmitted disease. All manner of scenarios played out in my mind on reading those scandalous words!

From the records held in Register house, I learned that William Scott Hay died in Newton Mearns in 1960, aged sixty-four. Intriguingly, his death certificate states that he was no longer married to my great-grandmother Elizabeth Ritchie McEwen but to an Italian lady by the name of Norah Ellen Vollar or Coia. Did that supposedly fine, upstanding gentleman, who I think perhaps may have turned out his own sixteen-year-old daughter for disgracing the family by becoming pregnant, actually bring shame on himself by having an affair while away from his family during the war? I looked but could not find any record of this new wife's death.

I was to find out, much later on, that my great-grandmother had in fact died and that there had been no secret affair after all. Had it turned out to be true, it would have provided a delicious slice of irony to the story.

Despite a rigorous search, I have failed to find any record of a marriage or a death for my grandmother, Muriel, within the Register Office. It is as though, after she handed over her baby and at the exceptionally vulnerable age of just sixteen, she simply stepped off planet Earth and disappeared. She must surely have gone on to live out her life after this traumatic time had passed. I could not allow myself to believe that she did not eventually go on to meet someone and get married and to have had more children. With this thought in my mind, it led me to wonder whether my grandmother ever spoke of giving away an illegitimate child at such a tender age, or if it was to be her guarded secret for the rest of her life.

Since I had gained so many certificates from Register House it raised my curiosity about whether any of the addresses were still in existence. So I bought a road map of Glasgow and began by looking up the address where my grandmother was born. Out of all the streets that were mentioned in the records, my grandmother's birth place sounded the most posh. I was right. I was completely astonished to find that it was in one of the most affluent areas of Glasgow. Impatient as always, I jumped into my car at the first chance I got and drove back to Glasgow to see for myself what the address looked like. I was stunned. The building was situated within a row of whitewashed, three storey, semi-detached houses in the opulent Claremont Crescent in the East End of Glasgow. The crescent had its own private, locked gardens. There were expensive vehicles in front of each residence and each one was flanked by pillars and personal placards flirting quirky names for their homes. I literally swore out loud as I stood in the street with my camera taking photographs to place inside my folder. This was where the cream of society lived and it bowled me over. I tried to imagine my grandmother walking in and out of the property and wished that I could walk right up to the door, ring the bell and find a relative still in residence there.

Since that day, I have used the internet to look deeper into the history of this property and have discovered, through the Royal Commission on the Ancient and Historical Monuments of Scotland, that in the year of my grandmother's birth the property served as Woodlands Nursing Home. The Home was run from three of the buildings on the Crescent. In confirmation of this, I also found another link on a website which held mention of a gentleman who had spent time there as a patient and who had died at the Home. All my imaginings of my grandmother having lived at Claremont Crescent were in fact false as it turned out that she had merely been born there, or at least this is the conclusion I drew from the fact that it had been a nursing home and not a place of residence.

I then used my map to find the address where my grandmother lived when she was pregnant with my mother. This was in stark contrast to the Claremont Crescent address where she had been born. She was by then living in Kirkland Terrace, an old red brick tenement building with a shared entry hallway and a communal area to the rear, where there were clothes lines and coal cellars. It was difficult to imagine how it would have looked back in 1934, but standing there now, I got the impression that it would not be so tranquil a place to live. I thought of my grandmother, heavily pregnant, walking in and out of that very door and I wondered how she must have felt. Was that poor girl put out by her parents? Did they cut all ties or did they provide the place where she lived? I suppose the answers will stay locked away, forever immersed in obscurity. While I stood in the street in front of the tenement, taking my photographs, two men were busy working in the neighbouring garden, an elderly gent and a younger man. For a while they watched what I was doing with a look of suspicion, eventually asking, 'You okay there, hen?'

I explained my presence and reasons for taking my photographs to which they replied, 'Gosh, it's just like that TV show, Who Do You Think You Are!'

Next I went to find the address where my own mother was born. This was situated right in the very heart of Glasgow near the Great Western Road and consisted of a row of grey brick tenements in Burnbank Terrace. I took my photographs and again used the internet to look up the history of this address, but unfortunately the Royal Commission on the Ancient and Historical Monuments of Scotland stated that there was no information to be found. However, they did provide me with an old photograph of the tenements, taken around the time when my mother would have been born, complete with an old nineteen thirties truck parked on the street in front of the address. Furthermore, I was very lucky some years later to be speaking with a lady who informed me that she knew for a fact that Burnbank Terrace was run as a hospital because she herself had been there many years ago as a child to have some dentistry work done. So it was confirmed for me that this address was the hospital where my mother was born.

The last address I visited that day, using my trusty map, was Edgefauld Road in Springburn, which is noted on my mother's death certificate as where she died. This time, the area had been completely transformed. The old tenement buildings had all gone several years before and were now replaced with grass and trees. All I could do was stop my car and try to get a feel of what it would have been like which, of course, was impossible but just being there in the same area where my own mother had passed away was poignant enough. Very close to this was a street once called Reidhouse Street, which was the address where my mother's adoptive parents had lived when they were given my mother as a tiny baby. This address was also gone and instead there now stood what looked like a modern nursing home for the elderly. This served to remind me just how long ago it was since my mother had died. As I am writing these words, I am aware that had my mother still been alive today, she would be turning eighty years old.

Once I had returned home after my adventure driving around Glasgow in search of those profoundly important addresses which were etched into the history of my family, I was exhausted. It was another challenge I had undertaken completely on my own, into areas of a large city which I was not at all familiar with, but yet always held a fundamental, eternal connection with me, silently drawing me back to where all my roots lay. Whenever I had found myself lost at various moments during my trip, I never panicked. I felt very calm and in control and would simply pull over, take a note of the name of the street I was in and follow this on my map until I reached my destination. I was suddenly very aware of how relaxed and at home I felt whenever I was in Glasgow, something which remains the same to this day.

Chapter Six

Since my difficult visit to the grave, I had been mulling over the idea of tracing my mother's eldest child, Rhona, who is my half-sister and who is fourteen years my senior. I had happened to be speaking to a friend about this particular issue, saying that although I did really want to find her, I truly had no idea how to go about it. My friend told me that she knew the Salvation Army carried out tracing services and I should give them a call. So when I returned home that very same day, that is exactly what I did. I spoke to a lady who, after establishing from me that my sister had not been adopted, said they would be glad to help and said she would post the appropriate form for me to fill out and send back. I explained to the lady that the only details I had on my half-sister were her name and the place and year of birth. The lady reassured me, 'Oh, don't worry about that. This is a lot more to go on than we often have.'

Despite my initial impatience to get things moving in my quest to find Rhona and thereby to be able to put the headstone in place, it was to take me one whole year after being in receipt of the form from the Salvation Army tracing service to actually summon the courage to fill it out and to send it off. I was learning something new about myself. Often when faced with a new idea to further my research, I would charge ahead without taking any time to think things through. Then, regardless of my impatience, the inevitable hesitancy would creep in. Always, I would end up needing the assistance of Jill or my husband, to ground me, to help me take a deep breath and to steady my racing thoughts. I had discovered that I have an impulsive streak, which is almost always over shadowed by self-doubt.

Once I had finally taken the plunge and sent off the form, I was filled with a renewed sense of anticipation. Rhona was indeed the owner of my mother's lair and that had been the foremost thing in my mind when I had first realised a need to trace her. However, the realisation was setting in that if found this person who, until that moment, had simply represented a name on a piece of paper, she was going to become flesh and blood. Moreover, it was very likely going to be the case that I was someone who she never knew existed. Also, there were no guarantees that she was going to want to know me, let alone assist in putting a stone at our mother's grave. All I could do was wait and try my best to be patient.

Astonishingly, though, I was stunned when it took only three months to receive a reply from the Agency. They had successfully traced Rhona. In their responding letter they stated that Rhona had asked me to send a letter to her introducing myself and inviting her to write to me in return. I could hardly believe it. She wanted to know me. I was on the ceiling! My heart was dancing and I could not stop smiling. A mountain of possibilities was opening up in front of me and my mind was racing with a hundred questions. It felt so incredible that I had managed to track down a half-sister who before then had felt so far removed from me. I had never dared to imagine that it would be possible to find her. I wondered if perhaps there might even be a chance that I would at last see a photograph of my mother.

'You are so going to have to calm down,' my husband said as I spun round the kitchen feeling deliriously happy.

By now the summer holidays were in full swing and we were preparing to have a barbecue that afternoon as the weather had turned sunny and warm.

'I refuse!' I replied. 'I have waited my whole life for this and I'm gonna celebrate.'

I wanted to rush out of the door, climb onto my roof and shout it to the world. Instead, I jumped into my car and drove to my friend's house. Almost bursting through her door, I blurted, 'I've found my sister, I never thought I would ever find her.'

She was speechless. She just hugged me tightly, eventually managing to say that she was 'so very happy for me'.

I was desperate to tell Jill that I had found Rhona as I was sure that she would be equally as amazed as I was. I had to bide my time, however, as she worked part-time hours and would not be in work that day. When I did get a chance to give her my exciting news her reaction was rather too restrained under the circumstances and I felt she was acting very cavalier, given the magnitude of what I was telling her.

'Wow! They were quick to find her and her letter sounds positive.'

I had to remind myself that Jill is a social worker, that she is a professional and while she has my very best interests at heart, she must encourage caution and prepare me for every scenario whenever she considers it necessary.

'Are you happy for me?' I asked, feeling a degree of irritation at what I perceived as a somewhat understated response coupled with the fact that I was not getting the satisfaction of sharing my joy with her.

'I'll be happy when I see that it all turns out well for you,' she said.

Jill did not always say the words that I wanted to hear!

My family and I were due to go off on our summer holiday the very next week so before we left I wrote my letter to Rhona and posted it off. I kept this initial contact a general one, talking about my family, how I had spent the first part of my life in a children's home and then in permanent foster care and then about where I worked. I asked her similar questions about her life and went on to say a little about the amount of work I had done so far in my research. I had such a good and very positive feeling about her and felt in my heart that it was going to go well. On our return from holiday two weeks later, the first thing I did was search through our mail to see if she had written back to me. Her letter had indeed arrived. My husband had not even had a chance to bring in the cases from the car before I ran out and showed him the envelope with her letter inside and the tell-tale Glasgow post mark at the top. I briefly admired her neat handwriting before opening the envelope, careful to use a letter opener so as not to tear the paper.

Rhona's letter was welcoming and wonderful. Excitement surged through me and again I simply could not stop smiling as I firstly scanned her letter and then slowly read her words again. Rhona confirmed that I was right about her not knowing anything of my existence. She wrote that she knew a little about the twins, Joanna and Edith, but said that she did not know that she had 'another little sister'. She went on to tell me that she too had spent time in a children's home in Glasgow and had then gone on to live in foster care. She mentioned that she had two grown-up boys of her own and that she was a grandmother to two little boys, who she stated are her 'whole world'. Her letter ended with the words 'I'm enclosing my phone number, please call anytime.'

Jill suggested that it might be best to start off by telephoning each other back and forth, once a week, to get to know one another a little before meeting face to face. Again she was telling me something I did not want to listen to. I was impatient and just wanted to set a time and place for us to meet.

Nevertheless, after sending a letter putting Jill's suggestion to Rhona and passing on my telephone number, I was absolutely elated when I received the very first telephone call from my own sister. Rhona was very softly spoken and had that strong Glasgow lilt I remembered noticing in

Joanna and Edith. She told me that the moment she heard she had another little sister she could hardly believe it. She said she immediately told her best friend and that the two women just cried and hugged each other. She then asked me if there were any more siblings who she was unaware of, but I assured her that I was definitely the last one.

The elation I was feeling was short-lived, though, when unexpectedly and rather hastily, Rhona told me about her unhappy, complicated early childhood with our mother and her father. Her father was a gambler and our mother suffered from a severe mental illness. This situation eventually led to her being put into care, aged just six years old. Rhona told me that the first set of twins our mother had were separated as babies, Avril being adopted and Sandra joining Rhona in foster care. She told me that she had met the twins Bruce and Hazel only for a brief spell in their adult lives and that as far as she could remember, they had been together in foster care in Aberdeen and had since moved to live in England. She said she had lost contact with them some years ago. Rhona proceeded to relay a childhood steeped in uncertainty, moving from the children's home, to one temporary foster home with Sandra and then another long term placement in Fife, where the two girls suffered intolerable cruelty and abuse. When she 'escaped back to Glasgow', Rhona was just sixteen years old. Rhona had managed to find Avril living in Glasgow and told me that when Avril's adopted parents invited Rhona to 'live with them', she had gone back for Sandra and brought her to live with her in Avril's home. As she spoke her voice did not falter. I was frozen.

This news completely broke my heart and made me cry for the sisters whose faces I had never seen. Rhona's words brought back the heaviness in my stomach. I was coming to understand, at this juncture, that my heart was going to be broken many times over as I trawled my way through my intrepid journey in pursuit of the truth.

With my sister's permission I have written her words here. However, to expand on this would be a betrayal of trust as I feel very deeply that to go any further would be to go into Rhona and Sandra's own personal stories and this is something for them to tell and not me.

Our lives were separate. We knew nothing of each other when we were all growing up. Now, no matter how close we may become in the future, our reality remains that we were strangers for a hugely significant part of our lives and may perhaps remain so.

I guessed that this was a potential reality which Jill was attempting to prepare me for when she was so hesitant at my elated announcement of finding Rhona.

After a few weeks of taking turns to call each other, Rhona and I met in Glasgow with Jill along as a support for both of us. This initial meeting with each other did not pan out quite as I imagined it would. In my mind, I dreamed of it being the way it always was in the movies—which I suppose was simply my imagination getting carried away again. What actually happened was that we literally bumped into each other round the corner from the hotel where we had planned to meet. The hotel was just outside the railway station and as Jill and I were making our way there, Rhona walked right passed us. We both had a fleeting glance at each other and immediately recognised one another from the photographs we had sent in our letters. It was surreal. After a small degree of awkwardness we hugged one another warmly.

It was mind-boggling to see that we were fairly similar in looks. We both have a long face, brown hair which was just past our shoulders and we were almost the same height and had the same slim build. The hotel was in George Square and the weather was hot and sunny. It was obvious that we were both feeling equally nervous and thrilled but also that we were exceptionally eager to ask the many questions we had, fuelled with the expectation of receiving all the answers we needed to hear. It was so special to be able, for the very first time, to share all the information I had found out about our origins thus far with someone who was a blood relation of my mine. I had taken photocopies of a lot of the information from my folder so that Rhona could look through it at her leisure and pass it on to Sandra and Avril whom she had told me she was in regular contact with.

In turn, the one unexpected and most beautiful item that Rhona had brought with her and was able to give to me was a letter which our mother had written for Rhona and Sandra when they were little girls in care. Having that letter in my hands was like holding onto a nugget of gold. My mother had held that same letter in her own hands. Seeing the words written in her very own unique handwriting was, however, like placing a brick onto my heart. What I felt was twofold.

I experienced an enormous rush of love for her. She had the most beautiful handwriting and her words touched a place in my heart that was reserved for no one but her. Nonetheless, at the back of this flooded an unforeseen darker emotion. Biting back my jealousy I slowly read and then re-read the words which she had written on the two small pieces of paper. Right at that moment it seemed impossibly hard for me to accept the undeniable fact that she had never written a letter for me. The very thought that perhaps it might transpire that there was a letter, somewhere, which my mother had written solely for me did fleetingly pass through my mind, but I dared not allow myself to believe it possible. I did not cry. What was inside my head I could not name and therefore I could not express it.

With Rhona's permission and typed exactly as my mother had written it, the letter read:

'My Dear Rhona and Sandra,
Sorry mummy has taken so very long to write to you both. I had not been very well for a while, but am wonderfully fit now and happy. There isn't very many times, when you are not both in my thoughts, wondering if you're well and Happy too. As you will see by the address on my letter, I have another house now with an inside toilet, its really nice dears.

It must be lovely where you two are on a small farm, I

hear, you must be both looking great. I wish I could see you. Send me a photo of you both, I'd love that. I'm hoping your taking good care of your little sister, Rhona, as Sandra's not such a big girl as you. Are you both eating well, and getting on well at school, I'm sure you are.

I'm hoping we might be able to see each other some time soon, wouldn't that be great. I want you both to be very good girls to the people who's looking after you at present, and say your prayers at night, mummy says hers too.

One day everything will be fine again you'll see Darlings. Meantime keep smiling. Write me a wee letter Rhona, I'll look forward to it.

Cheerio Rhona, cheerio Sandra.

God bless.

Love and Kisses

xxxx Mummy xxxx'

It was obvious that our mother was a loving person with real genuine warmth and care inside her. However, it was heart-wrenching to read her promising words that everything would be fine, as it was very far removed from their reality and that if Rhona and Sandra had received the letter when they were trapped with such brutal foster parents, it would have provided such a false hope for them of escaping their nightmare and of returning to our mother.

Rhona kindly provided me with my own copy of this precious gift and it is now placed inside my folder and will forever be a treasured part of my story.

Despite my own unique experience in receiving this letter, Rhona's own story behind her receiving it was quite the reverse.

Rhona explained to me that when she reached her forties, she realised that she had a need to find out about her family history and, similar to myself, she telephoned Social Services in the hope of gaining access to her file. She was then visited by a social worker at her home. Rhona said that the social worker stated that she had a letter in her possession which had been found hidden inside the file, held within the Social Work offices. She was informed that the letter had been written by our mother, many years before that time, when she and Sandra were small children living in foster care and that it was addressed to her and Sandra. The lady had then handed it over to allow Rhona to read it.

Rhona said that initially she had felt an overwhelming feeling of happiness at the words which our mother had written for her but said her happiness was very quickly replaced with a surge of anger.

'How come I have never seen this before now?' she demanded.

The lady informed her that she surely must have seen it because it would have been sent out to her as soon as it was received at their offices and went on to tell Rhona that at some time soon afterwards, it must have been returned to Social Work.

'I can assure you that if I had at any point in my life been given a letter from my own mother, especially when

I was so young, that I would most definitely not have ever returned it, not under any circumstances,' said Rhona. She told me that by then she was struggling to contain her mounting fury.

The lady then continued by insisting that the letter belonged to Social Services and that Rhona should give it back to her as it must immediately be returned to the file. Rhona told me that at that point she felt like shouting. She said to the lady that she felt no anger towards the social worker, that it was not personal between them and that she completely understood that, of course, the lady had a job to do but that the letter firmly and rightly belonged to her. Rhona told the lady that if she left Rhona's house taking the letter with her, that she absolutely guaranteed she would do whatever she needed to, which included contacting a solicitor if necessary, in order to have it back in her possession within a matter of days.

To Rhona's incredulity she discovered the letter sitting on her doormat the very next day on her return home from a shopping trip. It had been posted through her letter box. There was no accompanying note of explanation but it was in exactly the same condition as it had been the day before.

Rhona could only surmise that the reason why she and Sandra had not received the letter at the time it was written was because her foster parents must have secretly read it and instead of passing it to the girls, they callously hid its existence from them and sent it back to Social Work. Whatever the truth was behind its concealment, it would forever remain a mystery and to Rhona's credit, she did nothing more about gaining any form of retribution from Social Services but simply felt deeply grateful to finally have a letter from her mother.

Rhona introduced me to Sandra very soon after that first meeting. She said that she would arrange for Sandra to be at her flat and we organised a day that was suitable for me to come to Glasgow. I had previously spoken with Sandra over the telephone on a couple of occasions and I found her to be a very shy person. This was evident almost immediately as, despite Rhona passing on to Sandra my telephone number with an invite to call me any time, it took her quite a few weeks before she felt confident enough to do so. When we first spoke to one another, it was mainly me who had to do most of the talking as Sandra was very reticent, saying, 'Sorry it has taken so long to call you but I just didn't know what I was going to say. I'm a really nervous person.'

Sandra sounded lovely despite this initial awkwardness. Though she was painfully reticent, when she spoke she used a loud, strong voice.

It was not easy meeting with Sandra for the first time. I quickly realised that she was suffering some very deep-rooted and lasting effects of her difficult childhood. I could see it etched in the lines in her face, her eyes barely met mine before quickly darting away. It was clear that I was going to have to put myself forward as the confident one, which took me completely out of my comfort zone. I thought she was not even going to stand up to greet me or to shake my hand at first and when she eventually did, she was indeed very nervous. I wanted to hug her but held back as I did not want to add to her discomfort.

I saw the family resemblance in Sandra the moment I met her. She had the same long face, very slim build and was about the same height as Rhona and me. The atmosphere in the room was not at all relaxed. The air was charged, full of raw and overwhelming emotions. I attempted to keep the conversation flowing but found myself talking too much and too fast. When Sandra did begin to talk, she told me that their foster parents were 'pure bastards', and then she began to cry, quickly apologising for her language. She asked me if Rhona had told me anything of their experience as children. Up to that moment Rhona had been general about what they had suffered but now Rhona proceeded to share with me one awful, painful memory. While I sat in her flat at that very first meeting with Sandra memories of my own experience in foster care were spiking inside me. It was so very gruelling and excruciatingly awful to listen to Rhona and her words will stay with me forever. Sandra began to cry again and as she apologised for doing so, I wished I had some magically appropriate, soothing words of comfort to offer, but I had none. Our combined sadness was projected between us and was captured in our hearts, to be locked inside us forever.

It was to take a long time for me to process all of the heartache in the words I heard on that day. It was a day which I had planned in my mind to be so special and full of happiness. I wished so much that I could have been filled with excitement afterwards, longing to share it all with my friends and my family. Instead, the only two people I could bring myself to tell were my husband and Jill. The realities of tracing my real long-lost blood relations was turning out to be nothing at all like the joyous scenarios I had watched being played out on the television. It was just painful.

I met Sandra's twin sister Avril soon after that. Incredibly, it turned out that she lived in a town extremely close to where I was living. I could hardly believe it! I actually had a half-sister living so close to me and had probably done so for quite a number of years and yet neither of us had been aware of each other until now. Rhona passed me Avril's telephone number and told me that Avril was more than happy for me to telephone her.

Unlike Sandra, Avril was a talker and I had no trouble at all getting along with her in the beginning. Avril told me that she often travelled on the bus into the town where I was living to do some shopping. It was disconcerting to think that we might have walked right by one another in the street or stood side by side in a queue at a checkout and all the while we would never have known we were sisters.

As with Rhona and Sandra, Avril did not drive so it was arranged that I would drive the twenty minutes it took to her town, where we met at a local hotel. She looked very different from Rhona and Sandra in that she was much smaller than me, with very dark, short hair and small facial features and she was slightly heavier set. Through Avril I learned a little more about our mother and her poor health and state of mind. She told me that our mother's living conditions were dreadful due to her husband's gambling problem and exacerbated by our mother suffering from extreme depression. Just as I had heard from Gordon all those years earlier and subsequently from Rhona, our mother's mental illness had an inexplicable effect on her behaviour and rendered her incapable of taking care of herself, not to mention Rhona and the twins.

Avril spoke of her childhood as an adopted person. She told me that she was shown a great deal of affection and love and that she had really been very spoiled. Avril admitted that all she needed to do was ask for something and she would be given it. Listening to Avril relay stories of her childhood years, it was hard for me to get my head around the sheer extreme differences between the upbringing she had enjoyed and that of my other sisters and of myself.

She brought along with her a lot of photographs of herself as a teenager with Rhona and Sandra and one or two of the children they each had. In some of the photographs the three sisters were all dressed up for a night out together and in others they were abroad on holiday lounging in the sunshine. I felt a degree of envy looking at the pictures of them doing the normal things that sisters do. I told her how I felt.

'All those years when you had each other, you had never known anything about me. I feel a bit jealous.' I said.

'I have felt jealous of Rhona and Sandra in the past,' she suddenly confessed. 'I have wished that we had never been separated. Anyway, you and I now have all the time in the world ahead of us to do these things. All of us together,' she said.

Despite Avril's optimism for a bright future together, I have to admit that my feeling was one of pessimism. I could not foresee us ever making time to all get together on a regular basis, or get to know one another, never mind actually go on a holiday together. It turns out that my reservations were right, as I shall explain later in my story.

Avril was very different from my other two sisters in that she did begin by keeping in regular contact with me. When I say regular contact, what I mean to say is that Avril started sending me text messages every single day, sometimes more than once a day. When compared with the very occasional text message or telephone call which I received from Rhona and to the fact that Sandra was not keeping in touch with me at all, Avril was almost smothering. Unfortunately, Avril turned out to be a difficult person to get along with and our contact became increasingly pressured and eventually stopped. However, I did go on to hear how she was doing now and again through Rhona and I think she sometimes asked about how I was doing.

It felt sad for me to discover that each of my siblings had at least one other with them when they were young. Joanna had Edith, Bruce had Hazel, Sandra had Rhona and eventually Avril. I was the only one who did not have a blood link with me.

As time passed, Rhona and I spent a little time getting

to know one another and eventually, when I had visited her at her flat, Rhona felt able to tell me about her memories of our mother. One specific, difficult memory she had dated from when she was a little girl and Sandra was a baby, when they still lived at home with our mother and their father. She recalled a day watching in terror as our mother set fire to the bedroom curtains and doing this while she and Sandra were sitting helplessly on the bed. She went on to say how she could remember our mother kneeling on the floor with her head bent over a chair, sobbing her heart out. Rhona said she remembers having to heave Sandra off the bed and get out of the room to safety. It was very difficult to listen to stories of just how ill my mother was and how much she had struggled with life when Rhona and the twins were so young.

However, not all of Rhona's memories of our mother were bad. She proceeded to speak of another very separate memory where she was sitting on our mother's lap being lovingly cuddled as our mother put a letter to Santa up their chimney. I held on tightly to this image, packaging it away in a small corner of my mind so that I could never lose it. I needed to have this picture of my mother tucked safely inside me. I needed there to be no doubt that she was indeed a good person. A person who loved her children and that if she were in good health then she might not have willingly chosen to have us all put into care. I so badly wanted to believe in this lest I forget that in my own need, when my own faith in myself is stretched and fears overwhelm me, that real, good, honest, genuine love can prevail and conquer, at moments when I least expect it.

It emerged that none of my sisters had any photographs of my mother. Rhona confessed that at some time she was in possession of one photograph. It was one in which my mother was sitting on a park bench, head scarf on, wearing red lipstick with Sandra sitting in a buggy beside her. Rhona admitted she did not know where that photograph could be and expressed her frustration at having lost it. Sandra and Avril both confirmed that they could remember seeing this photograph but that it had been a very long time ago when they last saw it. I concealed my own frustration at being so tantalisingly close and yet so very far away from being able to look at my mother's face.

My mind was being railroaded through enormously confusing highs and lows and my emotions, without doubt, reached new peaks. For me this was a time of an inconsolable pain that ripped through me, right to my very core. I would not have managed these emotions had I not had Jill's steadfast support. She stayed right by my side through every arduous step and her belief in me never faltered. Without Jill I do not think I would have been strong enough to continue going into my work on a daily basis, or to conceal my heartache from my children. I did not for one moment wish for them to witness how distressed I felt, in some moments, during this time, or to put onto them any of the harsh realities I was discovering.

Chapter Seven

After taking time getting to know a little about my sisters, I got around to explaining to Rhona about my initial reason for tracing her. I found it very surprising to hear her say she was shocked to learn that she was the owner of the lair where our mother was buried. I prompted her to think carefully about whether she remembered ever receiving any title deeds in relation to the grave, to which she replied that she had no recollection of this whatsoever. I carried on by relaying that on visiting the grave myself, I had discovered that our mother had no headstone despite the fact that she had died over thirty years ago and that her own adoptive parents were also buried in the same lair. I expressed my profound sadness at the fact that the only thing visible at the grave was some muddy ground with a piece of wood marking the plot number and how, when I had been told of our mother's location, I had visited the grave with a huge desire to see her name written there. I continued by explaining that it sat with Rhona to put a stone in place and that if she wished, she could pass on permission for me to do so simply by signing an indemnity form which was held within Glasgow City Council. I described to Rhona the journey I had gone through in order to discover where the grave actually was and of how delighted I had been at getting the news that it had been found.

After that, Rhona and I spoke together on many occasions and made many varying arrangements that would be needed in order to put a stone in place for our mother. I suggested that it was perhaps something which all three of us could do together. Money was, however, a big issue between us as I was the only person who was working. At one point Rhona said that she had talked it through with Sandra and Avril and the suggestion was put forward that perhaps we could wait for a year in order to allow them this time to save. So, despite the fact that I knew I had sufficient money already saved and could go ahead immediately, I agreed with this idea and settled down, doing my best to be patient.

As years passed, with no mention of the headstone or any sign of action being taken to move things along, I became increasingly restless at being stuck in a position where I was unable to do anything about it. Moreover, it seemed always to be me who was the one to broach the subject. I thought I would explain to Rhona that, given that she lived in Glasgow, perhaps she could go into the City Council to sign the appropriate form. I again described how I had been told by the lady at the Council about there being an official form of indemnity which she could sign, passing permission to me to put a stone in place. This was something that was deeply important to me and which I felt sure also meant such a lot to her. I assured her that if she would allow this, I would consult with her on every step, that it would be a joint venture and that there was nothing I would do without firstly making sure that she and the others were in agreement.

Nevertheless, despite the fact that she said that she absolutely would go into the Council herself and sign the form and despite the fact that she did come across when speaking on the telephone to me as being equally determined to do so, it simply never happened. It made me wonder, not for the first time, if I was being selfish to ask Rhona to do this, because I wanted it so badly and I had the means to do it. Still it must surely have been clear to her just how much I needed to do it by the way I was bringing up the subject over and over. It was like I had an imaginary fist gripping onto my collar holding me back.

More years passed and although I continued to mention it periodically, it began to occur to me that it was something which was never going to happen. My sisters did tell me that they remembered visiting the grave a long time ago. Everything was very new and raw for me, however, for them a lot of what I was discovering was not new but something which they had for many years already known about. This made me wonder if this might be a reason why the headstone perhaps did not feel like something they needed to prioritise. Nevertheless, I could not find a place in my heart to rest this issue knowing that it was unfinished. I had promised my mother when I visited her grave that this was something I would do and I could not dispel my determination to see it through. The decision unfortunately was not mine to make and therefore I was eventually forced to stop mentioning it, as more and more time continued to pass by without the subject being brought up.

As I continued to work with Jill, going to many great lengths to find out all I could about my natural family, I was also building an awareness of my own strength and resilience. My journey was presenting challenges at so many different levels and I was finding constant changes in myself and a growing confidence in my abilities. For example, I was becoming quicker at bouncing back whenever I felt defeated at being faced with the many setbacks I encountered. Also, I was becoming better at being patient when having to wait for information to come back to me.

Moreover, my drive and determination has continued to grow and my inability to stop being impetuous has never waned!

Chapter Eight

In some of our conversations, my sister Rhona had mentioned a lady called Violet who had lived in the same tenement block, two floors up from our mother in Glasgow. Rhona described her as being a good friend of our mother and of the family. Auntie Violet, as she was known to my sisters, was someone who Rhona told me had spent a lot of time with our mother and it suddenly occurred to me that this was someone who, in all probability, would have known her very well and so might be worth talking to. All at once, I was gripped with a great expectation that I was going to find out so much more about my mother and understandably, with fresh hope of getting a photograph. Rhona passed me Violet's number and I telephoned her right away!

Violet was in her eighties and sounded very frail. She said she was pleased to receive a call from me and invited me to her house to meet her. Off I set once more into Glasgow, again using my map to find her address. Her home was quaint and very typical of an elderly person's house, with shelves cluttered with ornaments and photographs of graduations and weddings hanging on the walls. Violet spoke in a faltering voice as though measuring her words carefully.

When I showed her my list of questions I had come prepared with she seemed hesitant, unable, or indeed perhaps
unwilling, to provide me with very much information
about my mother. Violet said that unfortunately she had not
known my mother for as long as I had hoped. She was not
at her wedding nor did she know much of her life as a child.

However, Violet told me that she had known that my
mother was ill and was very vocal about the fact that she
regarded her as being an irresponsible parent. She told me
that my mother would sit at a table in the living room during
the evenings with Violet, playing cards and that 'she took a
drink'. Violet said she remembered the children being very
young at the time, practically babies. They would be lying in
the cot close by to them in the living room, often needing
to be changed and washed.

She continued by saying that she also remembered a lot
of laughter when she was around my mother. She told me a
little about my mother's adoptive parents, her father being a
gent's tailor and working nights at a fish shop but who also
suffered from arthritis. Violet told me that both my mother's
adoptive parents were very hard workers and that they were
good, honest people.

Then Violet proceeded to tell me a significant story. One
day while in my mother's flat, my mother had turned to
Violet and said, 'Does your friend still want to adopt, because
I'm thinking of giving her one of the twins.'

Although Violet must surely have been shocked at the
cold nature and blunt delivery of these awful words, she

calmly replied that, indeed, her friend—who was called Margaret—was extremely desperate to adopt a child.

Apparently, the two women proceeded to make arrangements for her friend to come to Violet's flat, on a certain day, at a certain time, when my mother confirmed that she would hand over the twin.

Margaret had duly turned up at Violet's flat, at the appropriate time. She described their impatience as they paced the floor, waiting with trepidation, worried that my mother might very well not bother to turn up. However, my mother did appear as promised and seemingly without any hint of emotion and with no words, she held out Avril for Margaret to take. Avril was just eighteen months old at the time. Violet said that my mother then simply turned around and walked out of the door. She never looked back and Avril never saw our mother again.

Margaret then charged on with the task of changing the baby's nappy and clothes and practically ran out of the door, in case my mother should change her mind and come back. My mother's mind was, however, very clearly made up and was never to change. I could not help but wonder why Violet had considered it fitting for my mother to give up Avril in such a cavalier fashion, without worrying that they might be breaking the law. However, she did reassure me that it was all done above board and that Social Services had been involved, although this I found very difficult to believe.

Avril was the first of my mother's children to be given over into the care of strangers.

When I went on to ask Violet if she ever knew anything of my father she scrunched her face and said, 'He wasn't any good. I think he was a drinker. He was not a good man to your mum.'

Just as I was starting to feel a familiar dark sense of foreboding closing in around me Violet suddenly threw me an unexpected new thread of enquiry to follow up.

'Of course, your mum did have an adopted brother,' she said.

My optimism was immediately sparked back into life. Violet said his name was George and he would by now be around seventy years old.

'He lives just around the corner from here,' she said, laid back as you like!

I could not believe it. The bright beacon of possibility had returned and fresh elation filled my heart. A brother! My goodness, surely a brother would have endless stories of childhood memories spent with my mother and, of course, there must be family photographs. I felt certain that this was it. I had cracked it. I was going to have my dream after all and at last be able to look into the face of my mother.

Before I left Violet, she told me that she was of the idea that after my mother had left her husband and met Gordon, she had gone on to live out an impoverished life with precious little and very often no money. Around the time of her split from her husband, my mother and Violet had lost touch with one another. Violet confessed that she had no idea that my mother had gone on to have another child after my twin sisters, Joanna and Edith, were born. She said that she did not hear very much of my mother after that. She confessed with regret that sadly no one had known at the time that my mother had died. It was some years afterwards that the news reached her and after asking me how she had died, she said that no one had ever known of the circumstances surrounding her death. Violet did not have any photographs. I left Glasgow with my heart torn. On one hand I felt immensely sorry for my mother, that it was becoming more and more evident that she had shut herself away from the world. And on the other hand, I had a fresh lead to follow. I soldiered home anxious to see where it was going to take me.

Around a year after meeting with Violet, I received a telephone call from Rhona letting me know that she had passed away. I think that I was meant to meet Violet that day. Violet will never know how grateful I am to have met her, nor of the important role she played in this journey of mine to find my past.

That very evening after meeting Violet I logged onto the internet to the British Telecom website to see if I could find George. I tapped in his name and place of residence and to my utter astonishment, he actually came up as the first person listed in that area. I felt unstoppable as I lifted the telephone and dialled the number. By this time it had reached nine thirty on a Sunday night but the late hour was the very last thing on my mind. A female voice came onto the line and holding my voice as steadily and as calmly as

I could, I explained who I was and why I was calling. The lady said that her name was Rita and that she was George's wife. I asked if she would kindly allow me to speak to George. Rita said yes, that she would just go and get him and as the line fell silent while she went off to tell George who was on the telephone, it was then when the thought occurred to me that ringing someone like this, out of the blue, nine thirty at night, shocking them with news of a family member they never knew existed, could very possibly give a person a heart attack! Nevertheless, there was no turning back now!

George quite understandably did indeed sound surprised. He told me that he and his wife had no idea that his sister had gone on to have an eighth child but had thought that her children had stopped at Joanna and Edith. Before I even had the chance to broach the question of a picture, he rather sharply and a little defensively said they had no photographs of his sister. He explained that he and his wife had passed all the photographs they had on to Rhona quite a few years before this, as they had believed that this was the right and proper thing to do. They had thought it best that her children should have them. A wave of despair that I was never going to see my mother engulfed me in that moment and I had to hold onto my tears as I felt my voice begin to waver. The last thing I wanted to do was start to cry over the telephone to these poor people.

I asked George if I may meet with them and he and Rita invited me to their house the following Sunday with the promise that they would tell me anything they could remember about my mother's life. The next day I wrote a letter to George and Rita thanking them for very kindly taking my telephone call so late on a Sunday night and saying how grateful I was to them for asking me to their home the very next week. I enclosed an up-to-date photograph of myself so that they would know my face when I came to visit them.

On to Glasgow I journeyed, yet again on my own and again with my list of questions, ever eager and this time keeping all my fingers and toes firmly crossed for something positive. George was a tall, slim man, who was smartly dressed in a jumper and jeans which I would say had him looking younger than his years. Rita, however, was much smaller than George and was wearing black trousers and a black polo neck top, which again I thought might well disguise her true age. They both greeted me warmly at the door and were very convivial, seeming happy to meet me, if also just a bit uneasy and embarrassed too. I asked my questions and waited for something, anything that would give me even the slightest ounce of fulfilment. By now, I was getting used to disappointment and had begun to expect it.

George told me that he had spent many years as a young man in the Army and said he had been away for a very long time. As a result, he had not been around at the time of my mother's marriage. When he had returned from the Army just after the time of their adoptive mother's death, she was by then living with her husband and had given birth to her first child, Rhona. His return from the Army, their mother's death and Rhona's birth all took place within the same year. George and my mother apparently did not spend very much time together after he returned home and so George was unaware of all the turmoil and strife that was going on in her life and of her increasingly ill health, although he said they did have some idea that things were not as they should be.

He told me that he and my mother had a good and happy upbringing and remembers good times with his parents. One memory he told me was, 'When I was a boy one day I was at the park with Irene. I had fallen and hurt my knee and Irene, being four years older than me, carried me right up the steep hill and all the way back home.'

George said he remembered good times on holiday visiting their grandparents' home and that he and my mother were both very normal, ordinary children living a happy contented life.

Being told of their happy childhood was positive news and I felt a strong internal wave of relief. It was good to learn that my mother had experienced a good childhood. However, despite these tiny pockets of information, I found George to be generally very reticent and unable to give me much information. I had expected an outpouring of endless stories. He told me that his memory was not as good as it used to be. The very words I did not want to hear.

When George excused himself to go out of the house for a cigarette, Rita imparted a small amount of explanation behind why George was so hesitant. She said that he himself had searched for his own birth mother but that though he was successful in finding her, his mother had wanted nothing to do with him. Rita said she felt this had left him with a strong sense of rejection. She said that he never spoke of his childhood, which again might indicate that it was not as wonderful and as normal as he was making out. I was glad Rita had told me this as I very much did not want to cause this kind, gentle man any distress but merely hoped that he would have given me a real, powerful image of my mother, whether it be in the form of a picture or of his memories.

Rita told me that my mother did visit with them on one occasion and that she had brought Sandra with her, still a baby at the time. She admitted that my mother did not look at all well and it was obvious to her that she was suffering some degree of ill health. Rita said my mother was painfully thin and came across as very nervous as she kept twirling her hair in her fingers. She said my mother was demonstratively loving with Sandra, petting her and cuddling her on her knee.

Rita told me that she felt the need to apologise to me for George's reticence and said she wished there was more they could give me but that her husband had not even told her very much of what his life was like before they met each other.

George and Rita were a normal couple who had been married for over forty years and had three grown-up children and five grandchildren. They were living in the same house in which they had brought up their own children. I felt a longing to be a part of their normality so very much and I quickly arranged another visit to their home, this time bringing with me my husband and children. I met my cousins and extended family members and even though they were not actually related to me by blood, still it gave me deep joy. I tried to convince myself that I belonged here, I was part of this family, that this was natural and right. Of course, I was only fooling myself, allowing fanciful ideas to trick me into believing something that cannot ever be real. Yes, we may keep in touch and perhaps every now and again even visit with one another, but there will never be that fundamental connection I so desperately needed. We were not blood related after all and it was the absence of this underlying bond that would keep us from having even a small resemblance of normality between us. Therefore, it is with realism that I admit that contact between us was short-lived and that being part of something that was never mine to have in the first place was always going to fizzle out and die.

Rita, however, did leave me with one small but significant statement for me to hold on to.

'You look like your mum. George, doesn't she look like Irene? I've put the photograph which you sent to us with your letter in a drawer and every time I open it and see your picture there, it is like looking at your mum's face.'

The enormity of all the things I was discovering about where I had come from was beginning to hit home. Some of my closest blood relatives were all around me, getting on and living their lives as best they could, some having come through the most unthinkable of circumstances. It seemed impossible to come to terms with it all. Our lives were so disjointed. We had spent so much of our childhood being distracted from what our real lives might have been, both through a lack of knowledge of each other and some of us by the very act of surviving each day. When I really thought about it, the one thing which I was initially so desperately searching for was a photograph of my mother and in endeavouring to do this, I had unearthed the roots of my past, with all the knots and coils of lives scattered and stretched along their own destined paths. Unlike the movies where 'happily ever after' always rang loud, my every discovery happened to be wrapped up in a tight weave of complexity and uncertainty.

Chapter Nine

Despite the fact that I was slowly putting into place huge pieces of the framework surrounding the circumstances of my childhood in care, I was feeling a deep-down sadness. What I was discovering served to lay bare the undeniable truth that I and many of my siblings had been let down by the very system that was supposedly in place to protect us. Social Services did not carry out their promise of a duty of care in providing us with a place of safety. Every one of us were entitled to be surrounded by suitably loving, nurturing people without feeling any level of threat from them. We all deserved to be in an environment where we could thrive in a healthy naivety and to grow fully furnished with the knowledge of our true selves. We were failed. It feels so very unfair.

Nevertheless, I have to confess that before I met Jill, I firmly believed that all social workers were negligent. I did not know that there were social workers who were committed to their jobs. Through Jill I have learned that there are social workers who do care and are sincere in their intentions to do their job to the very best of their ability. Meeting Jill has instilled in me a degree of trust towards those in authority who purport to care, as I have been lucky enough to receive this care from knowing Jill. However, my sisters Rhona and Sandra have not ever experienced this and so they hold no such good will towards Social Work Services and certainly have no ounce of trust towards them. I feel there is a responsibility to be taken for this failure and I live in hope that some day my sisters, myself and others who have lived through the same thing will gain some level of retribution.

When I reflected on all the people I had met so far who knew my mother, I could not bring myself to accept that there was not a single solitary photograph of her somewhere. There simply had to be. My heart and mind refused to allow me to give up. There is a big wide world out there and she was in it for forty-two years. Was there no one who cared enough to treasure just one priceless photograph? To keep it safe for someone who might in the future have the most basic of needs to have it? It was impossible to comprehend how anyone could ever let go of something so precious. Yet in spite of this, that hugely significant and tangible part of my mother seems to have been obliterated, as though she never existed.

By now, it was several years into what I was calling my lifelong research. I was now beginning to think that the work I was doing would never have an ending and that perhaps, when I was no longer around, my own daughter would take up the challenge and continue the search herself. I wondered if maybe it would be she who would successfully complete all the research, for our family.

I was still keeping in fairly regular contact with Rhona through telephone conversations and the occasional trip to Glasgow. She had eventually been able to admit to me that the sudden appearance of a sister, of whom she had known absolutely nothing, had really had quite an enormous impact on her life. There was so much of our past that she realised she did not know and with all the research I had done, I had been able to provide her with a lot of answers. Rhona could not believe how much work I had done on our background and confessed that she had always wanted to do something similar. She said that although she had done some work on her own a few years back, she had never properly put her mind to it and said that she was glad I was doing it now.

I had always lived with an awareness that facing the truth about our past would be the healthiest thing I could do, no matter how painful. I strongly believed that knowing is definitely so much better than not knowing, as at least I can then deal with it. I feel I am no longer in limbo. Being equipped with the facts of my past means that perhaps, when I feel that I am ready and have an opportunity, I will find it easier to talk about. I would like to be able to properly explore my most difficult feelings relating to my childhood so that they will no longer be a secret. With hope and in time, I might eventually reach a place where I can move forward from it.

I think it would be much harder to live out my whole life wondering and thereby perpetually yearning. When a person is not furnished with the facts, it remains something they cannot put a name to, like belonging to nothing or having a past with no purposeful meaning and so cannot be understood or reconciled.

The hardest part for Rhona, I think, was to hear of the conditions in which our mother had died. Rhona had wanted to know the full truth regarding the circumstances of her tragic death and because I had already heard this from Gordon, I was in a position to relay it to her. I felt very sorry for her as I could feel her pain reflected onto my own. On the one hand everything she had learned from me had rocked her world but on the other, it had strengthened the threads of our relationship and created the beginnings of a potentially unique bond. This I held onto very tightly and silently wished for it to last. However, because of my ever-present sense of mistrust, I was acutely aware that to keep any kind of relationship from dwindling takes effort on both sides and I felt doubtful of Rhona's strength of resolve to perpetuate this newly kindled sisterly union.

Rhona often mentioned Violet's friend, Margaret, who had adopted Avril. It just so happened that Margaret, who was now a very elderly lady, lived very close to Rhona. Rhona frequently told me how she did what she could to help care for Margaret, by assisting her with her weekly shop and her general wellbeing, popping in regularly to provide her with some company as Margaret's husband had passed away a few years ago. Margaret was now in her eighties and had grown to rely on Rhona. Rhona and Avril had told Margaret the story of how I had abruptly come hurtling into their lives out of nowhere and Margaret was apparently expressing to them that she was extremely interested in meeting me. Rhona would often tell me during our conversations that I 'should really go and meet Margaret' because every time Rhona sees her, she asks about when I plan to visit her. At first I did not see any reason, nor did I have any desire, to travel to this elderly lady's house to meet her. I could see no benefit in doing so for anyone, except perhaps to satisfy her curiosity. However, Rhona was persistent. So I agreed to come through to Glasgow to visit with Margaret purely to allay her futile fascination with me.

How bizarre it was to tell my husband, 'I'm off to meet my sister's mum!'

Meeting Margaret was like going to visit a very sweet old grandmother. She was insistent that we had lots of cups of tea and force-fed us sandwiches and chocolate biscuits. I had arranged to collect Rhona before going to the flat where Margaret lived, the same flat in which Avril had been brought up. Margaret's flat was literally right around the corner of the block of flats in which Rhona now lived. I had brought my children along with me as I felt sure that Margaret, being so elderly, would enjoy meeting them. I was right. The moment she saw them, she gathered them both in her arms and squeezed my children warmly.

Margaret's flat was small and quite cramped and at first it felt a little claustrophobic as we entered the poorly lit narrow hallway. The living room space was a bit larger and much brighter and was comfortable to sit in. Margaret was very small and frail, with a tiny frame. She had a kind face and warm manner. It struck me very quickly when she began talking that her memory wandered slightly and she clearly found it difficult to keep a hold of her train of thought.

Nevertheless, she did manage to explain to me that she had found great pleasure in providing Avril with a loving and very giving upbringing. She confessed that she had spoiled her adopted daughter, stating that she and her husband had enjoyed doing all they could to provide Avril with everything she asked for. I kind of understood why she would spoil Avril with material possessions. I suppose she was attempting to make up for the loss of our mother. Margaret went on to tell me about her own deeply personal struggle at being unable to have children of her own and how she so desperately wanted to be a mother. I could feel the sadness of that in her as she spoke and understood how it had reinforced her reasons for lavishing Avril with all the love she could give. She commented very generously on my own children, praising their good manners and asking them about school and what their hobbies were. I liked Margaret very much. She was a lovely, genuinely good person.

She gave me the warmest, motherly hug when it was time for us to say goodbye and made me promise to visit her again. I felt very glad that I had taken the time to meet Margaret. It was not long after meeting her that her mind and body deteriorated so that she could no longer live alone and Rhona and Avril told me that she had gone to live in a hospital so that she could receive the kind of intensive care she needed. After her mother had moved into the hospital, Avril also moved from her house in the town near mine, back into the city of Glasgow.

Rhona telephoned me when Margaret passed away. I thought of my three sisters' sadness and particularly of Avril's loss of a mother who had loved her.

In spite of finding living members of my true family, together with a lot of information pertaining to my mother's life, it genuinely hurt when it emerged that every single person I had discovered had known nothing of my existence. This knowledge compounded my core belief that I had lived my life never belonging to anybody, that any family I was ever going to have, had been created by me. My sense of being alone remained as intense as it had always been. Hypervigilance against the threat of rejection was ingrained and I possessed none of the emotional tools I needed to dispel this. I found myself wondering how my mother could have concealed the whole nine months of her final pregnancy from every person she knew and, of course, I questioned just how instrumental Gordon was in her apparent disappearance from the outside world. He must surely have kept her pregnancy hidden and must never have told a soul. It was impossible for me to grasp why anybody would do this. Of course, all I could do was surmise that this was indeed the way things had panned out because without the facts, it was only natural that my mind would conjure up a scenario, no matter how far from the truth it really was.

It was like heaping layer upon layer of invisible, unresolvable, painful issues one on top of the other inside my brain. Everyone around me expected me to carry on regardless. No one asked questions and no one saw my pain. I never let it show—that had been ingrained in my own upbringing. The only person who actually knew that I was hurting was Jill because she was the one person who encouraged me to talk about it.

Moreover, the glaring fact that not a single person had possessed any photographs of my mother was mind-boggling. Her life was ambiguous and inaccessible and the things I had learned made it seem so scattered that it was impossible to fit the information together to form a clear or precise picture in my mind. Frustration and disappointment were a very prevalent and recurring theme running through this long and exceptionally arduous journey.

Then, all of a sudden, I had a brainwave. I decided that I would place a small article in a Glasgow newspaper and see if this would perhaps be a way to catch someone's eye and hopefully jog a memory which someone might hold of my mother, during some stage of her life. I once again telephoned my mother's adoptive brother, George, this time to enquire which papers were local to their area. On speaking with his wife, Rita, she advised me to use *The Glasgow Herald* and the *Evening Times*, as they were the most prominent newspapers read by people in their area. Rita wished me luck and kindly said, 'I really hope that the next telephone call I get from you is with the good news that you have managed to get the photograph that you so deservedly should have.'

I carefully thought about how I wanted to word my message and once I was happy with it, I emailed both of the newspapers Rita had suggested. My little article was placed in the personal announcements section of the paper and read:

I have spent 4 years researching my family background. I have reached a point where I have no one else I know, to ask about my natural mother. I have no photograph of her. I am appealing to anyone who might have known her, gone to school with her, worked with her, or is perhaps related to her, to please get in touch with me.

She was born ELIZABETH HAY, in Glasgow, in 1934 to MURIEL RITCHIE HAY. My mother was adopted as a baby to a couple named CULLEN and her name then changed to IRENE CULLEN. I believe that she attended Wellfield Primary School, Springburn and perhaps went to Albert or Hydepark High School. At aged 23 she worked as a Hotel Waitress and she was married to a man named SMITH, MARCH 1957. Irene died in May 1977 aged 42.

I am hoping that someone may have a classroom, or wedding photograph of my mother. Or that she had any friends who may possess a photograph taken at any time in Irene's life. Please contact me: Elaine…'

The newspapers sent me a complimentary issue with my notice inside and once again I had to find some patience from within, while I hoped that it would grab someone's attention. To my utter astonishment, within a week, I received a call from a lady who had lived in the same tenement building as my mother had done at the time when Rhona was a baby. I was driving my car on my way to work when my mobile telephone burst into life. Luckily I found an appropriate place to pull over so that I could take the call and even though I knew it would render me late for my work, this call was more important to me in that moment and I pushed the thought of work aside. My job came second place to this!

I could not believe my ears. The lady told me that her name was Amanda and that when she had read my article she had instantly known that it was referring to my mother. I barely held on to my excitement as I listened, thinking that I must surely have cracked it this time.

Nevertheless, my hopes were once again instantly deflated. Amanda literally echoed everything that Violet had told me. She described my mother exactly as Violet had done, both physically and in personality. She could provide me with no new information and, unfortunately, she too did not hold any pictures of my mother. She told me that the moment she had read the message, she immediately began asking all the people she knew who would have been around at that time if they could remember my mother and whether anyone had some pictures. Amanda apologised that her attempts at gaining a photograph had been unsuccessful. She explained that on speaking to others who could remember my mother, that it had transpired that no one had known what had happened to her after she moved away from those particular flats. Amanda said that none of them knew that she had continued to have so many children, or that she had put all of her children into care. She expressed her shock that my mother had done this but confirmed that she did remember my mother's health being poor. She and everyone she had spoken to were only ever aware of there being just one child and that was Rhona. She expressed her sympathy and wished me luck in my search.

What an enigma my mother's life seemed to have been, I thought to myself as I listened to this lady's sketchy memory of her, because just like Violet and George before her, she too seemed to be extremely limited about how much she had to say, or indeed, how much she perhaps wanted to say.

However, Amanda was very kind and seemingly understanding of how it must feel for me to be searching for my mother in this way and she vowed that she would keep my details to hand, just in case anything should come up in the future. My heart told me that I would never hear from her again. This was the one and only call I received in response to my article but I did have a little peace of mind that at least I had tried and one person had wanted to help. That was that.

I had now reached a point where I could not think of any other way forward from my newspaper idea and so all I could do was to allow time to pass and wait for a new seed of hope to crop up. This gave me the chance to attempt to digest the mass of information I had gathered to date and to somehow order it inside my mind.

My folder was also expanding. It gave me a tangible way to logically collate all my clips and the pictures I had taken so that I could rationally take in the information without letting my mind race off on a tangent of what might be. Everything I had learned thus far was real and factual and my folder was proof of it all. It also gave me the means whereby I could show my children and talk to them about my discoveries in a way that was not burdening them. I wanted them to always know, unlike their own mother, where their roots lay so that they never need to question who they really are. Through my hard work, my own children will never have to go in search of their true identity. They would be able to live out their lives knowing where their origins lay and so would always feel complete. When they are grown, they will have the knowledge to pass on to their own children and will be able to tell their children that this knowledge came from their grandmother's determination for the truth.

The effect which everything I was learning was having on my self-esteem was quite profound. With the continuing support of Jill and for the very first time in my life, I was facing up to my past and confronting some of my most difficult issues with a new-found understanding and without fear of crumbling and of never being able to get up from it.

From the moment I met Jill, I knew that she had me. I was safe with her. That if ever I fell she would catch me and so although I was finding it hard to ride the emotions which were coming to the fore through this research, my growing self-awareness was enabling me to cope.

It took me a very long time to allow myself to cry in front of Jill. I physically could not let my tears fall. I was completely aware that this stemmed from my childhood. When I was a young girl I truly believed that no one loved me, in fact, I thought that most people detested me. Whenever things got too hard to handle as a child, I would look out of my bedroom window feeling sure that my mother was out there watching me and only then could I really cry. I thought that if she were indeed watching me, then she would see my tears and come for me. For too long I fought my tears back, keeping my feelings about my real mother secret, so that no one would ever know how I actually felt and firmly believing that so long as nobody saw my tears fall, then I would always have some ounce of control over that aspect of my life. When I lived with my foster parents and if ever I was seen crying, no matter what the reason may have been, I was literally ignored or made fun of or often threatened to be given something to 'really cry about'. I was certainly never, ever comforted. I was told that people would laugh at me if they saw me crying and on the occasions when I did cry in public, my foster parents would tell whoever saw it to just ignore me: 'She's only doing it for attention.'

I felt exceptionally small and insignificant.

As an adult, I learned from Jill that crying was not a shameful thing nor was it selfish or attention-seeking, despite what I had been taught throughout my childhood. In the very beginning, I confessed to Jill, 'I don't know what it was about me that made them hate me.'

Jill immediately cut me off and said, 'It wasn't you. It's never the child. It's always the adult.'

She taught me that, contrary to what I believed, none of it was my fault. Everything that had happened to me was a result of a rippling affect with its core originating from that one most primitive separation from my birth mother. Jill recommended books for me to read which were centred around people who had been adopted and the emotions and situations they had to cope with. One of these books was called *The Primal Wound*, by Nancy Newton Verrier. I was bowled over by the enormous amount of identification I gained from reading this book. When I finished reading it I said to Jill, 'Oh, my goodness, I think the author has been following me around my whole life documenting my every emotion.'

It opened up my eyes to the fact that I was not the only person who had the kind of experiences I had in my life and that everyone's story was unique to them but the emotional reactions were very often the same.

The heartache I found myself having to face up to added an agonising new twist to my quest. I used to believe that learning the full truth of what had happened to my mother and my brother and sisters would be crippling and that I would never be able to get over it. Instead, what took place within me was a kind of state of unrest. I refused to believe that there was no more about my natural family background out there waiting to be discovered. My desire to know everything I possibly could had revealed a deep-rooted stubbornness to never give up, at least not before I felt I was ready to.

I would not bow down, cower or be defeated. I was no longer quite so submissive or easily convinced as I had once been. I had not known that a person continued to grow even as an adult. Moreover, Jill equipped me with the tools so that I could now name every aspect of what I had lived through and in so doing, she had created in me the tenuous beginnings of a healing process.

During my years of searching, I have had people say to me, 'Don't you think it's time to give it up now? Maybe you should let it go. Look at what it's doing to you.'

To which I would always reply, 'Only someone who has their whole family intact and who knows exactly where they have come from would ever say those words. I will never give up.'

Chapter Ten

A year or two passed by with no more real progress being made or anything new springing up. Normal everyday life continued and my own little ones grew, physically and spiritually, full of innocence and happiness.

One day, during the school Easter break, I was out enjoying a lovely day trip with my family. We had planned to visit the old jail at Inveraray. The weather was perfect, with blue skies and bright sunshine. On that day, my own personal story was very much the furthest thing from my mind.

As we drove along taking in the beautifully diverse landscape through towns and mountains, my relaxed, laid-back mind was suddenly stirred to attention as I noticed that we happened to pass a road sign which read 'Helensburgh'. I caught my breath, turned to my husband and simply said, 'Look, Helensburgh.'

My husband smiled and nodded his acknowledgement but said nothing. I had spent the first three years of my life in Blairvadach Children's Home, in Helensburgh.

Neither of us made any more mention of it during our visit on that sunny April day and as we had planned the day around our children, it had slipped out of my mind as easily as it had abruptly entered. However, just as we were making a move to return home my husband unexpectedly suggested to me that we should go to see if we could find the Home.

'We could go back the same way we came,' he said. 'Or we could go the scenic route. Do you think you would know it if you saw it again?' he asked.

'Yes, I most definitely would. I can remember it from when I visited as a teenager with my social worker. It sits up on a hill overlooking the Clyde,' I said.

Although on the outside I appeared to be calm and collected, on the inside my heart was doing summersaults.

My eyes were trained on every road sign as we drove. I found myself feeling desperate and urging my husband to please slow down even though he was driving at the correct speed limit.

Then I saw it. Thankfully Blairvadach turned out to be surprisingly easy to find, sitting fairly close to the main road. We had driven straight past the sign.

'That was it. I saw a sign for it. It said Blairvadach. Turn around. Go back,' I said, failing to conceal my impatience.

As we slowly followed the steep driveway leading to the Home, my growing anticipation was near to bursting point. The road curved round tightly and suddenly there it was.

'You know I have to go inside. I'm going to go in,' I said as we parked in the space in front of the house.

'I know,' my husband replied.

I practically sprang out of the car. The house was huge and very imposing. It had a large black doorway, massive windows, small turrets and a tall dome. Part of the roof looked rather like a castle and I did feel like I was in a fairy tale at that moment. While my husband roamed the grounds, my children came inside with me. Before we entered the building I explained to my children where we were so that they would understand. They were already aware that I had spent some of my early childhood in a children's home and seemed excited about actually being there.

'Do you want to stay with Dad or come with Mum?'

'We're coming with you,' they said, and I instantly felt a kind of protectiveness within them.

I had to stand in the doorway for a moment just to steady myself and take in my surroundings.

We climbed a set of marbled stairs and stepped through a door which took us into the spacious main hallway. It was beautifully ornate, with high ceilings, a carved wooden archway behind which stood a wide staircase and the biggest stained glass window I have ever seen. A familiar feeling of being small and insignificant washed over me. I swallowed, put on a confident stance and went over to the man behind the desk.

Be bold, I silently told myself. I explained that I had lived there when it was a children's home and the man was immediately kind and understanding. Coincidentally, he told me that he himself had lived at the home for a spell but that he had eventually gone back to his parents. He offered to take us round for a look but said that the house had been changed into Argyll and Bute Council offices since 1996.

As we toured round, I was having flashes of familiarity which were difficult to clarify. The house was like a maze, with lots of stairways and murky corridors going this way and that, leading to hidden secret rooms. The rooms which we did go into were again very large, with huge windows overlooking the River Clyde. I tried to picture the rooms with rows of bunk beds along the walls, which was how I had always imagined it would have been in my dreams.

'It's just like Tracy Beaker', whispered my eight-year-old son!

All the while the man repeatedly asked me if I could remember this or that and although I had no firm memories I was aware of constant passing flickers of recollection. After all, I had actually lived there.

He asked me if I had seen my records of the time I spent at the home to which I replied that I had no idea that there were any records or that I had any right to see them. The thought had never crossed my mind. He told me that for every child who spent time at the home, there would have been a record kept. He provided me with the name and number of Dunbartonshire Council who had been the authority in charge of the home at that time. A glimmer of hope passed over me. If there was a record to be found then perhaps some unanswered questions might be resolved. Also, I quietly wondered if by some miracle it might even include photographs?

I thanked the man for kindly giving us his time and patience, asking whether it would be alright for us to look around outside. He said it would be perfectly fine. Then we went back outside to find my husband. Around the side of the house was a long rectangular-shaped garden and it was there that I had a jolt of emotion. My mind started to race and I could hardly talk. I had played there when I was just a little girl. I would have been so small and accepting of my surroundings and my situation.

I needed to step away from my family for a while, to be quiet and alone with my thoughts. I yearned to know how I would have felt back then. I would not have known anything except for this house with so many children around me and different carers coming and going. Unanswered questions flowed through my brain. Who looked after me? Did I have just one main carer or were there lots of people coming and going? Was I a good child? Was I happy?

Standing there in that massive garden, I sensed a tenuous connection. I imagined I could hear the haunting sound of constant chatter, feet bounding about, laughter and crying. My gut instincts were telling me that my time spent at the home was a good one.

'Mum, come here, come and see this.'

My son, whose voice emerged from somewhere at the very back of the garden where there were colossal fir trees and rhododendron bushes, brought me out of myself and back to the present. Along the right side of the garden there was a slight slope which I instantly imagined rolling down as a very small child. Down the left-hand side there were two neat rows of blossom trees which, when in full bloom, I think would form a long and very floral archway that people could walk through and which looked like it led in among the fir trees and rhododendrons, to where there was a small clearing and the remains of what looked like a seating area.

'Look, Mum, this would have been your den,' my little son said with great enthusiasm.

Gripped by a sudden flash of recollection, I turned to my husband and said, 'I have dreamt of this place. I have remembered it in my dreams. On more than one occasion I have had the same dream in which I am with another child and we are hiding. We are very little and we completely believe that no one knows where we are, even though we could clearly see the large house so close by through the bushes.'

There was a massive tree trunk, an old broken down, rusty bench and a half-fallen and extremely corroded iron fence.

'When I close my eyes right now I can see the bench as it was. I can remember, plain as day, that fence being our boundary and us not daring to cross it. I know these things.'

I could clearly see the picture in my mind and feel that little girl crouching in the bushes pretending to hide. When I thought back to my other dream of being inside a dormitory with rows of bunk beds, I felt positive that this was also a memory I had relived in my dreams.

Being back at Blairvadach Children's home was one of the most beautiful days I had experienced up to that point in my research and to share it with my own little family made it all the more special. My daughter took lots of photographs while we were there, which I have added to my folder of memories.

The small lost child within me was validated that day. I was really there in the place which until then I had only ever remembered in my dreams. This place had cradled me after the rejection of my own parents. It had been my mother, my father, my brothers and sisters. It had been my protector. It had sustained me and nurtured me and it had been my safe haven. As I stood there, I felt a loyal sense of gratitude for it.

When we returned home, I went right on to the telephone to call the number which the kind gentleman had given me for Dunbartonshire Social Work. I spoke to a helpful lady who confirmed that indeed their offices had been in overall charge of the home at the time I was there and stated that they do have records on all the people who had spent time there both as residents and as carers. She agreed that she would pass my request to see my records on to someone from their archives to look out and would contact me in due course once they had been recovered. I felt certain that the records would be found as the lady had sounded very confident in this and my patience was once again put to the test as the prospect of being able to read the notes that were kept of my stay at Blairvadach would surely provide some degree of fulfilment. I was a tiny newborn baby when I had first arrived and a small three-year-old child when I left and I was more than a little curious to find out what had been written about me. However, my patience would very much be tested as the wait was to turn out to be a long one.

A couple of weeks after putting in my request for my

records, I was on my computer when the idea came to me to type in the name of the Children's Home just to see whether there would be anything written on its history. To my sheer amazement I stumbled upon an online forum. This appeared to consist of past residents and carers who had all spent some time there in years gone by, sharing their memories and personal experiences of the home. I read through every entry on the site, which took a while as there were rather a lot to get through and as I did so, I was able to gain a real flavour of what life would have been like at the home. It emerged from the different entries that all the children were in groups of mixed ages so that each one would have felt like a family of brothers and sisters. Each group held the name of a Scottish Island.

Even though some of the stories were inevitably tinged with sadness at children having been separated from their families and some under awful circumstances, the stories of their time spent at the home were all very happy. I could not help but marvel that there were so many people all messaging one another and swapping their fond memories of each other and of the different carers. One person spoke of being rather naughty and a bit of a handful for the carers. He wrote that on a particularly bad day he had his mouth washed out with soap for using foul language. Another spoke of how much they loved a certain carer and another had responded that they too remembered this carer as being their favourite person. There were lots of stories of how the carers knew each and every child so well and of the house having a real homely feel. Several people wrote of how they remembered finding the gardener creepy. They spoke of different events and lots of things that had happened. One person wrote that they remembered how their friends at school called the children from the Home, 'the Blair kids'.

It was an odd but heartening feeling to be able to read those real-life accounts of a place where I too once belonged. I very much felt like I was part of it and that I was one of them; however, I also felt sad that I could not convey my feelings or memories of the home because I had been so young.

I showed my husband the site and asked him whether he thought I should write a message about me being there even though really all I could say was my name and age at that time and note the dates of my stay.

'Of course you should! You will never know what you might turn up, if you don't,' he replied.

I decided to be brave and write a little message on who I was at the time stating that I had no memories or photographs and that if anyone could remember anything at all of me, or if anyone may actually hold photographs of the home, that I would be delighted to hear from them. Then I waited.

You might well imagine my absolute thrill when just a few weeks later I received a reply from a lady called Isobel. I was ecstatic! This is the message she wrote in response, dated June 14, 2011:

Hello Elaine, I happened to go into the Blairvadach Childrens Home site and happened to be reading your message. I remember you when you were at Blairvadach as I was one of the assistant housemothers who helped to look after you. My name is Isobel and I spent a couple of years there, then had a break and went back for another year or so. I knew I had some photos of the children in the group and I knew you were in at least one of the photos. I thought I might spend a long time looking for them but fortunately they were still in an old album I kept. I knew they would be somewhere in the house as I would never throw out photographs. I have one of you with the other children in the group and also a few of you on your own as well as a couple with the two of us on a day out across the road from the home on the shore front. I was so pleased to see them and I'm sure you will be too. The group you were in at the time I was there was called Jura. I now live in West Lothian and have done for a lot of years now. I would be only too pleased to send on your photographs as I'm sure you will be curious to know what you looked like all these years ago. I often wondered what happened to the children I helped care for and hoped that their lives would turn out o.k.

At first I pondered over how I was going to pass my address on to Isobel as I felt it unwise to put such personal details onto a public website. Then it dawned on me to use the social worker at Dunbartonshire Council as an intermediary. I telephoned her that same day and relayed the whole story to her. She was amazed and expressed her delight at my luck in finding Isobel in such a manner. She confirmed that she would be very happy to act as a go-between and that it was perfectly alright for me to put the Social Work department's address on the site for Isobel to use. Isobel then duly posted the precious cargo on to Dunbartonshire as promised.

When the social worker telephoned me, on yet another sunny summer's day, I almost exploded with excitement and sheer glee. The social worker was so overwhelmed that she actually cried over the telephone when relaying to me the amazing news that she had received the package.

'Oh Elaine, you are so cute. I can't believe I am holding in my hands a piece of your life, from a time which you have no memory of,' she said.

What I wanted so badly to say was, do not go anywhere, I will be there in a couple of hours! Instead, the social worker promised that she would send them out to me by way of recorded delivery post that very same day. I could not articulate my gratitude as words failed me. I was just so very happy.

It was another one of the happiest days of my arduous journey when I arrived at the Post Office to collect my parcel. Outside in the car park, I opened it inside the car, too impatient to wait until I had driven home. When I first looked at the pictures, for the briefest of moments, I thought they had sent the wrong photographs to the wrong person.

'Aw great,' I said to my children. 'This can't be me, look, this wee girl's got blonde hair!'

However, as I then looked through the other photographs I could see that it was definitely me after all and that my hair had indeed started off blonde. I had just never known this before that day.

The pictures were so lovely and portrayed a very smiley, typical looking baby and little toddler. As I studied each of the pictures, it was clear how I had wispy blond waves which gradually turned dark brown and thickened as I grew through those earliest years of my life. I was plump and looked as if I enjoyed my food, especially as I was holding what looked like an exceptionally sizeable cake in one photograph and in another, when I had grown a little older into a toddler, I was cheekily looking up into the camera with a packet of sweets in my hands. There were two of me with blonde hair. In one of the photographs I am sitting on Isobel's lap cuddling in and looking quite coy. I look like I could have been around eighteen months old. On the back in large looped letters Isobel has written the words, 'You again on the beach sitting on my lap. x' It was lovely to be able to see what she had looked like at the time. She was very young, in her mid-twenties. Her long hair looked strawberry blonde and was tied into two loose ponytails. She was smiling at me as I snuggled into her. Anyone who might not have been any the wiser could have easily mistaken her for my mother. Then there is another of me slightly older, maybe nearer two years old. I am standing with a group of children of varying ages, with me being the smallest child, standing at the front of the group. In the picture, the boys have on shorts and bow ties, while the girls have on party dresses. It looks like a Christmas photograph. On the back Isobel has written, 'This is you right at the front of the group. You shared your time at Blairvadach with all the other children in this photograph. There was approx 8-10 children in each group. Your one being called Jura. Isobel x'. Then there were a few of me a little older still, perhaps closer to the time when I was due to leave to live with my foster family. On the back of one of these Isobel wrote, 'You were such a cute little toddler and we were all very fond of you.'

I was so surprised at actually receiving these photographs that afterwards I felt exhausted and practically had to go and lie down! I was due to turn forty years old the following year and this lady had kept a hold of these precious pictures all this time. She told me that she had moved down to England, then returned to Scotland, gone through a divorce and then remarried and in spite of all that, she had still managed never to lose them. She wrote that she very much loved working at Blairvadach Children's Home and that when she had moved back up to Scotland, she had also come back to work at the home, stating that she could not keep away.

I felt like the luckiest person on earth. I had been given back some fundamental missing years of my life. I have spoken to Isobel a few times through email and she informed me that the group I was in was called Jura and that I would have been very well cared for, especially since I was one of the youngest. I would have received lots of attention while the older children were in school. Isobel told me that the other children in my group would have been like my big brothers and sisters. I had hoped that one day I might be fortunate enough to meet Isobel, to talk with her and ask her some of my many questions. Questions like, who watched my first steps? Was I a good baby? Was I settled at the home? And much more. It would surely have been so nice to chat with her about that time. Especially to perhaps hear of any idiosyncratic stories which she might have had of me, as often it is those small pieces of a person's life which help to build a human story. Rather than merely reading what was necessarily written down solely as a record.

In my communications with Isobel I have many times suggested that it would be wonderful to meet with her but sadly, despite writing how she agreed it would be lovely to meet 'in the near future', given that some years have now passed, it looks like yet another thing which will never happen. It seemed to me that whenever I happily acquired some degree of success, I never actually retrieve the whole carrot.

The irony in finding Isobel was that during the entirety of my time in foster care, having no photographs of myself under the age of three, this lady had lived a mere twenty minutes car journey away from me. I had lived all those years having no knowledge of having ever lived in a children's home or of my true identity and this lady had held concrete evidence of this in her home, where I would have passed on countless occasions, completely oblivious. The answer was always just right there, forever within reach. Agonisingly inaccessible. Although it was another frustrating twist in this journey, ultimately it turned into a beautiful discovery.

I could hardly stop myself from looking at my photographs for the few weeks after receiving them. That unfamiliar, very small, vulnerable child was me. It gave me such warmth to be able to see what I looked like, to see myself looking so happy, so natural. I wanted to hold her, to talk to her. I wanted to tell her to keep strong. To reassure her that things were eventually going to turn out alright. Eventually, I found myself crying for the innocent, naive little girl in those pictures who had yet to learn of her own mother's sad rejection of her.

Some months had now passed by since I had contacted Dunbartonshire Council with my initial request to see the records of my time at the home. The telephone call I had been waiting for eventually came one afternoon some five months later and unfortunately the news was frustratingly disappointing.

The official who called me from the Department of Social Work informed me that despite a thorough search, there did not seem to be any records in existence of me ever having been at the home. She said that they had looked through the electronic records as well as scouring through the old boxed records held in their archives but that they had found nothing. It felt like a blow to my stomach and I immediately found myself bursting into unstoppable tears. I felt the need to assure her that I had definitely been there as a child, to which she confirmed that she already knew this as she had seen the pictures which her colleague had received from Isobel. Although she sounded sympathetic saying that she could hear how upset I sounded, she could only apologise, assuring me that she wished there was another option for her to look into but that there was nothing else that she could do. She was emphatic. On hearing the finality of her words, I ended the call abruptly, struggling to form any coherent response through my tears.

I got into my car and drove unannounced to Jill's office where I was grateful that she was able to see me without an appointment with her. I poured out my disappointment and frustration at Dunbartonshire Social Work losing my records. In my mind, I battled to suppress the old recurring feelings of being unwanted, unconnected, unworthy, which so regularly threatened to drag me down. It was very hard given that, despite concrete evidence being discovered by way of the photographs that I had been at the home for three years of my life, it was evident that the authorities did not care enough to keep my records safe. It was as if, to them, I simply did not count.

With Jill's unwavering and consistent support and validation I got through yet another low point and was once again reminded of how lucky I was to have her.

About one year after this, another person contacted me through the Blairvadach forum. She said she had read about my request to see my records and enquired about whether

I had been successful or not, as she had also spent time at the home and said she would like to see her own records. The only thing I could do was to be honest and tell her of my disappointment. I did not wish to put her off, however, and said that my own failure to retrieve my records did not mean that it would be the same for her. I gave her the name of the appropriate authority to contact and wished her success. I wondered whether this person had gone on to retrieve her records, but did not hear from her again. For a spell afterwards, I occasionally received posts from people on this forum and I loved reading of all their different experiences at Blairvadach. The forum had grown exponentially, over the years, since I first stumbled across it.

Chapter Eleven

Since meeting with Gordon all those years ago when I was a teenager, rightly or wrongly I had carried with me a huge amount of blame and anger for my mother's demise, aimed solely and squarely at him. My firm belief was that he was the root cause of all the horrible things that he had so coldheartedly told me had happened between him and my poor mother. For so long I had thought that if it were not for him and his self-centredness and had he not left it for so long to get the right help for his illness, then he might have been the person to have helped my mother and she would not be dead. I held a vice-like grip to the notion of good guy versus bad guy, my mother being all good and Gordon all bad. I could not let go of the idea that my mother must surely not have been able to help her situation and that, were she ever to have had the right person beside her, guiding her towards obtaining the support and assistance she so terribly needed in order to improve things, then she would have truly wanted and loved my sisters and me. I could not shake the notion that the only person who had stood in the way of my mother's love for us was Gordon. It was becoming apparent to me that the only person who could give me the answers to some of my most difficult questions regarding this, as well as holding any information about where my sisters might be living, was in fact Gordon.

Ironically, a long time later, I was to discover that the effects of his addiction on me were more direct than I ever could possibly have imagined.

It had been almost twenty years since I had walked out of Gordon's life. On the few occasions when I had met him, I was forced to listen to his endless stories about his horrendous drinking days and his disgusting behaviour during those twenty-five years and then he would eagerly list his resulting ailments, seemingly seeking some sympathy from me. He openly told me about the resentments he was still holding onto towards his own family from those appalling years. However, my final reason for my abrupt exit from his life was this. Gordon had sprung a surprise telephone call on me one New Year's night. It was at the time when I had left my foster home to live with my husband to be. We were living in a flat back then and were at that serene time between being engaged and being married. It was just after midnight when the telephone rang. My husband answered it and his face instantly registered surprise.

'It's your dad,' he whispered.

My dad? I thought. Feeling confused, my initial and understandably most natural reaction was to think of my foster father, although it made no sense at all, as I knew he would never normally telephone me. However, I flinched when it was Gordon's voice that came through the receiver.

Back then I had made it a very clear and strict rule from the very beginning that Gordon was not ever to contact me by telephone and that I would be the one to telephone him. It was a condition I had put in place when I had still lived with my foster parents and was keeping contact with Gordon a secret because of my fear of incurring their wrath. On this occasion, nevertheless, Gordon informed me that he was currently living with one of my twin sisters, Joanna, in her home and that it was she who had coaxed him into calling me, in order to say Happy New Year. I involuntarily recoiled when Gordon excused overriding my wishes by blaming Joanna. He explained that it was she who had told him that I would be fine about receiving a call from him, that it was perfectly innocent and a natural thing to do since we were entering a brand new year. Moreover, he continued by saying that as I was obviously not living with my foster parents any longer he assumed there must surely be no more need for secrecy. I felt so angry. How dare he have such audacity to intrude on my life in this way and presume he was right to do so? As far as I was concerned, Gordon had zero rights over me. He had crossed a line and I knew in my heart that I was not easily going to forgive him. Control over contact was something I had always felt very strongly about.

I tried to keep my cool, as it was after all the festive season and good will to all men! However, when I proceeded to make conversation by asking him how his wife was doing, I was taken aback when he replied, 'Aw, me and Jean are divorced. I just fell out of love with her, you know?'

My heart sank. I did not 'know'. This news completely compounded my belief that this man was incapable of actually having any true love for anyone and that his loyalty lay purely and solely for himself. It was going to be impossible for me to ever have any degree of trust in him.

When Joanna came onto the telephone I did my best to keep a handle on my mounting anger and barely managed to tell her in as calm a voice as I could that I was not at all happy with Gordon telephoning me. I explained to her the circumstances surrounding the arrangement which I had made with Gordon right from the very first moment of contact. I explained to her that it was of paramount importance to me that I be the one who was to hold control over how, as well as how much, communication went between him and me.

Unlike me, however, it seemed that Joanna did not share that same need to battle with any feelings of animosity or mistrust towards Gordon. Things appeared to me to be quite the reverse between my sister and Gordon and, instead, she freely invited him into her life. Although I could not understand my sister's resolution of her feelings for Gordon, I did respect them. I simply believed that Joanna must be a better person than I was and that her heart was evidently more forgiving than mine. I did not possess anything of the kindly attitude which she clearly had towards Gordon. I could not conceive of the idea of ever dispelling my anger towards him.

It was after this that I knew that something inside me had shut off, that I was drawing back and literally could not bring myself to have anything more to do with Gordon, from that moment on. Unfortunately, I also ended communication with Joanna.

Until now.

I decided to go back on to the British Telecom website as I had done when I was looking up my mother's adoptive brother. I typed in Gordon's name and the name of the town where he had lived at the time when he was writing to me, thinking as I did so that it was very likely going to be the case that, just as my sisters had done, he had moved away. This I especially expected given that so many years had gone by. However, once again I was astounded when Gordon's telephone number easily popped onto my screen. I could hardly believe that he was still living in the same town where I had visited him all those years ago.

I wrote the number onto a piece of paper and waited for the right moment when I had summoned the nerve to pick up the telephone and call him, exactly as I had done when I was eighteen, living in an altogether very different world. This time, of course, there was indeed no need for secrecy, although it was very hard to entirely remove myself from the feelings of concealment that had been so ingrained as a teenager.

Understandably, Gordon was shocked and angry to hear from me, out of the blue, after almost two decades of nothing. According to Gordon, I had purportedly sent a letter to him stating that I did not want him to contact me ever again. This I found very surprising because I had absolutely no recollection of sending any such letter, although admittedly, back then was an emotionally busy and at times turbulent time for me as I was moving forward with my life. It was not outwith the realms of possibility that my actions could have been rather irrational. I did not offer him any words by way of an apology as I could not find it within me to retract something which I could not recall ever doing.

'Do you have any idea how I felt when you came crashing into my life and then just bounded straight back out of it, in the way that you did?' he demanded.

I could hardly believe my ears. It seemed so hypocritical to me that Gordon should feel so indignant. I could not stop myself from replying, 'Do you have any idea how it felt when you abandoned me into the care of the authorities as a tiny innocent and vulnerable new born baby?'

He did not have a quick retort to come back at me with but instead he replied, 'Okay, I suppose I asked for that.'

Now, as I look back on this situation, I am very aware that I could have gone about things a bit differently, perhaps in a more mature and reasonable way and that through my somewhat brash attitude, I might well have put into motion a kind of battle of wills between us. For just a mere micro second, it occurred to me that Gordon and I may have some similar traits in our personalities, although this positively jarred against my every instinct.

Nevertheless, after a few more awkward words between us, we both managed to soften a little; enough so that we were able to at least talk, in a calm and civilised manner, one adult to another. As was always the case with Gordon, he wasted no time in expressing his view that we should meet face to face so that we could talk properly. Unlike my very earliest contact with him, when I was still a teenager, this time I hesitated at the notion of seeing him again. Yet at the same time to my pragmatic mind it was obvious that we would need to meet if I wanted to talk through all of my unresolved issues and perhaps gain some closure. Gordon said he was more than prepared to listen to me, to allow me to air my feelings and ask any questions which, he knew, I surely needed answered.

'Then afterwards, once we have covered everything, perhaps we could get to a point where we can decide whether there was any basis for us to strike up something of a relationship and maybe continue to keep in touch and really get a chance to know each other,' he said.

I went on to ask him whether he was still in touch with Joanna and if he had her address to which he said, 'Why?'

This response stunned me as it was curt and almost made me feel like an intruder into his private life, like I had overstepped my rights. I felt he was belligerent and somewhat immature.

He did not say so, but I took it that this was his way of accusing me of turning my back on her too. However, taking into consideration the fact that I very much felt I did not owe it to Gordon to give any manner of explanation, I did not rise to it. Although I knew in my heart that this held a massive element of truth and I did indeed

hold a large amount of guilt over breaking communications with my sister, I was most emphatically unwilling to
ever talk this over with Gordon. So when he continued by
questioning my motives for enquiring about my sister, my
hackles immediately were raised. The urge to tell him that
it was none of his business and that it was between Joanna
and myself was very strong and I had to bite my lip to stop
myself. Given the glaring fact that it was Gordon who could
actually furnish me with my sister's contact details, I once
again reined in my temper and said nothing.

The confusion I felt about Gordon's reluctance to pass
my sister's contact details to me and of why my sister had
always been happy to have Gordon in her life were to
become abundantly clear much later in my journey. Gordon
eventually and, it seemed to me, rather reluctantly, was able
to tell me that my sister had been married for some years
now. This news I was already aware of, given that she had
actually sent me an invitation to her wedding, but which I
had declined purely because she had told me that Gordon
was going to be there. I was not prepared to play a part
in their pretentious happy family celebrations. Again, I was
reminded at how selfish I would have come across. Joanna
could not possibly have had any idea of my reasons for not
celebrating her wedding with her, as I had not taken the
opportunity or made the effort to voice them. I would have
been consumed by my own feelings. Moreover, to air my
opinion at such a time of great celebrations might also have
been construed as self-centred and to decline without fuss

I believed was the only way. At that point, when I cast my mind back to that time, I was still unsure whether I was right in staying away from her wedding or for withholding my true reason for not attending. All I knew is that it definitely felt like the right thing to do at that time. I hoped that if my sister some day were to read this, that perhaps she would be able to understand that I was not intentionally trying to cause any ill feeling between us.

Gordon's next words were to shock me even more than his indignation had. Joanna was now living in Australia. He said that she, her husband and their daughter had emigrated to Brisbane two years ago. I could feel the power which Gordon evidently wielded at owning and coldly projecting this information down the line. He continued by purportedly having real concern for their welfare as it was apparently proving to be a struggle to get themselves established into a new country and work environment. He even said that he had sent them money in an attempt to alleviate their financial burden.

'I couldn't send much money over to them because I don't have much myself, but I sent them what I could.'

It was galling having to listen to this flimsy, sanctimonious gesture of care and concern.

The news that Joanna had moved to the other side of the world made me want to cry. She was so far away. I had envisaged us reuniting in Glasgow with me simply jumping onto the train to get to her. More important, though, was the news that she had a little girl. This would mean a full blood cousin to my own two children. I felt a tightening of the knot of despair inside me, as Gordon went on to tell me that Joanna's daughter would have been eight years old by then. So many years had gone by without my knowing what had happened and it was just one more exceedingly precious missed opportunity to add to my ever-increasing collection. I knew, in the depth of my heart, that in all likelihood my sister and I would never see each other again and my own two children would never meet their one real cousin. Another dream of mine was drowning in the dregs of reality.

What made this all the more hard to bear was that Gordon proceeded to boast at how he and Joanna had remained in touch via email. Again I felt that wielding of power he held over me with regard to me accessing Joanna's details and the inevitable striking up of communications that may bring.

When I asked if he knew anything about Edith, Joanna's twin sister, Gordon said that, as far as he could gather from Joanna, Edith was still living at home with her foster parents. This completely threw me. Wait a minute, I thought to myself! From what I could remember of the short time I had spent with Edith, she was the more domineering of the two. It was she who portrayed her self-confidence and independence. She had achieved her driving licence, when Joanna had said she could not find the confidence to do so. Edith was going out into the world, heading off to college, gaining employment, whereas Joanna had given me the impression that she did not possess the same motivation that her sister had and was far less outgoing. Joanna was in fact successfully working in a care home for the elderly but she told me that she could never emulate her sister as far as to put herself through a driving test. To hear now from Gordon that she had not moved away from her foster parents, given that she would be, by then, in her early forties, just did not add up.

Then again, if I were to throw down all restraints and freely speak, I would express my view that my twin sisters did not enjoy an upbringing of total equality. I always felt I was good at reading between the lines and innately hypervigilant at picking up on favouritism. On the morning after my sisters' twenty-first birthday party, their foster dad stood up when Edith stepped into the kitchen. Cupping her face, he had turned to my friend and me and said, 'Isn't she beautiful?'

This would not ordinarily have aroused my attention so vividly had it not been for the blatantly obvious fact that Joanna had entered the room but a mere moment before Edith and this man had not uttered a single sound at her appearance. At the time, as was always with me, I gave away nothing of what I had observed but instead I stored it inside my brain as yet more evidence of the way people might wish to be viewed as having good, kind, honest hearts—but that what you see is not always what is there.

Despite my desire to know, I held back from asking Gordon if he happened to know Edith's address. My intuition was barking at me that, of course, she would not be interested in being back in touch with me, under any circumstances.

I knew I had left it far too long and I felt another jolt of guilt. Almost as though Gordon were reading my thoughts, he started on another tack by saying that although he had not had any contact with Edith for a very long time, Joanna had mentioned to him that Edith had periodically been asking about him. He told me, 'Even though I don't have any contact with Edith, I know she thinks about me because Joanna's told me that she does ask about me.'

Gordon then went on to say that he now had a new partner. He explained that they did not live together because, 'I need to have my own space. I can't abide people living with me. I'm afraid that I am not the easiest of people to live with.'

To me, those words spoke volumes.

We spoke another few times on the telephone and eventually Gordon and I agreed that it would be a good idea to meet. I suggested it might be sensible to meet up in a mutually convenient location in Glasgow. I told him that I did not wish to come alone but that I wanted to ask my social worker to be with me, assuring him that she would be able to act as a mediator between us. His terse response was, 'Well, if you're bringing someone with you then I'll bring my partner along with me.'

So, the next thing I did was to arrange to go into Social Work to see Jill. I informed her that, once again, I had gone onto the British Telecom website and how easily I had found Gordon's telephone number and address. I told her that I, perhaps rather hastily, had telephoned him. I knew that she would be surprised by this because in the past, every time I had made any mention of Gordon to her, it had always been with a negative connotation and I was aware that Jill would caution me about my motives for contacting him. I went on to tell her of our small altercation and that although things were still slightly strained between us, that we had both agreed that the right thing would be to meet to have a proper talk.

I was very grateful when Jill confirmed that it would be a good idea for her to come with me for support and confirmed that she would indeed be able to be mediator to both Gordon and me. So, we travelled on the train through to Glasgow once again.

This meeting with Gordon turned out to be one of the hardest parts of my journey so far.

On arriving in Glasgow, Jill and I initially found ourselves wandering up and down the street in the pouring rain, looking for the hotel, as we could not find it. However, once inside we found the perfect table tucked away in a corner and because we had some time to spare, we were able to sit with a coffee and have a chat before Gordon arrived, which I was grateful for as it gave me a chance to attempt to steady my nerves.

When I eventually saw Gordon walk through the door, I recognised him immediately. He had not changed much: he had gained some weight and grown whiter and maybe a bit thinner on top. My reaction on seeing him again after so many years was exactly the same as I had experienced the very first moment I had seen him when I was eighteen. I felt guarded. My body involuntarily tensed up and I was unable to relax enough to be myself.

When he approached me, I instinctively drew back and courteously extended my hand. I did not want Gordon and his partner to think I was being impolite but hoped that they would sense that I did not wish to be hugged. Once we were all seated, Gordon proceeded, almost without hesitation, to roll off his version of the story, in the same seemingly well-rehearsed, draconian, unblinking way he had done when I was eighteen. It felt brutally harsh, just as it had all those years before.

He again focused heavily on the details of his alcoholism, being particular to remind us that this was something which was completely outwith his control. Gordon stated that alcoholism is a disease and, should we be in any doubt of this, this could easily be looked up in an English dictionary. I got the impression that his reason for putting so much emphasis on his alcoholism was purely for the benefit of Jill, given that she was, in actual fact, a social worker. Gordon kept his gazed squarely on Jill, deliberately bypassing my own eyes, despite the fact that I was sitting right next to him. It was very disconcerting and made me feel insignificant and almost as if I were listening into a conversation which did not concern me.

Something I also noticed very quickly was that Gordon seemed to fail to focus any real attention on the issue of discussing the effects that his actions must have had on my mother, as well as on his three children. Whether he had chosen to become a parent or not, he came across to me as being of the opinion that giving away his children removed all source of responsibility from him. He seemed to be saying that he was not at fault nor could he be held accountable for any real detrimental consequences on his children as a result of their being in care, as the onus would have been moved onto someone other than himself. He even went so far as to say, 'I just always assumed that you were all happy and well taken care of.'

The bare facts were simply that he had never taken any time to ask.

Moreover, he was very clever at passing the burden of blame over so that it appeared that he could not have helped the situation because of his inability to improve things. I got the distinct impression that he was implying that my mother perhaps could have done more.

I have since then come to my own conclusion that alcoholism is indeed an illness, but that with the right kind of support it can be effectively arrested and managed, should the person suffering the illness want to badly enough. Also, that while responsibility for recovery of alcoholism sits solely with the alcoholic, so then do the consequences.

Gordon spoke about my mother's poor health due to her depression and her inexplicable behaviour in the way she was not looking after herself. He emphasised that because she considered herself unfit to look after the children it was left up to him to care for the twins; he made sure to point out the increasing pressures which this placed upon him, being the only bread winner of the family as well as struggling with his own illness.

Gordon spoke of how at one point he was quite literally living on the streets, gravely under the influence of his alcoholism. He described how he had reached rock bottom. He continued by explaining how he had woken up one day, taken a long hard look at what he was doing to himself, and decided it was time to do something about it.

Gordon said he had fought long and hard to conquer his alcoholism and had now been sober for many years. He told us he was religiously attending Alcoholics Anonymous meetings in order to maintain his sobriety.

As Gordon spoke he was completely devoid of tact or emotion. To me, he seemed inordinately unperturbed when talking about the fact that he had chosen to put us, his own children, into care. He went on to express that he emphatically knew he had done the right thing by having us taken into care, as he had witnessed, through others, how raising a child within the house of an alcoholic could be disastrous. Gordon had apparently seen before the damage which alcoholic fathers inflict on their children and witnessed the destruction they leave behind. Gordon categorically stuck to his decision and stated that by putting his children into care he was doing his best by us and though I could not envisage what my life would have been like with my natural parents, the way their circumstances were, neither did I have it in me to feel any gratitude.

As I sat very still, keeping quiet as Gordon defended himself so righteously, inside my brain unsaid words were screaming at him. I could not comprehend why, at the exact moment when he was aware that he was going to become a father, he did not use that momentous and perfect miracle as his proudest reason to decide to stop drinking. Instead, all I could think was that he was not able to see past himself. Instead he selfishly continued on the same course, drinking the way he was, damaging every relationship he encountered, right up until I was thirteen years old. It was not until then, when there had reached no hope or basis for any kind of meaningful relationship to grow between us, that he chose to look at himself and do something to change his situation. His one and only reason for deciding to get the help he needed to become free of alcohol was solely for himself. He made the choice purely for his own selfish means. He had purportedly worked hard to gain sobriety and yet in his sobriety he did not work hard to see his children.

Although I did not say the words, I wanted him to explain to me why he never ever looked back, why he never took even the smallest glimpse. Never, during the whole time that we kids were growing up, did he take any time to stop, to turn away from what he was doing to himself and check up on us. Even just to make certain that we were all happy and well cared for. Even if he had gone on to decide that he never wanted to see us afterwards, he would have at least known if we were safe or not. I wondered for the hundredth time whether he ever had any real desire to know. Was it that he did not have the capacity within himself to ever care?

I had taken with me a list of questions but the piece of paper stayed inside my pocket for the whole of the time I spent with Gordon that day. He had been exceptionally rigorous at covering almost everything I had on my list without the need to read it. However, one question which I desperately needed to ask him was whether my mother had held me when I was born or had even wanted me while she was pregnant. Gordon's reply was harsh and callous.

'When I told your mother that I had made the decision that this baby was going straight into care, it was like lifting a burden off her shoulders. She did not hold you nor did she look at you. You lay in a cot at the end of the hospital bed and she did not go near you.'

It was like a sharp knife, targeted squarely at my heart, slowly slicing straight through it. I asked him if he had been present at my birth.

'Yes,' was his abrupt, defensive reply. 'I was there when all three of you were born. But it had been previously arranged that you were not coming home with us. I was determined that if it was not possible for me to have the twins back home, then there is no way that I'm having you.'

When I asked him if he had held me, he said, 'I shook your little hand, turned around and walked out of the door.'

He said this with his voice held completely steady and assured, without even the tiniest ripple of shame.

Gordon then moved on, delving deeper, going into the

tragic details of my mother's death. He firstly spoke of how he found the situation they were living in increasingly desperate. All of his children were by now placed into care, my mother's health continued to deteriorate and he himself eventually reached his lowest ebb. He said that it was then when he made a decision to visit his doctor regarding his own struggle and how he had been prescribed antidepressants.

He went on to explain that since my mother was literally hooked on Valium, this meant that there were now two lots of different medication inside the home and he said he had known that it was imperative for him to keep both sets separate so as to remove any lure of overdosing from my mother. Gordon told us that on the day it had happened, my mother had not only taken her own full prescription all at once, but that she had taken all of his too. In his haste to leave the house that morning and under the heavy effects of his alcoholism, he had forgotten to put them away as he would normally have done. He said that he felt guilty for not remembering to hide his pills from my mother but that, 'I'll have to live with it, for the rest of my life.'

At some point during Gordon's story, he mentioned the fact that he had also been a violent alcoholic. He explained that it was him who had discovered my mother's body and, given that she was covered in bruises from when he had last beaten her, the police had mistaken her death for murder.

'She already knows all this.'

This blunt remark was said to Jill but directed at me. The

whole time while Gordon delivered his story, he continued to keep his gaze averted from mine, looking squarely at Jill.

Jill attempted to excuse this need to repeat the story, explaining that I had been a mere eighteen years old at the time he had told me and perhaps it had been rather over-whelming to absorb back then.

'But she was an adult though,' was his hard-hearted response.

'An exceptionally young adult,' Jill reiterated.

'I have learned that there comes a time when you have to put it behind you and move on. Going over and over it doesn't help and just hinders any chance of progress. Shouldn't she be trying to do that instead of always asking me about it?'

'Elaine's doing that.' Jill said.

After this torturous stream of seemingly self-serving pity for having lived through this tragic life, as well as an evidently inward admiration for carrying out an act which he steadfastly believed was right, he finally directed his full attention towards me. For the first time since he had sat down next to me, his eyes met mine. He then practically demanded that since he had poured out his heart, that it was now my turn to do the same thing and tell him all about what life had been like for me when I was growing up. I briefly wondered if he desperately needed to hear me talk of a happy, healthy, wonderfully fantastic childhood and that perhaps in so doing I might provide him with some measure of redemption.

However, for me this had never been the purpose of our meeting. I believed that my childhood was completely none of his business and that he had unequivocally given up the right to hear any of that a very long time ago. When I made an attempt to express this, Gordon took exception at my reluctance to return his openness with my own. I felt defensive and my own hackles were immediately raised as Jill had to step in and do her bit to keep things calm.

Jill did manage to keep the situation civilised and cordial.

'I understand it must be stressful, feeling obliged to pore over painful events when you find them difficult to talk about and that you now feel that in so doing for Elaine's benefit she might owe it to you to do the same thing.'

'Yes.'

'But maybe it's a case of building a little trust.'

However, I had no trust inside me for Gordon and at that moment I just wanted out of there.

What I found to be very strange about this man who had spoken with such apparent determination about wanting to spend time together getting to know me, was that he did not seem to have any specific questions. He asked me nothing about my job, my children or about my husband or his job. It seemed to me that none of it was of any interest to him. He claimed to want a father/daughter relationship, but it felt to me like it was nothing more than mere words. Small, empty, apathetic words which, as far as I was concerned, did not come anywhere close to holding any real purpose because I could not see any common ground between us on which to base any kind of meaningful relationship. I did bring this up with him during the conversation and his answer was, 'I want to get to know you first and hopefully establish a relationship between us, then afterwards we can see about whether it could be possible for me to maybe meet your husband and kids and get to know them.'

I just could not lift the barrier inside me. I could not allow him to get close and so I carried on pushing him away, so much so, the distance between us remained wide.

I had met Gordon that day in order to be given the unadorned, unadulterated truth and that is precisely what I came away with. The whole experience was like stepping into the mouth of a cave. The more Gordon had spoken and with each answer he gave me, the deeper into the darkness I went, further and further away from anything that provided me with light. And even though I was afraid, I grew more and more compelled to hear the truth and so I continued to wade. And when he was done, all that was left was so dense, colourless, airless that all I could hear were my own thoughts echoing around inside my head. Alone. Abandoned. Unwanted.

Jill must have sensed that enough was enough.

'I think that probably this should be enough for now, there's been a lot said and it's probably a good time to end things here today.'

However, Gordon was clearly not pleased. He fumbled with a menu, making attempts at suggesting we could eat, evidently feeling reluctant to call it a day and instead wishing to prolong our meeting. Nevertheless, it very much did feel a good time to say our goodbyes and having no desire to stretch things out further, I reiterated that indeed a lot had been discussed and it was definitely a good idea to stop for today. I was so very glad to have had Jill along for support on that day.

It did not feel right for me to hug Gordon and so I once more offered my hand as a parting gesture. Despite this, he asked, 'Can I at least have a hug?'

I felt obligated to deny my natural impulse and simply acquiesced. His partner, on the other hand, embraced me warmly. She had remained politely reticent throughout the afternoon and only when appropriate, had she expressed her sympathetic opinion.

'It must be very hard to hear Gordon speak of your own mother in this way,' she had said.

I surmised that her sympathy came from her observation of Gordon's distinct lack of emotion and that she had felt a need to attempt to soften the blow.

'Don't worry, Elaine, everything will turn out alright, you'll see', she whispered kindly in my ear while she held me tightly for a moment.

I instantly liked her and quietly prayed that, despite Gordon's past record, he would be able to hold onto their relationship.

Jill and I left the hotel and stepped back out onto the busy Glasgow streets where the rain had now stopped. We walked along the path which lead us into the opulent George

Square in all its glorious representation of the wealth and power of the city.

I tried to set my mind to the task of separating myself from the darkest, truest grit of the devastated lives of people who, albeit imperceptibly, were undeniably a part of who I am, but it was futile. I was consumed by all of the heartache Gordon had just relayed to me. All of a sudden I felt a tightening in my throat. I was choking. The weight of all the pain that I had just listened to was crushing me and I wanted the world to halt at that very moment so that I could scream it out.

Thankfully Jill just carried on walking, keeping things calm; even as we sat together for more coffee and something to eat, she kept the conversation light and uncomplicated. She even ended up having us joke about putting the events of my research into a film and which famous Hollywood celebrity would take each of our roles. Jill considered Meryl Streep would be a suitably feisty actress to play her! I thought Julia Roberts could play me! Jill then made the image all the more comical by suggesting Bob Hoskins could act as Gordon!

It was not until I had returned home and some time into the evening when an uncontrollable, unstoppable crying began and continued for a further three days. I cried myself to sleep and then would wake in the night crying. It continued as soon as my eyes opened in the mornings. Despite the fact that I was obviously utterly exhausted and distressed, I did not allow myself to take any time out in order to grieve.

I reined in my tears enough so that my children did not see them and I continued to go to work every day. In the mornings once my children had left the house for school and before I left to go to my work, I was sobbing so hysterically out of control that I continued crying in the car on the way there and again, like a switch, the tears began as soon as I was back inside the car ready to drive home.

I was devastated.

Once I stopped crying I decided I would not see Gordon again.

I then began to look back on what Gordon had said about my mother. It seemed inconceivable that my own mother never wanted me. That all I would have been was a burden to her. That she could not even bring herself to look at me, never mind to actually hold me. It was unbearable. My worst fears of rejection had been realised and it completely reinforced my core belief that I was unworthy.

My own mother had broken my heart.

Now, she had well and truly fallen off the proverbial pedestal where I had resolutely held her for the entire duration of my life. I had set out on a quest to have the truth and now I knew it, I found it impossibly hard to endure.

My feelings towards my mother underwent a shift from longing and aching to love her and have her love me, into a state of anger. How could a mother be unable or unwilling to hold her own child? How could she not even have looked at her tiny creation? Although she had put every child she had into care before me, I wanted so badly to believe that she had pined for us and that surely at some time during those years, she had held some love and that she actually had yearned to get us back. I think the hardest part for me was feeling unwanted. Hearing Gordon say I was a burden to her and this while I was still inside her hit very hard.

My idealistic image of my mother had totally shattered and all my dreams of her vanished. My determination to have the answers I longed for had revealed the truly despicable reality of total rejection and that eternal elusive love which I believed I had so badly needed was never mine to have.

When the crying eventually subsided it was replaced with rage. I felt that I no longer wished to put a headstone at my mother's grave. I decided to break my promise to her that I would do this good deed for her. Looking back now, I think it was a kind of immature feeling of redemption I was having towards my mother. She had hurt me and this was the only way I felt that I could hurt her back.

Now began a different journey. I was on a new path to acceptance. My deep inner void, I now knew, would never be filled and my pain might never heal, but I was aware that I had strength and that, in being a mother myself, I was now also aware that I did possess a huge capacity to love. When I was a young girl, I used to believe that I could not love, that I had no capacity within me to hold real love for another person. I actually believed that I would never survive into my adulthood because of this inability and because of the struggles in foster care. Whenever I watched a mother cuddle and kiss a child, it made me jealous because this very natural, primitive entity had completely evaded me and therefore I could not be normal and live out an ordinary adult life.

I now considered it possible that perhaps in being a truly loving, kind and caring mother, that this goodness could somehow penetrate the swirling pool of poison inside me and that my anger would dissipate. Perhaps in time the damage could be repaired and, one day, I could learn to forgive and in so doing, maybe I could find peace.

From this time on what ensued was a time of slowing down for me. I had never stopped chasing my dreams, leaping from one hopeful lead to another, following different trails and thinking up countless ways to uncover any thread of information that was possible to find. It was all in desperation to reach that one important and ultimately most elusive goal—to hold a picture of my mother. This was a time to draw breath and to take a step back from it all.

Of course, stepping back categorically did not mean I was backing off completely. That, for me, was impossible. Whatever I had inside me, driving me on, would not rest and I was poised, forever ready to pluck the next seed of discovery just waiting to sprout its foliage my way. This break simply provided me with some space in which I could try to piece it all together and come to terms with the many unexpected twists and turns I had encountered along the way.

It was a natural lull in my intrepid journey.

So I took out my precious folder which contained all the bits and pieces of information and pictures which I had gathered along my journey so far and carefully added the facts and photographs I had most recently gained. I had also been making sure that I typed up a record for myself of the few relations who I had discovered so far, with their dates and places of birth, how old my mother would have been at the time and keeping a note of where they were now, insofar as I had been able to acquire any information at all. It was extremely good to now be able to begin to form my family tree, which was a great way of easily seeing precisely where each individual fitted in, through the years.

Chapter Twelve

One day as I was thinking things over, I remembered that I had managed to obtain Joanna's email address from Gordon. I felt a shiver run through me when I recalled the tense telephone conversation which he and I had at the time and his reluctance to divulge her whereabouts to me. Whenever my thoughts turned to Gordon, I felt a tightening in my stomach. I came to the conclusion that he might forever be a source of so much conflict within me. I wondered if I would ever reach a place where I felt nothing but serenity towards him, when his words no longer bit into my soul and the germ of hatred, planted so long ago, would cease to grow.

Now, holding Joanna's details in my hands I considered the idea of making contact with her. So many years had passed and so much had happened since my sisters and I were last in touch with each other. I had now been married for quite a few years, with children of my own and I knew that she too was married. I had heard from Gordon that she also had a child. I wondered whether the fact that these were hugely significant things which we now held in common could perhaps be a foundation upon which to form a new relationship and hopefully build some bridges between us.

With some degree of apprehension and a large amount of positive thinking, I wrote a message by way of email to her. I imagined that Gordon probably would have already alerted her to my sudden appearance back into his life and my interest in having contact once more with my sisters. I was careful to keep this initial communication short but also wanted to make sure I was honest. It felt right and proper that I should inform her of some of the research I had done and of the living relatives I had found. After all, it was all relevant to Joanna too. I hoped that she would hold the same intrigue and desire for the facts that I held and would wish to know everything I had discovered so far about our past. I suppose I was hoping that because I held so much information on our natural background this would entice Joanna to want to get to know me as the person I had now become and to forego the person she had met when we were teenagers.

I was wrong.

Although Joanna's reply took me by surprise, it was not entirely without merit. She wrote that she felt confused and dejected by my actions, all those years ago. Joanna explained that she had written to me many times, wanting to know what had gone wrong between us and asking me to write back to her but that she never received a response. I raked through my memory trying to find any recollection of reading these words in any letters from her but I could not remember receiving correspondence to that effect nor of making a decision not answer them. I went back to my case where I had been methodical at keeping every single letter I had ever received and, taking the bundle pertaining to my sisters, held together by an elastic band, I painstakingly read through each one. None of the letters I read from Joanna held any questions regarding my sudden absence from her life or any requests urging me to write back to her. I could only surmise, given that I would have been living with my husband by then and she would not have my new address, that for whatever reason, the letters were never forwarded to me by my foster parents.

Joanna wrote in her email that at the time, she had thought that I did not want to know her. I could absolutely understand why she would think this. I knew then that my sudden disappearance had caused her pain and I was sad for her and ashamed of myself.

I sent another email to her attempting to do my best to explain a little of my circumstances and going over my reasons for not keeping in touch with her. I apologised that I had made her think that I did not want to know her, assuring her that this had never been my intention. I explained my struggles with Gordon and how impossible it had been for me to accept him into my life as she had done. I reminded her of how she had wanted us all to come together at her wedding. As I wrote this I was thrust back into the moment. Joanna in her idealistic world of us three sisters with Gordon happily reunited and me having absolutely no desire to participate in such a falsehood. I was becoming very aware that his presence had been, and was still, putting a wedge between us. The thought ran through my mind that perhaps everything might have been so much easier to manage between my sisters and me, back when we were in the throes of discovering each other, if our mother had survived. I wondered about how differently it would all have panned out if our mother had recovered and returned to our lives. Would she somehow have been the one to hold us all together, unlike Gordon who had separated us from each other as babies and still seemed to be so instrumental in keeping us all apart?

Nevertheless, Joanna went on to say that she was very happy and content with her life as it was. She said she hoped that I had found some peace and contentment in mine. All I could really do now was take from these words that she was letting me know she held no interest in any information I held on our natural background, and nor did she wish me to pass on to her all the discoveries I had made. She had made no mention of any of the work I had done to uncover where we had come from, nor did she respond to my explanation behind why I had held back so much from them when we were teenagers. I did my best to explain about the difficulties in my life in foster care and about my lack of any kind of real support. However, this too did not seem to warrant a response from her.

So now it was my turn to feel confused. I just could not get my head around why my sister was not as eager as I was to learn of her origins. I had been so excited at the prospect of sharing all my findings with her. It seemed impossible to fathom why anyone would shun the opportunity to know where their roots lay. What I later learned from this was that because our earliest moments and childhood memories were so entirely unconnected, there was no undoing of what was already done. We were strangers at the beginning of our lives, strangers as we grew, and strangers we may well remain.

Joanna and I continued to keep in touch for a short time simply to exchange the trivialities of our family lives. I told her that I would be happy for her to pass on my being back in touch to Edith but have heard nothing at all in reply. I fully expect that I may never hear from Edith. My sister's silence made me feel that to pursue the idea of us having contact would be an intrusion and so I did the only thing I could do: I respected her wishes. Perhaps this is exactly what she felt about me all those years ago.

Despite Joanna's emails to me being limited to cordial conversation, she always ended her messages with an outpouring of kisses and hugs, making sure she extended her seemingly abundant love for me and my family. This is something I had a real difficulty with. Why is it that a person can convey their apparent love for another person in this way without evidencing it with their actions? Love is easy and exceptionally empty when just a word. However, I believe that when genuine love is present it can be seen. It is tangible and it is unmistakable. Real love within a family is boundless and impossible to deny.

It is in this vein that the one thing I feel compelled to mention is that, in my communications with my newly found half-sisters, there have been a lot of words stated from them, packed with expressions of extensive love. Too often, they would say they had a great longing to know more and to be involved in the work I was doing to uncover our past. However, there never seemed to be any evidence of the appropriate actions to back up those words. I was putting in a lot of effort to keep contact going with my sisters but if I were to be really truthful with myself, I would have to admit that I was receiving no effort from them in return. It was never a two-way thing. I seemed to be chasing the notion of having my siblings in my life and the dream of how wonderful that could have been, but my reality was turning out to be very different.

Boldly facing up to the most difficult stuff and doing what was, to me, absolutely imperative for my own peace of mind and sense of true self, had always been something which I had done by myself. I was never used to leaning on anyone. It was something that had been drummed into me as a child. I had learned how to shrug off people's insincere words, blurted out in a mere moment. I had witnessed their words evaporate into nothing too many times. It is something which I had become accustomed to. However, this did not mean that it was always an easy task. Sometimes I desperately needed to believe that I was not alone. This categorically did not apply to the help I was receiving from Jill. Her support was steadfast. These feelings of isolation were part of a set of core beliefs which I fought hard against each day. I had brought with me into my adult life the negative and irrational feelings of being a small, insignificant nobody.

Chapter Thirteen

Failing to locate a single picture of my mother at any stage of her life continued to plague me. The thought of living out my whole life having never seen her face deeply troubled me. It was a constant reminder that I did not feel complete. Each time I found an answer to even the smallest piece of my family background, I experienced such a tremendous high, because it felt like I had come another step closer to finding her. Sadly, this elation was always short-lived because the gaping hole where my mother should be seemed to widen every time I was told by someone who had known her that they held no photographs of her. It was like a knife to my heart. I truly believed that if I managed to get a photograph of her, to be able to hold it in my hands and to look at it, any time the feelings of being alone were especially strong, it would equip me with the knowledge that her existence was real and important and I was actually never meant to be alone, even though I never had her in my life. I would be able to hold the evidence of this in my hand.

Instead for me my own mother was purely just a name, written down onto certificates and records. A mere word on pieces of paper. To me she did not seem like she was ever a whole being because I simply could not see her image in my mind's eye. There was no profile to recall. No voice to hear or scent to trigger a memory. No touch of comfort to remember.

For me, my mother is as intangible as the particles of dust you can see dancing on the air whenever the sun shines through the window.

One day, I was visiting with one of my closest friends at her house. Our children were all outside playing in my friend's garden and we were sitting indoors, talking and drinking cups of tea together. I was in the gloomiest of moods and my poor friend was doing her best to be patient with me, ever attentively listening while I trudged through all my disappointments and the many dead ends I had come up against in my quest to find a photograph of my mother. I was shamelessly feeling rather sorry for myself and was in the most negative frame of mind, when suddenly my friend stood up, went over to where her computer sat on a ledge in front of the window and after logging on, she turned to me and asked,

'Right! Where in Glasgow was your mum from?'

Initially stunned by her burst of energy and her forth-right question, I answered, 'Springburn.'

Unperturbed by my disconcerted reaction to her audacious intrusion into my world of misery, my hugely personal and up until now very private mission, Suzanna googled the word Springburn. She started sifting through the websites which came on screen under this heading.

This particular friend of mine had always been such a pragmatic and straightforward person, someone who was grounded and had very little time for fanciful ideas. She was one of those people in my life who was always generous, whose door was always open and who was always right there, ready to listen and offer help.

'Oh, look at this,' she suddenly piped up. 'It looks like an online forum. It's called A Reminiscence of Springburn.'

I was initially wary of using the computer to search public websites in this random way. However, at first glance this forum seemed almost too good to be true and certainly managed to capture my attention and snatch me out of the weak minded, poor me routine I was in. My friend and I had a brief scan through what appeared to be an immensely copious website. Though, given that it was a school night and the hour was ticking quickly by and we both had our children to bath and put to bed, we were forced to halt proceedings at that time. The little I did see, however, was enough to stir my inquisitive nature and rouse my tireless instincts to never let any new avenues pass me by. Suzanna wrote down the details so that I could follow it up for myself once I was at home and when I would have more time to properly absorb the information. I think I might have got my children washed and into bed in super quick time that evening!

This rather fabulous friend of mine had been someone who had always remained steadfast in her encouragement of my research and was one of the few people in my life who was constantly telling me never to give up and seemed sincere in her desire for me to succeed. She showed a great interest in how things were proceeding and was always ready with advice and suggestions. She also expressed her admiration in my determination and said she could not imagine being in my shoes. Suzanna refused to allow me to become defeated and whenever she saw me downhearted, she would always be ready to cajole me back to what was looking likely to become my lifelong quest to find a photograph of my mother.

'There must be one out there,' she would say. 'Your mum cannot have gone through the whole of her life without someone taking her photo. We just have to be sure that we are thorough and careful and look in all the right places.'

I was fortunate to have exceptional friends.

Once I was home and my children were both tucked up in their beds and the house was quiet, I switched on my computer. I typed in the name of the website, 'A Reminiscence of Springburn' and began reading. It was an amazing website consisting of past residents and old friends reuniting with each other through the forum and sharing their memories of Springburn, swapping old stories and displaying their old photographs. It listed lots of local schools right the way back to around the early 1900s, as well as shops and businesses. There was information written on the history of the town, famous buildings and landmarks, churches and so much more. It had old photographs of families and neighbours all gathered together out on the streets, groups of children with their long shorts and dresses dirty from play, each taken in different parts of the town. It had lots of old school class photographs with the old school buildings which were long since gone. It also had old maps showing the layout of the old town. The information contained in their website encompassed a whole lifestyle that was antiquated and rather sadly unheard of nowadays. It described a community that was united through a common need to share with each other the little that each family had, such as communal wash facilities where the women would gather on a specific day of the week to do all their laundry. Suzanna and I immediately thought we had hit the jackpot. We were sure we were going to come across someone enrolled in this forum who would remember my mother and her family. My expectations were soaring that I was surely going to get a photograph.

I was now, unexpectedly, propelled down the alternative route of using the internet as a tool for researching. Up until now all I had achieved had been by sheer leg work alone and this exciting prospect of finding answers simply by staying at home and sitting at my computer was completely new to me. I should confess that, although I had always been rather cautious of using the internet as I never quite trusted it to be completely safe, given that I was out of any alternative ideas at that time, this did hold a large element of hope for me. Unlike myself, however, my friend was not at all shy of getting stuck right in and before I knew it and with Suzanna providing me with a nudge in the right direction, there was no holding me back. There was no way

I could resist chasing my dream down such a wide avenue of opportunity. I was off again.

This particular online forum completely bowled me over. That very same evening, I proceeded to type in a message about my own connection to the town through my mother, along with some details of who my mother was. I made sure to add in the appropriate dates when she would have lived there both as a child, with her adoptive family and later when she had moved back into the area when she was married and would have had my eldest sister, Rhona.

With a new-found optimism lifting my spirits high, I eagerly waited to receive the news that at last someone held something, anything of my mother. I felt so sure that I was going to hear some good news this time. There simply had to be someone who must remember her, or at least had heard of the family. It was so intensely probable and potentially so viable that I was positively brimming with anticipation.

What in actual fact happened was that the proverbial carrot was once again dangled just outwith my grasp. I received lots of replies from people who purported to have lived close to her during the same time she was growing up, but not one person who could remember her. A lady even sent me a message saying that she would have played in the same patch of grass which separated their tenement blocks and that she would also have been around the same age as my mother at the time, but that she had no memory of the family living there. It was incredible to comprehend how a whole family could have gone unnoticed.

It was almost as though the thing I wished so badly to achieve was laid out in front of me and I was being invited to simply take it, but the very act of doing so seemed to change the dream into a delusion.

Another person replied to my message saying that they might have gone to school at the same time and asked whether I knew which school my mother and her brother had attended. With frustration once again dousing that initial spark of hope, I replied that at that time I held no information of the schools they would have gone to. Then this same lovely stranger kindly suggested that I tried the Springburn Library and even offered other alternative routes for me to try. He told me that he remembered that there were two families by the same surname as my mother living in the Springburn area at around that time.

I wondered, not for the first time, whether my mother had simply been invisible. Did she hide herself away or was she just someone who was painfully shy and so did not ever stand out in anyone's memory?

The people who I conversed with on this amazing website were more than kind. They would have been spread out all over the world by now, but even though they could not furnish me with anything concrete, I did feel very deeply that they wanted me to succeed. They provided me with a great image of what life would have been like in Springburn when my mother was a child.

A thoughtful and clearly very caring lady sent me a beautiful message which read:

There was indeed a strong community spirit the likes, probably, never to be seen again. Both addresses you gave were four storey tenements and part of the community spirit was that we all shared the same toilet on each landing. We shared a common clothes line and took turns cleaning the stairways, usually on a weekly basis. We shopped in the same stores. For most of us, we took our weekly bath at the same public swimming baths close by. Most family's incomes were much in the same region as each other so we all had much the same standard of living. We all took our vacations at the same time and lots of times to the same places as our neighbour's. Hopefully someone or some new member will remember your family.

This stunning message from a person whom I had never even met, although providing me with an invaluable picture of the kind of life style my mother would have had, also, inevitably, served to intensify the sadness I felt that no one could remember her.

Nevertheless, the genuine willingness of these complete strangers who selflessly gave up a small amount of their time to offer their help is extremely heartening. All the strands of deeply welcoming information which they have passed on to me has in turn assisted me in piecing together the jigsaw of a life to which I am fundamentally connected and ultimately an extension of. They have also kindly suggested larger, more wide-ranging sites for me to explore such as Old Glasgow Board, Virtual Mitchell and Friends Reunited.

Through the Old Glasgow Board's online website, I received information from a man living in Canada which was just amazing. Just like another person on the forum, this man thought that he might have attended the same school as my mother's adoptive brother but I unfortunately later discovered that they had gone to different schools.

I have discovered that indeed a lot of the people on these forums have emigrated all around the world but still hold onto the old-fashioned community spirit and who seem to sincerely want me to find what I am looking for. Not only have these considerate people provided me with some precious answers, but, as I have already stated, a few have also given me a real flavour of life in the old Glasgow tenement blocks in the thirties, forties right up to the seventies. I have even been lucky enough to get some pictures from the forum of the actual tenements where my mother had lived during her life in Springburn, including the block of tenements where she was when she died in 1977.

Moreover, by taking my time to read through the different available websites, it has especially moved me to see the great number of individuals who are also searching and are simply aching for something, anything that would fill the gaps in their lives.

The World Wide Web is truly a wonderful thing. The power it has to inflict pain is in equal measure to the power it has to bring joy. My wonderful friend who opened my mind to this line of enquiry will remain someone who I think so much of in a deeply grateful way and although I have told her this, I do not believe she fully comprehends just how important she is to my journey.

I would mention here that with the encouragement of Jill and my husband, I wrote an article regarding my experience of using the internet to further my research and of the kindness of the strangers on the different websites and forums who assisted me along the way. My article was published in *Family History Monthly* magazine and won star letter. By way of a prize, I received from them the folder which I have mentioned, which now holds all of my documented research and pictures. I was also written to by a lady from Canada in response to my article. She wrote:

> *Hi Elaine,*
> *Greetings from Canada.*
> *Thank you for writing to the Family History Monthly, it gave me some ideas of where to look for some of my answers to my questions. I will need time to study and process some of the information as I only received my magazine today…*

I have also written an article about Jill, my amazing social worker, which was published in *Your Family History* magazine and also won star letter. I also wrote an article about the children's home and about receiving the photographs from the lady who had helped to look after me which was published in the Christmas edition of *Family Tree* magazine.

These successes very much helped inspire me to write my story.

Chapter Fourteen

As my husband and I were sitting in our living room one evening mulling over all the things I had discovered from the Springburn forum, he came up with the suggestion that he and I could travel to the Mitchell Library in Glasgow to see if we could track down my mother's school records and perhaps from there we would manage to obtain a school photograph. Thanking him for his ceaseless belief in me, I hugged him tightly, feeling loved, extremely happy and proud to be married to someone who I considered to be such a caring man. My husband is a practical man who, although is not always as aware of human emotions as I would like, did seem to possess the ability to come through for me at moments when I least expected it.

My husband did not usually encourage me to open up to him when it came to my natural background and my life in foster care, and given that I was brought up never to talk about it to anyone this did not feel alien to me. In fact, it felt easier not to speak about it, as I had been conditioned to do. Whenever I spent time with my social worker, he did not ever ask me any questions regarding what was discussed or how I was feeling, or indeed how he was feeling. Unlike my foster parents, however, he was very interested in knowing the technicalities, but never wanted to hear the bare specifics. A lot of people have told me that this is simply down to the fact that he is the male of the species, but I have never been able to accept this as an excuse to disregard or turn away from one who is emotionally in need. Unfortunately, it has come to my mind that, like so many situations in life, it is only when things reach a point where taking action is paramount that appropriate attention is paid.

The day we travelled into Glasgow together was pivotal to us coming together in my research rather than me going about things with his support firmly fixed to the sidelines. It was different to the time we had all visited the Children's Home in that this time it was completely planned and thought out beforehand whereas visiting the Children's Home had been an out of the blue, on the spot decision. My husband had expressed a keen desire to go to the Library and I could tell it held some interest for him to come with me.

The Mitchell Library is an impressive building. When I first arrived, it struck me how I had spent many times in years gone by looking up at its huge expanse as I travelled along the motorway. It stood out from the surrounding buildings, with its opulent yellow stonework and large green dome. It had never crossed my mind before then that it held a hive of information and would some day prove to be essential to my own research.

Sufficiently tooled up with the details of my mother's date of birth and the approximate year she would have started school, we approached the lady behind the desk and enquired about whether it was possible to see her records. The lady tapped the details into her computer and confirmed that the records did indeed exist in their offices. She then asked us to take a seat while she looked them out for us. Adrenalin coursed through me. The room was very large, with tall windows, wall-to-wall shelves of antiquated books and centred with huge desks. Although the atmosphere was very hushed and calm, a scattering of people all sat squirrelling away at their own research, I was feeling charged with energy. My husband and I sat down at one of the desks and again, I willed myself to be patient while my heart was positively leaping in my chest. In no time at all, the lady returned with two very old-looking, large books which she carefully placed onto the table in front of us, confirming that they held the appropriate records. She then walked back to the main desk, leaving us to sift through the pages of children, schools and dates, in search of my mother's name.

We opened the first book and very quickly came to the relevant pages. The records were written in neat rows according to the appropriate dates. Running our eyes down the list of names, suddenly it was there, in front of us, my own mother's actual name, as real as I ever could dare myself to imagine. I think my heart might have skipped a beat or two as I felt so incredulous at seeing it. To be able to look at her authentic school records, handwritten in the large archaic volumes of that time was very moving and it touched my heart. I felt extremely privileged and sensed that seeing her name, written at such an important time in her childhood, had somehow brought me a significant step closer to my mother.

As we slowly read through the records pertaining to my mother's school attendance, however, the information it contained was ultimately mind-boggling. This is the information written.

My mother started at Wellfield Primary School on 3 September 1940. She then left to go to Albert School two months later on 11 November 1940. Two months on she was re-admitted to Wellfield on 6 January 1941. But she left again almost one and a half years later, this time to attend Keppochhill School on 11 May 1943, aged nine. However, she was again re-admitted to Wellfield two years later on 26 February 1945.

My mother left Wellfield on 1 September 1947 aged thirteen, having 'qualified' for Colston Junior Secondary— but spent just two years there, leaving on 1 November 1949, aged fifteen. The records had a small after note which stated that Colston closed as a "special" school on 2 April 1947.

None of it made any sense to me and yet there it was, written down in black and white. It was a good thing that I had my husband with me at the time because when I read all the different schools she had attended my mind quite simply shut down and I literally could not take in what I was reading.

'I'm confused,' I said to my husband.

'Just write down what I say, I'll read it out for you.'

I stated earlier how I had, before now, always insisted in carrying out all my research alone. However, this time I was very grateful that my husband had come with me. He not only took control and proved to be a great help on the day but having him on board went a long way to lifting the stigma of secrecy regarding my being fostered which I had carried all my life and which was now firmly opened up between us. It enabled me to use the moment to open up a little and talk to him about how it felt for me. Moreover, he seemed to be extremely interested and full of anticipation on my behalf and even said to me, 'It isn't right that you don't have a photo of your mum. You shouldn't be having to go to these lengths. Someone should have been able to give you one. You just couldn't make this up. You should be writing this, Elaine.'

Later that day, once I had returned home, I decided to telephone my mother's brother to ask him what he could remember about his school years and to find out whether he knew why my mother had moved so often and between so many schools. Once again, I found him to be very reti-cent. He could not provide me with any direct explanations, blaming his lack of knowledge on his poor memory. I could not help feeling that he was holding something back from me. The only piece of information he could relay to me was, 'We did move to Keppochhill at one point.'

However, he was unable to confirm whether the move was due to schooling, housing or down to some other reason. It just felt very obscure and much like he was being obstructive. I struggled to conceal my frustrations.

While at the Mitchell Library, I had asked the lady at the desk as to whether they held an archive of class photographs from the schools in Springburn. She immediately directed us to the School Museum on Scotland Street in Glasgow. The lady told us that all the photographs which had been brought to the Mitchell Library from the Springburn Museum when it had been closed were subsequently sent on to Scotland Street.

So, with determination pushing us on, that very same day my husband and I travelled straight from the Mitchell Library to the Museum on Scotland Street. However, on arrival we were instantly faced with yet more wearisome news to the effect that although the photographs had indeed been sent on to the Museum by the Mitchell, none of the photographs had in actual fact been kept by the Museum but had, for some inexplicable reason, been sent straight back to the Mitchell. The good lady at the reception desk passed me the name and telephone number of the Social History Curator from the Burrell Museum, confirming that this was the person who was originally set with the task of logging each photograph which had been received from the Springburn Museum and so would be the appropriate person to assist me. By the time we left the Museum in Scotland Street the day had stretched late into the after-noon, the sky had turned dark and the rain was coming down. How apt, I thought to myself, feeling the inclement weather very much reflected my despondency.

The next day, feeling more than a little exasperated, I

picked up the telephone and punched in the number for the Curator of the Burrell Museum. The telephone was answered very promptly as a female voice with a softly spoken English accent came down the line. She listened attentively to my story and promised that she would do what she could and get back to me. After taking the time to consult her records, she returned my call, stating that she had indeed found a record of at least one class photograph from Colston Junior Secondary which tied in with the same year in which my mother would have been in attendance. The lady confirmed that the photograph was held at the Mitchell and gave me the code which she herself had put onto the back of the picture.

With mounting anticipation I once again telephoned the Mitchell Library, giving them the number of the picture which the Curator had given me and requesting that they kindly order up the photograph on my behalf. I was told that this would take time and that I would receive a telephone call from them once it had been recovered. My patience was once again put to the test.

Around one week later, the call duly came from the Mitchell Library confirming that they had managed to retrieve the class photograph and stating that I needed to come into the Library in person to collect and pay for it. Armed with the number and year of the picture and brimming with fresh hope, I again took another trip into Glasgow's magnificent Mitchell Library and this time my darling daughter accompanied me. After making our request to the lady behind the reception desk, we were directed to sit down at the same large table my husband and I had sat at and, as you might well have guessed, once more I struggled to wait patiently. As we sat, I silently wished over and over in my head, 'Please let this be it, please.' I tried to keep my breaths even as my anticipation was almost bursting out of me.

'I can't believe I'm here in this place right now,' I said to my daughter. 'This might be it. I think this photo is going to be the one. I can feel it. After everything, today is the day that I'm going to hold a picture of my mother in my hands.'

Of course, what I was actually conveying was a measure of the reality of my grappling. I was abundantly and, albeit reluctantly, aware that I would have to take the photograph to my mother's adoptive brother and his wife in order for them to verify that she was really in the picture, given that I had never actually seen my mother's face. However, I refused to allow the pragmatic nature of this detail to in any way dispel my dream of achieving my ultimate goal. There was a part of me that so badly wanted to believe I would instantly know her if ever I saw her, that her image would have an unspoken, fundamental familiarity which only exists between mother and child.

What happened next, we could not ever have been prepared for.

The fire alarm suddenly burst into life, sending the staff into instantaneous action, ushering everyone through the emergency doors and out into the street round the side of the building, while the fire brigade were called. I could not believe it. On this of all days, for the Library to be on fire would be catastrophic. No sooner had this thought registered in my brain when my daughter tapped my arm and said, 'This would not be a good day for the Library to burn down, just when you could be about to get your photo!'

All we could do was watch as two fire engines arrived. My eyes darted all around the building, looking for any signs of smoke or flames, but I could see none.

'This cannot happen,' I said to my daughter. 'It's got to be a false alarm.'

I tried to keep my spirits up by smiling and making light of the situation.

'Well, at least the sun is shining!' I piped up. 'Wouldn't be any fun having to stand out here in the rain.'

Thankfully my instincts were proved correct and after an agonising wait of about forty minutes, the fire engines eventually left and the all clear was announced. Everyone was allowed to re-enter the building.

On our return to the room, I was very relieved to find that awaiting me on the desk was an A5 brown envelope with the photograph inside. I held on to it tightly, once again silently praying that please, at last, let this be it. I turned to my daughter and said, 'This is the closest I have ever come to having a picture of my mum. Can you believe that right here, in my hands, could be my chance to having the one thing I have always wanted.'

My daughter squeezed my arm and smiled.

'It would be amazing. After everything you have been through.'

Impatient as always, as soon as we had stepped back out into the street, I carefully opened the envelope and removed the black and white class photograph. It felt like holding a precious, fragile gem. The children in the picture looked like they were of varying ages. The boys were dressed in the old-fashioned long shorts and the girls all wore dresses and had their hair tied back, some with ribbons. I gazed at each face, trying to pick out any features which were similar to my own, concentrating on the girls whose hair was darker, long and wavy or were tall and slim as I had been during my school years. Nevertheless, how could I possibly pick out my mother's face without ever having seen it, without having a single memory to base it on? Even though I realistically already knew this would be the case, the brick of disappointment weighed heavily inside my stomach, but I did not dare to say the words out loud. Instead I placed the photograph back into the envelope and went home, clinging to the tiny fading shred of hope that my mother's adoptive brother would tell me what I desperately wanted to hear.

After I had gained a note of the schools which my mother had attended from the records at the Mitchell Library, I went back into my computer to have another look at the A Reminiscence of Springburn website. The site displayed photographs of two of the primary schools as well as the secondary school which she had gone to and I was able to print off pictures of the relevant schools as well as some of the class photographs, taking particular care to be certain that each picture had the appropriate dates pertaining to my mother's attendance noted on them.

Thereafter, I went straight to the telephone to call George. I explained how I had managed to acquire the photographs of some relevant schools in Springburn and that I would be very grateful if he would allow me to visit him and his wife and bring along the photographs so that they could confirm for me whether or not my mother was in any of them. George agreed for me to come through, saying that I was welcome to visit with them and that they would be happy to look at the photographs.

So I found myself once again travelling back into Glasgow, this time on my own. George and Rita gave me a warm welcome, as they always did, and I passed the photographs over so that they could scan the faces to see if they could pick out my mother. Adrenalin coursed through me once more as I sat on the settee opposite, observing their expressions for any glimmer of recognition, my mind silently begging them to announce that she was there. First of all George looked, then he passed them on to Rita, then back to George, but I could tell from their body language, before they even uttered the words, that it was fruitless. I could feel George and Rita positively willing her to be on the page as they even resorted to the use of a magnifying class, meticulously studying each face, but it was not to be. The answer was yet another no.

'I'm so sorry for you, Elaine. I really hoped that this would be it. You're sure Rhona hasn't got any photos? We definitely gave her all the photos we had of your mum because we thought it was right that she should have them,' said Rita.

I did not have any words left to say. We had been through all of that before and I could feel the energy for it ebbing away. Although my head was reasoning that George and Rita were not deliberately obstructing me from having a picture, my heart refused to allow me to accept this. My mother's brother, the very person I wholeheartedly trusted to surely have so much of his sister to share with me, her last born child, his niece, evidently had nothing. It felt intolerable that this should be the reality I was being forced to face.

I drove home unable to cry. It was one more let down to add to my list. I felt like shouting, 'Why, why can I not have this?' It felt like there was a hand pressing against my chest, pushing me back whenever I was getting too close, holding me firmly in my place. That whenever there was even an ounce of hope, that same hand would always be there, ready to snatch it away. It was as if there was some force, higher than me, saying that I was unworthy of ever having anything of my mother, that I did not deserve her. 'I was her daughter, yet I was not allowed to see her or to have any part of her life.' There were all these people who were living right there, so easily accessible, who had seen her, spoken to her, touched her and had the privilege to be in her world and yet, despite this, I could never have what they had of her because she was not important enough a person for them to have kept her memory safe. It was so unfair.

Chapter Fifteen

After my success in gaining my mother's birth name from her adoption records in Glasgow Sheriff Court I was now managing to tie together many different threads to her own natural background. I now had the names of some distant relatives from the records I had gained from my visits to Register House. I was managing to piece together a significant portion of my family tree. However, the information I had obtained was full of holes and because of this, my family tree was far from complete. I felt frustrated at myself for being too hasty when I had last visited Register House. In my sheer delight at being able to go farther back to my ancestor's lives, I had not been thorough when taking notes of the names and dates of some of the births, marriages or deaths or of the other details held on those vital records. I decided it was time for another trip to Edinburgh.

I had, by now, a much better idea of exactly what information I wished to find and so was able to make sure that I was properly organised. I put together a list of the precise questions I wanted answered and took along the family tree I had managed to set out thus far.

This was my third visit to Register House and I had by

now obtained a good knowledge of how to go about using their computers to obtain the information I was looking for. This time I was led into a different room, which was set out almost like a high school Information Technology classroom, with rows of desks lined with computers and swivel chairs and each allocated with their separate login and password. It seemed that Register House was always busy. So many people searching, just as I was, beavering away at their own family research. I paid the standard fifteen pounds required for carrying out a day's research, was allocated my desk and I eagerly set to work.

Every time I had visited Register House, I had always enjoyed the experience and got a real thrill at being able to acquire facts about my own family history. The task of trudging meticulously and laboriously through the endless lists of dates and names was something which I relished. I found I enjoyed a sense of euphoria whenever I was successful at finding a member of my family among the hundreds of similar names which the records hold and on that particular day I had great success. I was able to gradually tick off every question on my list. Each time I hit on the correct relative's details, whether it be their birth, marriage or death, I was struck with an overwhelming urge to celebrate. I wanted to jump to my feet and wave my hands in the air proudly announcing in my loudest voice to everyone in the room, 'I've found them!'

It was that much of a rush.

Being prepared with a list of the specific information I

required meant that I could direct my focus more closely to precise tasks without allowing myself to drift into those wider details, which inevitably came up during my search. That day, I managed to gain all the dates and names I wanted and, more importantly, I was also able to print off all the relevant records so that I could examine them in more detail and at my leisure, once I was at home. I brought home eight different records that day. I was very happy and excited to see how my family tree would look once I had put in all the new information. I had reached as far back as 1846 to my three times great-grandparents on both sides. I had fun rewriting my family tree in much more detail. I felt a sense of duty as I did this, to myself, to my children, to my mother. I was aware of a tenuous connection to those people whose names I eternalised, as I proudly placed my family tree at the very front of my folder.

I found it exceptionally fascinating to read about all the various occupations my ancestors had, their places of work as well as where they had lived. All this was on the certificates which I had printed out in Edinburgh.

I shall now attempt to give an overview of what the records said. I must warn that it is rather complicated, but is also, I believe, very intriguing.

Beginning with my ancestors running down the right-hand side of my mother's family tree there was my three times great-grandfather Peter Ritchie, Police Constable, and his wife Rhonaine McCallum, married in Glasgow in 1856. The Ritchie family were resident at 15 Tobago

Street, in the East End of Glasgow, and this is given as the address where their daughter Agnes Ritchie was born in 1874. Agnes's birth record states that her father was present at her birth and I believe this would have been very rare in those days. The original Police Station was also situated on Tobago Street and very probably was Peter Ritchie's place of work. I discovered by way of the internet that the original police building still remains intact today and I printed off a picture of how it had looked then from the website; this now sits in my folder. My husband and I have since taken a trip along to Tobago Street and were able to see the actual building for ourselves. It was surreal to be able to stand in the same doorway which my ancestor would have walked through every day, all those years ago, during the course of his employment.

My other three times great-grandfather, still keeping to the right-hand side of my family tree, was James McEwen, a coachman and domestic servant and his wife Helen McNeillie, married in Stoneykirk in 1846. The McEwen family were resident at 55 Cubie Street, also in the East End of Glasgow and very close to Tobago Street. This address is given as the place where their son William McEwen was born in the year 1873.

When their respective children, my two times great-grand-parents William McEwen and Agnes Ritchie, were married in the year 1894, Agnes's family were by then stated to have moved to 27 Soho Street, which at that time sat back to back with Cubie Street and, living in such close proximity to one another, this is very likely to be how William and Agnes would have met each other. Their marriage record gives 7 Cubie Street as being William's residence while 108 Cubie Street is given as being the place where William and Agnes were married. Peter Ritchie was by then a Superintendent Fire Brigader. An interesting fact to come to my attention, once again by way of using the internet as a tool for gaining my information, is that the fire station which serviced the whole area happened to be situated in Soho Street and is very likely also where Peter Ritchie worked.

At the time when William and Agnes's daughter Elizabeth Ritchie McEwen, my great-grandmother, was born in 1895, William was working as a sewing machine factory operative. Once again, the address 7 Cubie Street is given as being the place where Elizabeth was born.

Cubie Street had now appeared on four separate occasions in my research and my interest was very much roused as to why this should be. Using the internet proved to be a very enlightening tool as, by simply by typing in the street name, I happened to come across an historian by the name of John Robertson who had carried out his own study of Cubie Street some years earlier and who was more than happy to provide me with some great information. He sent me an email stating the following;

Number Fifty five, had been demolished in the year 1892 to make way for Annfield Primary School. It would be easy to surmise that Elizabeth would have attended Annfield

Primary. This would have been why the family had moved to number Seven by the year 1895, the year of Elizabeth's birth. [...] It would have been fortuitous that Elizabeth was born at this time, because in the year 1897 toilets and a wash house had been added to the building. The address sat above the Shandon Bar or Shandon Bell's as it was locally known.

This same person very kindly managed to provide me with a photograph of this building with the pub on the corner and the dwelling above, which was taken in 1967. He went on to state that 108 Cubie Street (which was noted on the marriage certificate) would have been a tenement building at the time and so, as far as he was concerned, it seemed strange that it was stated as a place of marriage. I was also very grateful to receive a photograph of the Soho Fire Station where my ancestor had worked.

The power of the internet in its ability to assist me in the most informative way and at such a personal level with these fascinating facts about places and people so intrinsically connected to me was truly astonishing.

I have also managed to find out that all those years ago when my ancestors were alive, that being born, brought up, then married and working all within close proximity of each other was not unusual in those days, as people did not tend to have the means to travel far in the same way that we do nowadays. The historian who contacted me from the Cubie Street website has been able to tell me that there is only one original building still remaining on the Cubie

Street site—the Post Office. My husband and I have visited the street but, as I was informed, there is nothing left of the original buildings apart from the old Post Office. It was impossible to gain any impression of what it would have looked like back then, which makes receiving the photograph of the original street all the more precious. I also discovered that some past residents are campaigning to keep the Post Office in place and that, at some time, there had been a Cubie Street Exhibition, put together by the same gentleman who had emailed me regarding my queries on the Cubie Street addresses. It was also pointed out to me that the streets in Glasgow's old East End were described as slums and that the people who belonged there would have lived an impoverished life. This I was able to witness for myself in some of the old photographs which had been on display at the Exhibition. The grime and squalor was clearly evident and I felt a pang of sadness for those distant relatives having to survive in such conditions, although I sensed a strong community spirit in the eyes of the people in the pictures.

Moving on to the left-hand side of the family tree, pertaining solely to my mother's family, there is my three times great-grandfather William Hay, a bleach workman, and his wife, Margaret Gilmour Craig, married in Newton Mearns in 1855. The Hay family were resident at Netherplace in Newton Mearns at the time of their son's birth: Dugald Craig Hay was born in 1864, by which time William Hay had moved on to become a retired bleach work manager.

Again, sticking to the left-hand side of the family tree, there is my other three times great-grandfather, James Scott, master baker, and his wife Jeanie Craig, married in Newton Mearns in 1858. Their daughter, Helen Clement Craig Scott, was born in Newton Mearns in 1864.

Their respective children, my two times great-grandparents, Dugald Craig Hay and Helen Clement Craig Scott were married in Newton in 1896. Their son William Scott Hay was subsequently born in Glasgow in 1896. I would surmise from William's birth record that Dugald and Helen had eventually moved the family into the city of Glasgow.

One other very interesting address which frequently appeared in the records was Baltic Chambers, 50 Wellington Street, Glasgow, which sits right in the centre of Glasgow, very close to George Square. This address is recorded as the building where my great-grandfather, William Scott Hay and his wife Elizabeth Ritchie McEwen were married in the year 1917. Even more significant is the fact that this address is also given as a place of residence for Elizabeth and her parents at the time of their marriage.

I once again looked up the Cubie Street and Wellington Street addresses on the internet and found that Cubie Street was listed on a local Glasgow news website pertaining to the Cubie Street Exhibition. I left an enquiry by email to the editor, giving details about my interest in this address and also enquiring about the Wellington Street address. To my surprise, around three weeks later I received a reply. A lady called Grace, who was the editor, was very interested in my story. She wrote that she had passed my enquiry on to a man who she knew had information that would assist me and that she would get back to me in due course. She mentioned also that it was odd that Wellington Street was noted as a residential address for a private individual as she had always known it to be a rather prominent office building. She said that today some Glasgow Members of the Scottish Parliament have space there. She continued that it was possible that the building, like so many in the city, had a resident caretaker who would have been provided with his own flat in the building. Such flats were usually situated at the top of the building. She wrote, 'This being so, we would have called it the penthouse suite if it were current day.'

The very next morning, after reading this email, I woke in the small hours with a start. I put on the light and ran down the stairs to look at the records I held from Register House. There it was. One of the records stated that when Elizabeth Ritchie McEwen married William Scott Hay in 1917 at 50 Wellington Street, Glasgow, Elizabeth's father's occupation was by then listed as caretaker and electrician. Indeed, it looked like Elizabeth's father, William, had managed to escape the slums of Cubie Street in the East end of Glasgow and saved his young daughter from living out an impoverished life and in so doing, had successfully provided improved living conditions for them all. Unbelievable!

It felt really good to be able to tie up another loose end. It would have meant that the family could enjoy a much healthier and more prosperous life and would have provided the means for William, who was a Lieutenant in the Royal Air Force and Elizabeth to meet one another and to be married. It would have been more unlikely, I would presume, for their paths to have crossed should Elizabeth have stayed resident in the slums of Cubie Street.

The building still stands today right in the centre of Glasgow and still serves as offices. I have managed to obtain photographs of the building's exterior and entry hallway from the internet, but, also took another trip into Glasgow to see the place for myself, along with my husband and daughter, who had her camera with her and got some fantastic pictures from the street in front of the building for me to add to my folder. I could not resist going into the building while we were there, even though it looked rather grand and extremely private. The interior was very lavish, with huge fireplaces which I could see from just inside a room where the door had been left ajar. The hallway had a high ceiling, ornately decorated in cream and peach colours and a large staircase which positively enticed me to climb to satisfy my curiosity. There were three small, colourful, stained-glass windows on the bend of the first staircase. At the bottom of the middle one it read Baltic Chambers, 1912. I would have loved to see the attic space to gain some idea of what it would have been like for my ancestors to live there. However, when I stepped inside, the doorman immediately approached me and it was obvious that a tour was definitely out of the question. I told him of my reason for being there and he confirmed that he knew that many weddings and other ceremonies had taken place there over the decades and that indeed there had been a lot of visitors from all around the world who had come to see the place for themselves and who had their own ancestral links to the building. He confirmed that the building would have looked the same except for the contemporary decor although he confirmed that some of the rooms did have the original fireplaces.

I wondered about why the building was named Baltic Chambers, but very quickly observed a common theme occurred in the area. Baltic Chambers sat on Wellington Street, next to Atlantic House which was round the corner from Waterloo Street.

One very odd fact which I came upon was that when I looked again at the military records for William Scott Hay dated 1918 (which I had managed to obtain from the National Archives in England), his address was noted as 10–14 Barrhead Road, Newton Mearns. However, his wife's address was given as 'care of McEwen, Baltic Chambers, 50 Wellington Street, Glasgow. McEwen was Elizabeth's maiden name. This was very confusing: why would the records give two separate addresses for a married couple? I have so far been unable to establish the reason for this but perhaps some person may in the future be able to give me an answer.

It was inspiring to learn that I came from such a long line of strong, hard-working, decent people. My ancestors had strived to gain responsible jobs and to provide the very best they could for their families. The very fact that they had at one time lived and eventually broken free of poverty-stricken lives makes me feel so sorry, given that my own mother had ended up living in such abject poverty and had to endure all that she had done. Her demise is all the more devastating knowing that no one had strived to better things on her behalf when times had been hardest for her.

Chapter Sixteen

As I reflected on my last visit to Register House and meticulously studied the details on some of the records which I had acquired of my ancestors, I noticed that there was a strong link to Newton Mearns. William Scott Hay, the Lieutenant in the Royal Air Force, his brother, his parents and their parents are all mentioned as resident in Newton Mearns. I also noted that the family had run a bakery in the same town under the name Hay. Moreover, my grandmother's name was Muriel Ritchie Hay. Register House had failed to supply any record of my grandmother after my mother's birth.

I now wondered if there perhaps might be some of the family by the name of Hay still living in Newton Mearns.

With this thought in mind, I went back onto the British Telecom residential website and tapped in the words, Hay and Newton Mearns. It flagged up eighteen people with that name who were resident within the Newton Mearns area. I printed out the list. Feeling ambitious once more and with my usual impulsive nature spurring me on, I turned to my husband and said, 'I plan to telephone every one of these numbers because any one of them could be a living blood relative.'

To which he replied, 'Aye, that's okay with me, so long as it's after seven in the evenings and at weekends!' This was due to the fact that we received free calls in those hours.

Therefore, with my husband's albeit emotionally detached approval, over the next couple of weeks I did indeed telephone every person who was noted as having the name Hay and living in Newton Mearns. I meticulously worked my way down through the list, crossing off each name as I went.

Keeping my voice even and being sure to avoid the words, 'I am not trying to sell you anything', I stated who I was and my reason for calling, giving the names of my grandmother, Muriel Ritchie Hay and great grandparents, William and Elizabeth Hay and explaining their connection to the area. Unfortunately, my efforts proved unsuccessful as, perhaps rather unsurprisingly, it turned out that no one on the list was in actual fact related to me. A few people were rather rude and immediately dismissive saying they knew nothing of my relatives and abruptly hung up, whereas there were some who, at the very least, extended me the courtesy of attentively listening to my story before confirming that they were of no relation to me and then showing a little compassion by wishing me luck. However, I did manage to speak to two individuals who were evidently genuinely kind and who were interested enough to offer me their help.

Firstly I spoke to a lady who said she had a relative whose husband's name was Hay. After listening to me, she promised to write a letter to her relative—who had since moved abroad—saying she would explain to her relative who I was and said if I gave her my address she would ask her to write a letter to me. This lady mentioned that her relative had carried out some family history research of their own and so should be very interested to hear from me. Despite the good intentions behind what she said, I did not feel any confidence in her words as I knew it was a tenuous promise.

Nevertheless, to my utter astonishment, some two weeks later I did indeed receive a letter from her relation. The lady's name was Sheilaann and she had written to me all the way from Washington State in the United States of America. She wrote that she was the granddaughter of a lady who also had the name Ritchie Hay, which happened to be the same name as my own grandmother. In fact, the coincidences were too big for me not to sit up and take notice and enough for my hopes to be stirred. She said her father's name was Hay, that he was born in Aberdeen and that he had then moved into Glasgow. She herself was born in Glasgow and then moved to America in her twenties. Our two families had shared the same name and were both connected to Glasgow. My anticipation soared. Could it be possible that I was about to discover what happened to my grandmother and to find more relatives in this random way?

Amazingly, this complete stranger, who herself at once became absolutely convinced that we must be cousins somewhere down the line since we evidently had such strong similarities in our family trees, then proceeded to do her own research from across the Atlantic, based on Muriel Ritchie Hay. This kind-hearted lady coincidently happened to be currently in the middle of looking into her own family history, just as the woman in Newton Mearns had told me and because of this, she was very keen to find out if we were connected in any way. She went to great lengths to research her Glasgow roots, determined that she would find a blood line between us. She contacted sources in Aberdeen as this was where her ancestor had originated from and she looked into Parish records. She even mentioned that there was a link in her family to Newton Mearns.

However, I had already delved into the history of where my ancestors were from which, in my case, was mainly the Newton Mearns suburb of Glasgow and then from right within the heart of the city. It was looking less and less likely that we were related.

In the end there proved to be no connection between us; she informed me that her own ancestors appeared to hail from Aberdeen and I had found no one from my family having been recorded as living there. All my instincts were telling me that we were not related. I wrote that I thought we may not be of the same blood, despite there being the name Ritchie Hay in both our families. I said that finding a living relative in America would have been amazing and how it was so wonderful to be in touch with someone who possessed the same drive and ambition as myself to find out everything possible of their origins and extended family members. It was exciting while it lasted.

I stayed in touch with this lovely lady by email and it turned out that we have some wonderful things in common.

One of those things was to do with my plan to give my mother a headstone. Sheilaann told me that she had learned that when her brother had died in Scotland some years ago, no one at the time could afford to put a headstone at his grave. She told me that she had made plans to do this when she next visited Scotland.

Sheilaann told me that she would like us to meet up together when next she comes to Scotland. Although I think this would be fantastic, it is probably unrealistic.

The second person to offer me help was a lady called Thelma who was still living in Newton Mearns. Thelma patiently listened while I told her that I was looking for the addresses in Newton Means where my relatives had lived and how I had hoped to find a relative still living there. I also explained that I was having some difficulty finding one particular address, Manse Lane, which was stated in the records as being where my two times great-grandfather William Scott Hay had died. I explained that on his death record it is written that his own brother was the informant, was present at the time of his death and that he too resided in the same town, at Barrhead Road.

Thelma seemed to find my story interesting and very kindly made some suggestions for me to follow up, such as going to the local library to check if they had any information. She went on to mention that she knew of a local historical society who she was certain would surely be able to help me. She even said that my story had intrigued her so much that she herself wanted to know how it was going to turn out for me and that she wished me, 'all the luck in the world' and to be, 'in touch again to let me know how things go'.

I was once again utterly astonished when, a few days later I actually received a message left on my telephone from Thelma saying, 'Elaine, can you give me a call back whenever you get this message? I think I might have something.'

I telephoned Thelma immediately, feeling the old familiar rush of anticipation churning inside my stomach. It turned out that this very generous lady had contacted the Mearns Historical Society on my behalf and told them of my research and a little about who I was and what I was hoping to find. I was flabbergasted! Not only had she genuinely taken a note of my ancestor's names and the names of the streets I was interested in, but she had also passed these details onto the Society and asked if they could help. Thelma instructed me to telephone a lady called Anne who belonged to the Society and who had told her that she might hold some relevant information for me.

I could not believe how kind Thelma had been to do this for me. I told her that sometimes all it took to get a little piece of good news was to keep my faith and tenacity strong that one day I would find the right person to help me. Thelma again asked me to keep in touch with her and to let her know how I got on. Also that she would love for me to come to Newton Mearns and meet up with her some time soon. I could not express my gratitude enough.

I wasted no time at all in dialling the number Thelma

had given me and, oh my word, the news was mind-blowing! This great lady, Anne, knew a lot about my ancestors due to the Society's hard work in compiling a book based on the history behind every headstone in the Mearns Kirk Graveyard. She told me she had the actual book in front of her and proceeded to read some extremely amazing details regarding my ancestors straight from the pages. I could not stop myself from gasping every time she mentioned a relevant name or other correct piece of information which I had already gleaned from the various records I had gained from Register House. Snippets of information such as the fact that my ancestor Dugald Craig Hay and his father-in-law James Scott had been bakers. It made her laugh to hear how utterly ecstatic I was at having someone offer me validation of the information I had worked so hard to acquire. This was the first time that someone was actually able to hand me the information instead of me having to painstakingly pick away at any tiny threads and clues which happened to come my way.

Anne invited me to visit her home in Newton Mearns so that we could have a chance to go over everything she had. I had literally experienced a real life, 'Who Do You Think You Are?' moment. All that was missing was the television crew!

She asked me to her house and offered me lunch. I took her up on her offer and while I was there she spoke of how my ancestors had founded a bakery and made a massive success of the business. She handed me a copy of the Society's book, which held the details of my relative's grave, for me to keep. It showed a picture of the headstone itself, underneath which was noted exactly what was written on the stone and a page detailing some history of the family.

The inscription on the stone was as follows:

Erected by James Scott, in memory of his son, David, who died 3rd October 1883, aged 20 years, also my wife, Jeanie Craig, who died 8th February 1914, aged 76 years, his son James, died 11th July 1920 aged 62 years, the above James Scott, died 18th December 1923 in his 90th year. Life is short, death is sure, sin the wound, Christ the cure.

The pages in the book entitled Mearns Kirkyard Project 2008 read:

This very obviously Victorian style monument was raised in memory of the family of a local baker in the village of Newton.

James Scott was born to parents John Scott, a gardener to trade and Janet Pollock and came from the district of East Kilbride. He met and subsequently married a young servant girl by the name of Jeanie Craig. Jeanie, who originally had been born and raised in the village of Eaglesham, was the child of a local builder called John Craig and his spouse Ellen Finlay Clements.

The marriage between James Scott and Jeanie Craig took place, not in the bride's village of Eaglesham as would be expected, but in East Kilbride. The reason why there was this break in tradition is unknown, but the couple celebrated their marriage on 13th April 1858. At the time of the marriage the bridegroom was twenty-four years of age while the bride was nineteen.

The couple through time settled in the village of Newton where James Scott set up his bakery business which was successful enough for him to have to employ staff. The fact that he did so entitled him to acquire the title of Master Baker.

The family soon arrived but, unfortunately, one of the sons was born with a condition then described as Potts Curvature of the Spine. This degenerative condition is nowadays diagnosed as Tuberculosis of the Spine. The effects of this condition in this case resulted in the softening of the spine which effectively put an end to this young man's life prematurely. This son, David by name, had, despite his condition gained employment as a clerk in the Apothecary Hall in the village which was today's equivalent of the chemist's shop. David expired at the tender age of twenty years and was first to be laid to rest in this plot. The parents and another son James joined their relative to rest under this monument in due course.

James Scott, the Master Baker, lived to the very advanced age of his ninetieth year.

After lunch, Anne drove me to the Mearns Kirk cemetery to visit the grave which had been written about in the book. It was beautiful. Very tall and ornate. The wording was incised and though it had been erected in 1883 it was still extremely clear to read. I felt very proud to be able to stand there in that ancient cemetery and read their names, the very same names I had discovered at Register House and which I had at home printed on the records which now sat within my folder. The weather on that day was bright and sunny and I took my own pictures of the stone as well as the lovely whitewashed Mearns Kirk, which stood with a commanding presence at the head of the cemetery set against a perfect blue sky. Anne was exceptionally knowledgeable and told me more of the history of the Church. It gave me a real genuine warmth inside to be there where my ancestors had been laid to rest.

Anne and I then returned to her house. She and her husband had prepared for my visit by looking out appropriate old books which detailed the history of Newton Mearns and contained old maps which showed the addresses where my ancestors had lived, including the Manse Lane address where William Scott Hay had died. The address no longer existed, which explained why I could not find it. It also marked exactly where the bakery had stood, and included some pictures of the actual street as it had looked back in the 1890s when James Scott was the Master Baker.

It felt good to be able to carefully put all my photographs and maps evidencing my connection to Newton Mearns, into my folder.

I was so happy. I felt ill-equipped to properly convey how deeply grateful I was to meet them and for all the things they had done for me. Anne and her husband were strangers to me yet they were so welcoming, helpful and encouraging that I felt as if I had always known them. They really made me feel quite special. I had enjoyed a lot of wonderful experiences along my journey and this day was right up there with the best of them.

Anne had one more surprise for me before I returned home that day. She took me along to meet an exceptionally nice old gentleman called David Arthur who was aged eighty-six and who Anne's husband and I think we have worked out would be my cousin three times removed. He was so interested in meeting me, and I was equally delighted to meet him. David explained to me that we were related by way of his father's sister's marriage to my two times great-grandmother, Helen Clement Craig Scott's brother, Alf Scott.

David shared a common interest in his ancestry and had employed someone a few years ago to do some family research on his behalf and because of this, David was able to hand me pages of information he had uncovered, which travelled some years further back from my own research. In these pages were the names of the parents of my great, great, great-grandparents from the left-hand side of my mother's family tree, and also where they were from—which, I had previously read from the book Anne had given me, was in the district of East Kilbride.

The information in the pages confirmed what David had already told me, that his Aunt, Margaret Boyd Chalmers married my great, great-grandmother's brother, Albert James McIntyre Scott.

In further detail, my Newton Mearns ancestor who had started the bakery was my great, great, great-grandfather, James Scott, born on 11 May 1834 in East Kilbride and his wife Jeanie Craig, born on 12 May 1838 in Eaglesham, whose family grave I visited. In the pages David had given to me, it was stated that James Scott was awarded the great privilege of becoming a 'Freeman of Glasgow, in honour of his standing as a successful baker in the city'. James Scott's daughter, Helen, married Dugald Craig Hay and the Hays eventually took over the running of the bakery from the Scotts, hence it was called 'Hays the Bakery'.

From the records which I had gained from my visit to Register House in Edinburgh, I found out that when Dugald and Helen married in 1896, they were both aged thirty-one and Helen was three months pregnant with my great-grandfather, William Scott Hay, at the time of their marriage. I believe this would have been quite a scandal in those days!

In one of the old books which Anne and her husband showed me, there was a little caption relating to the bakery which read:

The best rolls ever came from Hay's …. you bought them round at the bake house at the back to enjoy the lovely smell any time from 5 o'clock in the morning …. and on Bank of Hope nights you hoped to get a fern cake or a pineapple cake as well as a bag of buns.

Interestingly, it was brought to light from the information in David's research that his aunt, Margaret, was awarded Decree of Divorce from Alfred back in 1915, which would have been very rare and quite a disgrace at that time. In the pages it is stated that 'he possibly ended up residing at an unknown address in America'. My husband and I came up with our own conclusion that it may well have been that her husband ran away from the trenches during the First World War, which was something apparently not unheard of.

This just goes to serve that it is worth keeping an open mind when researching your family history as you just never know what buried secrets you might unearth.

I have been lucky enough to have been able to gain all this massive and crucially important information because of the help and good, honest, kindness of these perfect strangers. Anne and her husband George are lovely people. Real-life Samaritans. They have asked that we keep in touch and said that I am always welcome to visit them any time in Newton Mearns.

My distant cousin David Arthur was a very interesting person who was happy to talk with me about what he knew of our ancestry. He was also very keen that I keep in touch with him and said he would love to meet my own little family. This, we duly did as not only did I take another trip through to Newton Means with my husband and children, but we also invited David to our home for a meal on New Year's Day the very next year. David told me that he felt a connection as soon as he met me and was extremely complimentary towards my little family.

I took home with me a very new and genuine sense of belonging that day. Everything I had learned had true substance and meaning and was to become such a significant part of my journey.

The one piece of information I failed to get from my links to Newton Mearns, however, was that of the whereabouts of my grandmother. David Arthur confessed to knowing nothing about Muriel Ritchie Hay and there was no mention of her within his own research. My lack of success in finding her only served to fuel my determination. This person cannot have vanished off planet earth the moment she had given birth to my mother aged just sixteen. She must surely have gone on to have a life somewhere. Not for the first time, the thought occurred to me that she very well might have left Scotland and if this were indeed the case then I was completely at a loss on how to go about finding her.

Chapter Seventeen

Visiting the grave of my ancestors in Newton Mearns and being able to see their names and read the words on the stone had cast my mind back to the old morose feelings I had about my own mother's grave and the lack of a headstone for her. I had decided to tell Anne about it while we drove back to her house. I told Anne how desperately depressing it had been to stand at my mother's grave where the only thing marking her existence was a piece of wood planted into the muddy ground. I expressed the helplessness I felt at being unable to put a stone in place even though this was something I positively ached to do. I explained all about Rhona being the owner of the lair.

When we got back to her house to collate all the information we had attained, Anne turned to me and said, 'Tell George about your mum's grave.' At first, I felt a little taken aback by her forthright request as although I felt able to freely talk to Anne, I felt shy with her husband. However, being put on the spot I decided there was nothing else to do but to go ahead with the story. I openly told him how sad I felt that there had never been a headstone put at her grave and explained that this was something I very much wanted to do but was held back from doing so due to the simple fact that I was not the owner of the lair. I told him that all that was required for me to be able to go ahead with the stone was for my eldest sister, as owner, to authorise her consent. I told him, all that was needed from Rhona was for her to go into the Glasgow City Council offices and sign an indemnity form passing permission to me.

I went on to tell them all about how it had been around five years since that first heart-breaking visit to the cemetery and of how I had vowed on that very day that I would put this right. I explained that I had talked to my sisters about it many times over those five years, that I had all but pleaded with Rhona for them to carry out their promise after a wait of one year to give them an opportunity to save up some money, so that it could be something which we could all do together.

I continued to relay to Anne and her husband the fact that, when I could see that so much time was passing by with no mention of a headstone being made by them, how I had then asked Rhona if it would be possible for her to take the time to go to the Council to sign the form herself, since she was living in Glasgow and was very close to the Council buildings. I told them how I had felt the smallest nudge of hope, when she seemed to assure me that she would do this and then of my gradual realisation that, because time was passing with no evidence of any effort being made, it was never going to happen. I told them that I felt forced to accept that there was nothing I could do, except to give up.

Anne's husband looked me square in the eyes and said in a purposeful voice, 'You go to Glasgow City Council and you get that form. Then you take it to your sister and get her to sign it. Then you go and put the stone at the grave of your mother.'

Those commanding words revived my determined spirit. My tenacity was firmly kicked back into action. I could not believe that this was something I had never thought of doing so many years ago.

In keeping with my impulsive nature, the very next morning I telephoned Glasgow City Council, just as I had done almost five years ago when I first set out in search of my mother's grave. The lady I spoke to was kind. However, she informed me that they were unable to hand the appropriate indemnity form directly to myself, for me to then pass to my sister. Rhona needed to come into the office, in person, to sign the form.

With determination and perhaps a degree of desperation, I telephoned Rhona. I knew I was going to have to be assertive. I announced that I intended to come through to Glasgow that very day to collect her so that together we could drive to the Trongate area in Glasgow where the appropriate section of the Council was situated where she could sign the indemnity form. I was also sure to be sensitive to her feelings and explained that I was prepared to be there with her when she signed the form and that I had already telephoned the Council and that a lady would be waiting on us with the form. I said that this would mean that the stone, which our mother so deserved to have, could at last be put in place. I tried my best not to come across as pushy but I definitely wanted to be emphatic with her so that she would know that I was serious about this happening and to leave no opening for weak excuses in order to put me off. In honesty, I would have happily bundled her into the car if I needed to. However, to my huge relief, she readily agreed to go.

I was positively buzzing with anticipation and impatience of this dream of mine actually coming true. However, I was in equal measure struck with bewilderment at how easy it was proving to be. I was quite fearful that at any moment something would go wrong. Rhona had mentioned over the telephone that she would have to consult with Sandra and Avril to make them aware of what was happening and to check with them that they too were happy for us to go ahead with Rhona's signature on this decisive form. I thought perhaps one of my new-found sisters might feel aggrieved at my audacious bombardment of a task which must surely have been buried so deeply and for a longer time into their own hearts. After all, once the form was signed, the power over this extremely sensitive task would legally and irreversibly be transferred into my hands. Nevertheless, my fears were allayed when Rhona telephoned me back with the reassurance that Sandra and Avril were happy for us to go ahead. The question crossed my mind about whether, in actual fact, they had anything of the desire in them to make this happen, as I did.

I instantly instructed my children to get their shoes and coats on and drove to Glasgow to collect Rhona, as I did not want to give her any time to change her mind. Once I had Rhona in the car, we then had some fun negotiating Glasgow's grid system in our quest to find the Trongate area where the Glasgow City Council building stood. Although Rhona had lived in Glasgow her whole life, she had confessed in previous conversations that her sense of direction was virtually zero. This was evidenced when I had once suggested, 'If I came to pick you up, could you direct us to Sandra's house?'

Rhona's answer was, 'No! I always just jump into a taxi to Sandra's.'

I admitted that my own sense of direction was only a shade better than Rhona's and so we had to rely on my road map of Glasgow and my twelve-year-old daughter's navigational skills since she was the one holding the map. This involved her holding the map upside down so that she could follow the roads, literally, while she read out the names of the streets as we came upon them. It was a good thing that we all had our patience and sense of humour fully intact, as we had our mini road trip drama. I constantly ordered my daughter to please turn the map the right way up.

'It's easier to follow holding it this way,' she protested.

My ten-year-old little boy could only sit in wonder at the comedy unfolding in front of him as he sat in the back seat. Who knows what he must have been thinking? In all probability he was wishing he was still at home quietly in front of the Playstation.

After a few wrong turns and a little difficulty in finding suitable parking, we managed to park somewhere close by, in what turned out to be an extremely muddy space full of puddles and potholes which we were forced to jump over in order to reach the pavement. When we eventually arrived at our destination the rain had begun. I was beginning to think that there was some kind of negative power in full flight against us. To top it all, the office was actually closed for lunch and was not due to reopen for another hour and fifteen minutes.

'Right, we'll sit here and wait,' I announced. 'I've not come all this way to stand out in the rain getting wet for over an hour.'

We all sat down on the cold, hard, stone steps and we waited.

I had brought along my folder with me as there was so much I had done which Rhona had yet to see. I talked her through all the photographs and information I had collected during my years of research and told her all about the most recent discovery of our Newton Mearns link. Rhona was incredulous at all the work I had done and I could see it was difficult for her to properly absorb it all in that small space of time we had sitting in the cold stairwell. On reflection, I think this was especially so given that she was probably already feeling the pressure of the rather weighty task impending on her and I felt that she was holding in some amount of emotion. I had to remind myself that on the one hand whatever Rhona was feeling in those moments would not be what I was feeling and it was important that I should respect this. I, on the other hand, was extremely impatient to see her signature put onto the form and, unlike Rhona, I struggled to hide this. I think I may have bombarded her in my excitement.

At last, the door duly opened at one thirty on the dot on that rainy Tuesday in October. The helpful lady I had previously spoken to over the telephone was there, with the form ready to be signed. I gripped my daughter's small hand as I witnessed Rhona's signature being put in place. Such a small seemingly insignificant act yet which held a massively important meaning. At last! My heart soared as this simple task was finally going to break down the barriers keeping me from carrying out my quest to firmly and permanently mark my mother's existence in the world.

I was elated. I had climbed a mountain to get to this cathartic point in my journey. Along the way there had been so many times when I had despaired that it would never happen. I had honestly believed that this was a point I was never going to reach. I had thought that I was going to have to break the promise I made to my mother a full five years before.

By now, my mind had stretched some way beyond the agony of having my heart broken, beyond the anger I felt when Jill and I last met with Gordon and beyond the searing pain I felt listening to his story about my mother's apparent rejection of me. Truthfully, I did not believe that there would ever be any kind of levelling off for me, that I could arrive at a subdued equilibrium regarding Gordon and my mother. If

I were to compare myself to a spirit level, then I would say I was sometimes too high and sometimes too low but never dead level. There would never be true peace, acceptance or contentment towards them. My emotions had tripped and stumbled down a very long path, enduring many bumps and at times reeling from the hardest of knocks, but had now set me onto a stronger and slightly more balanced road down which to travel. I marvelled at how things can sometimes turn, just at the right time and in a way which I could never have imagined.

I was now equipped and very ready to put my mother's headstone in place and I was massively grateful to my sister, the catalyst to making it happen. As I drove Rhona home that momentous day I expressed my gratitude.

'Oh, Rhona, thank you so much. I can't believe it's finally going to happen. You have no idea how far I've come to get to this point. I'm so happy. I just can't believe it. I absolutely promise you that we'll do this together. I will not go ahead with anything without consulting you beforehand. This is going to be for all of us.'

It was clear from Rhona's response, that day was just as big a step for her as it was for me but in an altogether different way. I wondered how she was feeling as I could not clearly read her from her facial expression or body language. All she could manage to say was, 'I don't know how I feel. It's just all a lot to take in, I suppose.'

When we arrived back at her flat, I gave my sister the warmest hug. In that moment I truly loved her.

Rhona and I discussed a little about how hard it would be to find the right words for the stone as I myself had never known our mother and she had only known her for the first seven years of her life. Moreover, Rhona once had (and unfortunately proceeded to lose) some photographs, whereas I had never seen any pictures and the little I knew of my mother could only come from what people had told me. We could not use the kind of words which would normally be seen on a headstone such as 'remembered always' or 'in loving memory of', as these were not appropriate to our situation. I, however, was in no doubt whatsoever that I definitely wanted her birth name, Elizabeth Hay, to be the first and most prominent words on the stone. Following this would be her adoptive name and, of course, her adoptive parents' names as they too were buried within the lair. This way, I could bring her true identity full circle, right back to my mother for the rest of eternity. Then, whenever I needed to, I could go there and place my hands over her name, just as I had longed to do all those years ago when I had first visited her grave. Perhaps in doing this I would at last feel a tangible connection to my mother. This was something which I was not only doing for my mum, I was also doing it for myself and for my siblings too.

I was feeling so excited about my successful day in achieving permission for the headstone that I telephoned Anne in Newton Mearns to tell her all about it and to thank her once again for all that she had done for me. I asked her to kindly pass on my gratitude also to her husband George for suggesting that I go to the Council myself to collect a indemnity form. Anne was happy to hear my news. She went on to say that she did not believe that Rhona had been purposefully trying to obstruct me from putting the stone at my mother's grave for all those years. She must have heard a tone in my voice when I was telling them about how much I needed to do this. Her words reminded me that not everyone possesses the same level of determination or perhaps the means for carrying out something so intensely important. I think Anne had sensed my frustration and perhaps a measure of annoyance within me at being held back from erecting the stone for such a long time.

While sitting with my children one evening, talking with them about the possible wording on the gravestone, I confessed to them that I wanted to have the words: 'Erected by Elaine, her daughter, who searched and eventually found her.' To my sheer amazement my little ten-year-old son turned to me and said, 'Mum, don't get upset right, but I don't think you should say those words. It would be like rubbing your sisters' faces in it. I know it's you who's done everything to make this happen but she was their mum too.'

I asked my daughter if she felt the same way and she said, 'Every time I heard you saying it I kept wanting to tell you that it just didn't seem like the right thing to do. But I didn't want to hurt your feelings.'

My children had shown me, once again, just how massively in touch they really are with real, deep-down human emotions and my heart swelled with pride for them. I had always taught my children to speak openly about what they were feeling and never to be afraid to show their emotions. This served to show that I was right to instil this in them. My own upbringing had been the absolute reverse of this. My foster family had taught me exactly how I wished things not to be for my children.

After hearing these wise words from the mouths of my innocent, beautiful two children, I felt so torn. They made me stop and really consider the enormity of the task. I knew that there was truth in what they were saying and that they were being pragmatic about it, but it also could not be denied that it was me who had done all the hard work and it was my own long-saved money that was going to be used. No offer of support in any shape had been made, after all the years having to wait. I wanted it written on the stone in order to validate the journey I had undertaken to get the stone in place and felt that it was going to encompass everything which that journey had involved. I wanted to see my name next to her name.

In that moment, I came to the realisation that I was going to have to take my time, seek appropriate advice and make sure I got it right. I would have to keep an open mind and be sure to accommodate the feelings of everyone involved. I was going to make it perfect for our mother, for all of her children and for their children, forever.

The next morning when my husband came home from working a night shift, I told him what the children had said.

'Wow!' he replied. 'What such grown up, clever children we have.'

Right then my emotions over flowed and I sobbed. The gravity and fundamental significance of what I was doing came crashing down on me in a fresh torrent of unbearable pain. My husband had always said to me that it was 'not right' that I should be having to go to such great lengths and through so much pain to achieve the answers and goals I 'deserved' in my life. I knew what he was saying was correct. Nobody should have to put themselves through this. Everything once more felt so unfair. It made me cry. Then, once I was calm and my emotions had subsided, just as it had always been with me, I pushed them to the side and I charged on.

My children and I went to a local cemetery to look around for inspiration. From this I gleaned the idea for the design which I settled upon for the stone. It was to be a triangular column. The words I eventually decided on were, running down the left side of the triangle:

For Elizabeth, whose name was changed through adoption to Irene and who died Sixteenth May 1977, aged Forty two years.

Then down the right side:

Annie Cullen, who died July 1958, aged Sixty two years, beloved wife of William Cullen who died April 1960, aged Sixty one years, Elizabeth's Adoptive Parents.

Then along the rectangle beneath the triangle, the words:

The mum we had but never had and yet will have forever.

At the top, sitting within the slope of the triangle would be her birth name *HAY* in large bold lettering.

The stone would be black, smooth and shiny with the wording in gold letters. I gave my children a piece of paper and some coloured pens and I asked them if they could come up with a design of their own which could be placed onto the stone. What they brought to me was just perfection. They drew below her birth name in the V-shape of the triangle a yellow flower which looked similar to a tulip, which sat in front of a rainbow of eight different colours. The flower symbolises our mother, painted in my favourite colour and the rainbow represents all eight of her children.

In life, we were all separated but in this simple yet deeply symbolic way, we are all united. My children's contribution to my mother's headstone would remain an inspirational and uniquely visual way of keeping us all together in the minds of all who see it.

'We added white as the last colour of the rainbow. That colour is for you,' they told me.

I felt so privileged to be the mother of two most thoughtful, kind and exceptionally caring children.

In November of the same year my daughter came home from High School and said, 'Mum, you know how November is the month of remembrance? Well, we all had to write the name of someone who we would like to remember on a piece of paper to be placed in the Oratory. I wrote Elizabeth Hay. Although I know I could never have any memories of her, I will always think about her.'

When she had finished telling me this, she came over to sit on my knee and I hugged her as she had a little cry for the grandmother she would never know. I held her tightly, loving her.

'What a wonderfully thoughtful, sweet, sweet child you really are.'

So, I ventured for the second time into a funeral director's office and once more I poured out the story behind my wish to place a headstone at my mother's grave. After I had described the design I hoped to go for, the two ladies who took on my request were emotionally overwhelmed. They told me they had 'goose bumps' just listening to me. They went on to confirm that they would be 'very privileged' to carry out the work and promised that the firm would do their absolute best for me.

'It is always when I hear such unique stories like yours I get the truest satisfaction in the work we do,' the lady told me.

Chapter Eighteen

I woke up very early one morning fully alert with an idea buzzing inside my brain. I was remembering how I had been so successful in tracing my sister Rhona through the Salvation Army Tracing Agency. The thought suddenly occurred to me about using the same agency to trace my grandmother, Muriel Ritchie Hay. I had had no luck finding her through the Newton Mearns link or from my trips to Register House, despite carrying out a laborious search in both areas. As soon as the idea was in my head, I was as impatient as always to get right onto it. I telephoned their London office that very same day, sure I was on the right track this time. However, I spoke to a very kind lady who informed me that unfortunately, because my grandmother had put my mother up for adoption, incredibly, it would be against the law for them to do a trace on her. The lady confirmed that, 'Anything to do with adoption, we are unable to touch.'

I could not hold back my disappointment. I had no other ideas on how to find my grandmother. The lady was very understanding and told me that she wished this was not the case, saying that there had been many occasions when she had thought this law was very unfair. With welling tears of despair about ever finding my grandmother, I asked the lady if there was possibly any other organisation she might know of, for me to try.

She suggested I contact an adoption charity called Norcap who were based in England explaining that she knew that they did searches on behalf of adopted adults who wished to find their biological families and thought that there was a strong possibility that they could help. I telephoned them immediately and again spoke to a nice lady who was attentive and expressed an eagerness to help me. However, she wanted me to be aware that the fee they charged for their services was six hundred pounds. I could not believe my ears.

'I absolutely realise that this is rather a large sum of money and thought it appropriate that I mention this early on so that you can perhaps take some time to think it over.'

Thanking her for taking the time to listen to me, I took down the details of their website and agreed I would definitely need time. On their website, there was mention of a Scottish equivalent by the name of Birthlink, based in Edinburgh. Norcap's website advised that anybody who was based in Scotland and wished to use their services should contact Birthlink in the interim. Although I took down a note of their address and telephone number my irrational, impatient mind had already settled on Norcap. Before I did anything else, I spoke with my husband. Although he did not completely disregard the idea of using Norcap's services, he did express some caution given the size of their fee. My husband knew the kind of person I was: once I had set my mind to something, there was very little anyone could do to put me off. However, I did promise him I would speak with Jill before taking any action and I could see that he was relieved that I was not being my usual impulsive self.

Jill's reaction was, perhaps unsurprisingly, not what I had hoped to hear. Like my husband, she was quick to express caution at my putting such a large investment into something that could very well have a slim margin of success. She also expressed some concern about the fact that I was thinking of going ahead with another search, especially since, this time, it was for a more distant relative. This frustrated me as I thought that surely she, of all people, knew me well enough to know not to say that, for why would I not search for my own grandmother? After all, she was about as close as I could get to my mother, not to mention the chance that there may well be more information to be found should any trace be successful. I did not find it easy to accept advice which was contrary to what I wished to hear. I knew Jill was being professional by doing her job which involved not only giving invaluable support but also advising me on what she considered was best for me. She did go on to say, 'I think that it doesn't matter what I say to you though. I know that if you want to do this badly enough, you'll go ahead anyway, in spite of what you hear from me.'

Jill did indeed know me well!

Once again I picked up the telephone and this time I rang the number for Birthlink. The fact that their establishment was set up for adopted people meant that the person who initially answered my call was required to query with her manager whether their service was available to me, given that I had never been adopted. As I impatiently waited for her to call me back, a familiar feeling of being unworthy turned over in my mind. I then found myself speaking to a well-informed lady by the name of Jennifer. After explaining my reasons for calling and providing a brief history on how much research I had already done, Jennifer agreed to take on my search. However, before acquiescing, she did question whether I might consider the possibility that, given that my own lengthy search for my grandmother had been rather thorough and without success, that I could be grasping at something which was not realistically going to happen. I discussed with her my inability to do a search outwith Scotland as I had no means or knowledge on how to go about this. Also, given that I could not find any record of her at Register House after the birth of my mother, it was highly likely that my grandmother had left Scotland. Jennifer's casting of doubt had me thinking that she obviously had no idea of the strength of my determination but, I thought to myself, she will, in due course! Despite her misgivings, I assured her that I was definite about wishing Birthlink to go ahead.

Happily their search fee was a much more equitable amount of eighty-six pounds. I arranged a meeting with Jennifer to go over everything I had found out so far and to pass on details of my grandmother, along with my request of what it was I would hope to gain from them. I stated that I would like them to attempt to establish whether she was still alive and if so where she was living, whether she had ever married and whether she had gone on to have any more children.

Ironically, this central Edinburgh-based agency was situated in a street which I would have walked up and down a thousand times during my twelve years working as a legal secretary. I had worked in Edinburgh from the time I left school aged sixteen right up to when I had my first child the month before I turned twenty-eight. Had I known of the existence of this agency all those years ago, I wonder whether I would have had the same drive and determination. Would I have possessed the same courage to open that door as I have now? There is something to be said for timing and although I do not believe in destiny or fate, perhaps it would not have been right for me. My social worker has always told me, 'Things happen for a reason.'

Maybe the reason I found out about Birthlink at that time was because, as my life stood by then with all the stability, support and security I had, I was ready and mature enough to handle it. For eight of those twelve years working in Edinburgh I was still living in my foster home and my life was, in many different ways, being very much controlled.

When I showed Jennifer my folder containing all the evidence of my research, she was impressed with how meticulously I had worked and at the help I had received. She marvelled at the success I had achieved. Although she

expressed again her reservations about succeeding in tracing my grandmother, she ultimately agreed to go ahead. So
began yet another time to be patient.

Jennifer acknowledged how sad it was that, despite
everything I had done, I had never managed to find the one
thing I had set out to acquire—a photograph of my mother.
She then suggested that I find out what local papers were
around at the time of my mother's wedding in Springburn.
This brilliant idea sent me off running again.

I opened my computer and tapped back into the
'Reminiscences of Springburn' website which I had previously found to be exceptionally informative. I wrote a
message asking if anyone was aware of what the local newspapers would have been in the year 1957, which was when
my mother's wedding had taken place. I actually received a
response later on that very same day listing the names of four
different newspapers: *The Daily Record*, *The Glasgow Evening
Times*, *The Evening Citizen* and the *Springburn Pioneer News*.

Armed with this knowledge I journeyed with my husband and my daughter back into Glasgow to visit the
Mitchell Library. After stating my request to the lady at the
desk, we were shown to two machines which were used
to look through the microfiche archives of old newspapers.
Then, working as a team, my husband and I set to the task of
methodically searching through each newspaper, with my
daughter looking over our shoulders making sure we would
not miss a relevant photograph if one were to materialise.
Of course, we were careful to remember to look closely at

the names pertaining to any appropriate-looking pictures because, as with the school photographs, it would be impossible to recognise my mother's face having never seen her before then. We each found lots of photographs of brides and grooms but we had no success in finding the one we needed. All the wedding pictures were of prominent members of society, such as head teachers of prestigious schools and highly accomplished sports people.

My daughter told me some years later that she had wondered, as a twelve-year-old at the time, how the newspapers got into the machines!

When we had spent what we all agreed was a considerably adequate length of time painstakingly sifting through the archived newspapers, we decided it was time to stop. As we were leaving I looked at my husband and said, 'I think I'm running out of options. Maybe it's time to accept defeat. How many other avenues can there possibly be for me to explore? I'm just not meant to ever have a photo of my mum, or to find my grandmother and the family she must surely have gone on to have.'

On the drive home from the Mitchell Library that day, I felt a desperate despondency drape heavily across my shoulders like a dank shawl.

Sadly, an indisputable fact which I have encountered time and time again throughout this journey is there seems to be an abundance of support in existence purely with the adopted person in mind. I have found support groups and charities, even books written extensively delving into the feelings and emotions of the adopted person. I have watched television programmes where professional family history researchers and genealogists have travelled the whole world over to obtain personal, detailed family information on behalf of adopted people. Not to mention the impenetrable confidentiality surrounding the adopted person which I have encountered throughout my research with Register House and the Mitchell Library, as well as the Salvation Army Tracing Agency who, as I have already stated, do not 'touch' adoption for 'legal' reasons. Moreover, according to Jennifer at Birthlink, I had been exceptionally 'lucky' to be granted permission from the Sheriff Court in Glasgow to view my own mother's adoption papers. She told me that she had heard of many people who had been denied this privilege.

I had even made an enquiry with the Mitchell Library to view any documents which they may hold in relation to my mother's adoption. However, despite the fact that I was channelled through the appropriate Social Work office, I had submitted all the pertinent forms concerning confirmation of my identity, I did not ever hear anything back from them. This, in spite of their promises that I would hear back from them in due course and their guarantee that the Mitchell did indeed hold such documentation on my mother.

With this in mind, I had decided to take the opportunity, while in the Mitchell Library looking for her wedding photograph, to ask the lady behind the desk about my adoption enquiry regarding my mother. The lady was most officious and said, 'Oh no, you are not entitled to see these documents.'

I felt exceptionally put out by her abrupt and emphatic response, which only served to raise my determination to get what I wanted. I went on to inform her that I had been directed through the proper channels and had already been told that papers did exist within the Library. She then gave me her own email address and told me to send her all the details I had of my mother, confirming that she personally would look into the matter on my behalf. This I duly did as soon as I had returned home and lo and behold, my message went unanswered. I did not even receive the courtesy of an acknowledgement of receipt. It felt like a slap. All I could think was that it must be because of the fact that my mother was adopted and I was not. Permanent foster care means absolutely nothing.

People have asked me, when I told them that I was in permanent foster care, why my foster parents had never adopted me. However, I simply had no answer to give them. I can only remember one occasion when I had plucked up courage to ask my foster mother about this, and by that time I had left home and was married. She did not have any reason to hand. All she told me was, 'It never came up.'

When I was getting married, the mere act of signing the marriage register meant that I had to firstly legally change my name by deed poll on my birth certificate, so that I could sign with the name I had used all my life. It hurt me to think that everyone, including myself, had always known me by my foster family's name and yet my foster parents had never gone on to adopt me. They had never wanted to claim me as their own. It really hurt. To me it was as if they were sending out the idea that they had adopted me. Yet I was not legally part of their family. The authorities were paying them. Whenever I heard someone saying they were adopted I always felt that word carried so much more weight to it than having to say I was fostered. Adoption was solid and emphatic. Being permanently fostered was nondescript. It intensified my feelings of abandonment and of being an unworthy person. It kept my feelings of being alone very raw.

Adoption falls into a precise, firmly placed and well-recognised category. However, there does not appear to be any such place for the non-adopted, ever-fostered person, nor the poor soul who finds themselves shunted from place to place. We do not slot into any defined category. What rights or support can be sought for our wellbeing? Where and to whom do we turn for assistance?

I did go along to an adoption support group for one of their meetings. I felt on the periphery. I sat among a group of people who all had that one fundamental thing in common. Although I was assured that I was very welcome and I did feel that it was a positive experience, I could not shake the feeling that I was not one of them. I felt a little like an intruder. On that occasion I was an extreme minority in an organisation whose motto was, 'group run by adopted people for adopted people'. It would have been wonderful if their group was outwardly open to those who were fostered or who were in care.

These thoughts have reinforced just how exceptionally fortunate I am to have found invaluable support through a social worker who has shown true empathy. Yet I wonder how many people do not know that there is such a service available to them within their local Social Work Departments. I certainly had no idea that this service existed and that I was entitled to use it until I was fortunate enough to meet my ultimately amazing social worker. I am highly aware that I could never have come this far without Jill.

Chapter Nineteen

While I waited the few months it would take for the headstone to be ordered and placed, Christmas arrived and with it came the routine dip in my emotions. Christmas symbolises the gathering of family. Listening to stories among my friends and colleagues of travelling home or coming together for their festive family fun once more became a test of emotional endurance. At this time of year the reminders of my own situation are ubiquitous.

As my sadness threatened to engulf me, I took a chance opportunity while I was with my friend Janice to lower my guard and I told her about how I was feeling. This lovely person helped me to see that I was more than my past. I had, until that moment, fully believed that the bad and hurtful things from my past had very much defined who I was. This friend told me that I was who I was that day and who I will be tomorrow. She then, after listening to the story of my long search and failure to find a single, solitary photograph of my own mother and of how this was something which so 'devastated me', said, 'Why don't you see if you can get an artist's impression drawn up of her, using all the descriptions you've been given from the people who knew her?

Even if it was sixty percent her, at least you would have the one thing you need, which is to have a picture to look at. I think it would provide a real sense of control and comfort for you.'

'Wait a minute, hold the boat. You are a genius,' was my response.

What a brainwave. This was something which would never have occurred to me to do. I jumped to it with gusto. With my seasonal dip forgotten, I plunged straight into browsing the internet to look up the availability of professional portrait artists. On coming upon a reasonably sized list of seemingly reputable artists, I chose six to read up further on and sent each a general request, which read as follows:

My name is Elaine and I have spent the past seven years researching my natural background as well as searching for a photograph of my mother, who I never knew. Along the way I have found actual family members, have studied my mother's school records and searched at Glasgow's Mitchell Library for a wedding photo and much, much more, however, I have been unsuccessful in gaining a single picture of her.

Nonetheless, the people who I have met and who knew her have been able to provide me with a description of her and everyone has told me the same thing. And so my question to you is:

Is it possible to create an artist's impression of what she would have looked like from simply following a description of

her? I would be happy if even it was just sixty percent close
to what she looked like.

It would provide me with a great deal of healing and validation of all of my hard, hard work, if this was something
which could be done.

I would be very grateful to hear your advice on this.

The first response I received was from a professional
portrait artist in England. Though I initially felt a surge of
excitement, the reply turned out to be a cold one which
was largely centred around her costs: 'My charges start at six
thousand pounds, which I know for some may be a little
out of their range.'

She then questioned the possibility of such a request
being carried out, given the absence of any photograph and
stating that it would need to come from my own image
of my mother which I had inside my head. The artist then
went on to enquire: 'How could anyone know if the finished product was a sixty percent or even ten percent accu-
rate image of what she looked like since there was no pho-
tographic evidence of this?'

Her flippant words struck a blow to a vulnerable place
inside me and I floundered for a mere moment. I wondered
whether this person's longstanding and evidently massive
success had literally rendered her completely devoid of
empathy. This artist would never know that her audacity at
issuing such a heartless response to someone who she had
never even met had set in motion an anger and frustration

within me. The very act of writing it at this moment in my story has literally served as a convenient outlet.

Nevertheless, after her initial cold response, she did come back to me in a softer tone. She told me she had done something similar before, but given that her fees were extremely high, she would advise me to take the time to think hard about it. Despite this person's frosty professionalism, my irrational, impatient heart just wanted to jump on it. The prospect of having an image of my mother felt so close, it was hard not to run with the first person to respond. However, my instincts were nudging me on and really in my head I knew that this was the wrong person to do the painting.

I now poured all my belief and energy into achieving the painting. I was determined to look seriously into every possibility of making it happen. As regards to this artist's comments, I notched them down as a minuscule setback in my longstanding quest for a picture of my mother. This alternative route to achieving her image was another unexpected and exciting twist in my journey and I was grabbing it.

It was not long before I received a reply from a much more enthusiastic and understanding artist. He informed me that he would be 'only too happy to take on my request but that because his work predominantly entailed very real life and meticulously detailed art, mostly from a live model or a photograph it would be a challenge.' He continued that although perhaps he would not be the best person to carry out the task, he wanted to give me his reassurance that I should return to him if I did not have any success in finding a more suitable portrait artist to do the job. This exceptionally kind man wished me great luck and told me that he admired my confidence and determination in doing this.

Receiving such a positive response, gave substance to the fact that in my heart and my mind, this was without doubt, something I truly needed to do.

What happened next was extremely heartening. I received a response from an amazing lady. She informed me that her name was Annabelle Valentine and that she was a professional portrait artist and had owned her own gallery in Dorset for two years. Annabelle's reply could not have been more encouraging.

'Regarding your request,' she wrote. 'Wow, what a quest, I would love to get involved. This is something which can absolutely be done.'

Annabelle appealed to me because she spoke in the kind of language which reflected my own. She seemed very much to understand the importance and significance of doing the portrait. We began by emailing back and forth and very quickly I could see that she was someone who could potentially give the task the justice it deserved.

She emailed me some examples of her work, one of which was a piece of still life filled with items of sentimental, very personal value and which were all symbolic to her own life's experiences. She explained that everything in the picture held enormous significance to her and each thing, such as her mother's scarf, had a pertinent story attached to it. It felt like this total stranger had climbed inside my life and taken a good long look around it, as she seemed to instantly touch on exactly the thinking behind what I was looking for.

This picture, and Annabelle's explanation of it, very much echoed the kind of image and effect I was hoping to create of my own mother. It made me think about my folder with all the pictures and documents encompassing my journey thus far and how perhaps I could do something similar with the portrait using those most precious items. My compulsive instincts were once more nagging at me to pounce and this time I did.

So began my new quest. A shift down a different path towards seeing my mother. I felt energised by the prospect of working with this artist, of being involved in a process to create a profoundly sentimental piece of art, which would be entirely unique to me. I had an idea that having this portrait painted of my mother might, in its creation, hopefully calm my soul, settle my heart and bring me peace.

An arrangement was put in place whereby I would travel down to the town of Blandford Forum in the County of Dorset with my husband and children so that Annabelle and I could meet face to face. Annabelle assisted us by letting us know of the various hotels and guest houses available close by and also told us of the many tourist sites and things of interest for my husband and children to do while she and I worked together. It turned out to be one of the most wonderful experiences on this journey of mine. My husband booked us into the most prominent and expensive hotel in the very centre of Dorset, saying, 'This is a one-off, out-of-the-ordinary event so we are going to indulge ourselves.'

He meticulously planned our route, driving us all the way there, an almost ten-hour journey. Once we had settled into the hotel and had something to eat, Annabelle and her boyfriend joined us in the evening. We had already spoken on several occasions over the telephone and from the moment she walked in, she absolutely lived up to the eccentric, flamboyant image I had conjured in my mind of her. She was a beautiful, upbeat person and very much projected her positive aura onto us and the people she greeted around her.

Her studio was an amazing feat in itself, as she had literally spent every waking minute applying all her vivacious energy into its creation. All her artwork was quite mesmerising in its professionalism and I quickly realised that this was someone who was going to inject her magic into my painting.

Annabelle and I spent a whole day together, while my husband and children went off on a tour of the area. When I got up that morning, I took my time getting dressed. I had bought a completely new outfit solely for this day. I slowly did my hair and even put on a little soft, subtle makeup, which was a rarity for me since I do not usually wear makeup. This painting was something which was materialising from a voracious yearning, a primal predisposition to have visual validation of the person who, with veracious loyalty, I call Mum. And I was determined to give it the time and care it deserved.

Annabelle's studio was a mere five-minute walk around the corner and up the street from our hotel. Blandford Forum was to my mind a typical old English town. It was like a market village, with its narrow streets and rows of quaint shops enticing you in with an array of archaic paraphernalia. When I arrived, Annabelle was already there waiting for me and fleetingly I could not equate my surroundings and situation to myself. It felt surreal that I was here, about to do this huge thing which was going to have a massive meaning to my life. At first we simply sat and had a long chat about my research. I had taken along my folder for her to look at as I talked her through my story. Then as we moved on to talk over the painting, I described my idea to Annabelle of having my mother in the centre of the painting with some pieces from my folder placed around her. After she had listened, Annabelle then told me what she had thought of for the painting. Her suggestion was that she painted my own portrait and then positioned the image of my mother beside me. After the shortest discussion on how this could be doable, I wholeheartedly agreed.

Annabelle prepared her studio by closing the curtains in the large front windows to darken the room. She then set up a small desk and chair, placing a lamp high up, so that it shown down onto the desk. Annabelle asked me to fetch my laptop computer from the hotel in order that she could set it up on top of the desk along with my folder and some pertinent items such as my mother's letter and records. I was glad that she had suggested I brought everything with me when I travelled down.

She then took a whole host of photographs of me sitting at the desk, positioned in a relaxed, natural posture so that it looked as though I was beavering away on my computer, logging all my information just as I did with every new piece of information I had gathered. Annabelle and I examined all the photographs and then carefully chose a number of them, which she printed off in large A3 size. We mulled over where we could position my mother, somewhere in the background, either from the light of a doorway, or standing behind me watching me work. I loved the idea of my mother being right behind me and settled on this position for the painting. Annabelle began to sketch my mother into the printed photographs she had taken.

As I watched Annabelle work her magic, a gauzelike image slowly, subtly materialised of my mother and it was then that I had an idea.

'Since I can't provide specific details for you to form precise facial features, would it be possible to paint my mother in an almost transparent, ghost like appearance?'

Annabelle most confidently agreed, with her infectious enthusiasm positively emanating from her. She even wondered if I would like my mother's hand to be resting on my shoulder, to which I most definitely agreed.

'I want people to look at the painting of me with my laptop etcetera and to feel a need to question whether or not there is actually another person with me,' I explained to her.

The painting, I felt, would very much symbolise how it has been for me to grow up having my real mother absent from my life. I have felt her presence throughout my whole life, particularly at certain specific moments, for example while I was pregnant with my own two children and during the earliest stages of their lives. The feeling that my mother was close was also very palpable during some of the more difficult moments of my life and especially so as an adult when I was at one stage very ill and had a spell in hospital.

When I told Annabelle this, she had tears in her eyes and said she 'loved it'. She said she was very excited about 'making this happen for me' and that she had 'never had a request like this before'. Annabelle expressed how 'privileged' she felt that I had 'chosen' her to do the portrait. What she did not know was that it was I who was feeling so very privileged to have found such a uniquely talented artist who positively emanated benevolence and enthusiasm.

Once the photographs had been taken, pondered over and my mother's image sketched, Annabelle was satisfied that she had everything she needed to begin painting the portrait. She told me that she would keep me updated by sending regular pictures of the progress she was making and of course would be in touch as soon as the portrait was complete. I had previously settled on the size of canvas I wished to be used for the portrait; however, Annabelle told me that she would be happy to upgrade my painting to a larger size but keep to the originally agreed price.

'Since you have travelled such a long, long way to visit me from Scotland,' she explained.

Annabelle asked me whether I needed the painting to be done within a specific time scale, but I genuinely did not mind how long it would take. I was just filled with gratitude by the fact that this amazing venture was actually possible to do. With that, Annabelle confirmed she would take her time with it, but would commit herself to it and that I should expect to receive regular progress reports.

When our work was done at the studio, Annabelle invited me round to her house. During our many telephone conversations leading up to our journey to Dorset, she had talked to me about how, once she had created her own studio, she then moved on to renovating her own home. Annabelle gave me a tour round her home and I certainly gained a good idea of the extent she was going to in order to infuse her own personality into her home. She was doing everything, from laying the slabs in the garden, to laying the real wood flooring. She had put beams into the ceilings and tiles onto the walls. All the materials she used were recycled from railway sleepers, to the old parker flooring from the very same hotel in which we were staying. Even her kitchen cupboard doors were salvaged from the renovations carried out on another local building.

We really spent time getting to know each other and when it was time to say goodbye to her, I knew that I had met someone truly inspirational who had left an exceptionally positive and lasting impression on me.

Throughout this emotionally arduous journey towards achieving my dream of one day seeing my mother's face, one of the many lessons I learned was that I was never too old to learn more. This prolific portrait artist very much played a hand in teaching me this. There were so many moments when I had no choice but to be brave. Equally, there have been times when I had needed to be more bold than I ever realised I could be. I have been forced to gather my so -called inner strength, to bring out courage from a place that at times seemed like an emptied pot. And there I was, once more, reaching deep inside. Another most prominent discovery I had made at that time was that I possessed a resourcefulness that I did not know was there. I was literally about to delve into an exceptionally unknown world and I would be lying if I said I was not a little anxious.

I have mentioned a few of the wonderful friends I had around me while I searched and researched, some of whom I feel I am in debt to for their tolerance, patience and abiding friendship. I feel compelled to mention at this juncture that I did not see my oldest friend for seven years while I was looking into my background. This was due to a particularly nasty confrontation from which I was left no other choice but to walk away. This happened right at the point when I was making the decision to meet up with Gordon, for what turned out to be the last time.

Relationships for me have always presented a challenge. It has been eternally difficult to hold onto friendships without doubting their integrity. When I was growing up in foster care, being hurt, controlled and bullied was something I was used to. I believe that it is those around you, in childhood especially, and the experiences you have during those crucial early years, which shape you into the person you are going to be. We are all products of our upbringing and our environment in one way or another. The ever-prevalent and unrelenting sense of hypervigilance which I had developed as a child in foster care had been something which until recently I had confused with paranoia. I felt as though a threat lurked around every corner and I was perpetually braced for it.

At times, forming relationships was like being alone inside a dark, narrow tunnel. I felt trapped and very isolated. I could vaguely make out people freely passing in the brightness at each end of my tunnel. Then, every so often, someone would change direction and come along my passageway and we would meet. Then the drain and misery of incertitude would again be set in motion. We would get along, a friendship would kindle and my heart would soar. Yet, this elation would be brief, as I would know that for them it was merely a wrong turning and eventually they would have to turn back. I would be left alone once more, inside the tunnel watching people pass me by. I would see the spurning even when it was not actually there to see.

As a young adult and beyond, I consistently questioned why a person liked me. I remember, on many occasions, having fun with friends yet all the while keeping my guard high against any real belief that I actually deserved to be there. I thought, if they knew the real me I would be shunned. I therefore shielded myself from the threat of rejection by being vigilant to any warning signs. I kept these feelings and my real self a secret. Years ago when my husband and I first moved into the house where we live now, I was getting to know the people in the surrounding houses. One day I spent the afternoon with a very good friend who lived a few doors away. On leaving to return to my own house I could not stop from smiling as I almost floated home, I felt so blissfully happy. Nevertheless, once the door closed the old well-known doubt swept in. I looked at my reflection in the mirror and silently asked, 'Why does she like me?' 'I don't even like me.' I then waited, fully expecting the rejection, which I knew would inevitably come.

Although I find that low self-esteem still comes knocking, in time I have learned to open up with my friends about my feelings and emotions, through the support and guidance of my social worker and eventually of others.

With my oldest friend whom I had known since High School, it had very much begun in that way.

In school when we were first getting to know one another, we sat together in our classes chattering and laughing with ease. We hit it off immediately. I felt comfortable enough to express how much I really liked her and one day said, 'I told my neighbour that I've met you and that I think you are a really nice girl.'

'I think you are exceptionally nice,' was her response and that was enough for me. I was happy.

My friend was someone who I admired because of her free spirit and strong will. She was very frank when it came to stating her opinion and she definitely was not afraid to speak her mind. These things I wholeheartedly leaned on. In my friend I discovered an ability to cope with the most difficult of my life's experiences and I think I lived in her shadow a lot of the time. She conveyed a strength of character which was lacking in myself and I wanted so much to emulate her. However, whenever I attempted to broach any of my past, it was evidently not within her realm of understanding, as she would square up to me and come full pelt with that sharp tongue, no matter how shocking or potentially damaging it might be. Consequently, it was this which was the final undoing of our friendship.

The fact that I was headlong into researching my family background with all its emotional highs and lows was very much something which she did not wish to hear about or in any way be a part of and in the end it proved too much for my friend. I was, for the final time, to be faced with just how closed off she was to that significantly defining part of my existence.

I had been holding back for some time from revealing to my friend that I had opened up my research once more. Then one day, while she was over visiting with the children, I decided to tentatively bring up the subject by telling her that I planned to make contact with Gordon in the hope that he might know where Joanna and Edith were living and perhaps provide contact details. I was very aware of some degree of underlying vexation from her towards the subject of my past and this had often made me hesitant to say anything about it. Nevertheless, this was my oldest friend and I thought it right to let her in on what was going on. My friend's face was fixed as she blatantly ignored what I had said.

'What do you think.' I asked.

'I have no opinion on the matter.' Her brittle words jarred and I fell passive, just as I had always done.

A few months passed during which we did not talk or see each other. My friend's acrid one-line assertions were always followed with me drawing back from her for a spell. By then the festive season was upon us. We had arranged to meet up in a café for coffee with each other to exchange presents for the children. When I arrived my friend was there with one of her children and had already ordered coffee for us. I removed my heavy winter coat and sat down, thanking her for the coffee. We must have had a brief discussion about our lives, though I have no actual recollection of this because what happened next rendered any initial pleasantries obsolete. My friend erupted into a protracted, bitter and pugnacious account of her judgements over my quest into my past. At first I sat back, shocked into stunned silence. I felt feeble, unable to defend myself. Yet despite this I found myself standing up, slowly putting my coat back on. My friend's demeanour instantly altered as she seemed to flinch at my actions to leave.

'What are you doing?' she asked.

'I'm going to have to go now. I don't think I can take any more.'

By the time I had returned home my friend had already messaged her apology and her concern that I was alright. The strangest thing was that I was absolutely fine. I felt nothing. My friend's outburst was not new to me and I think I had come to accept that I had been pulling away from her for some time. Without knowing it, I was already moving forward with my life in a positive direction and beginning to remove myself from those who caused me pain or upset.

Although at first I did not miss my oldest friend, a few years had passed by and I found myself thinking of her every so often and sometimes with sadness, wondering how things would be if we were ever to attempt to build bridges between us. Would it be possible to somehow engage with the same energy which had once bound our friendship? We truly did have some fantastically happy times together and those memories will always remain. Could it be possible for a person to change so much that what was once inside them could eventually dissipate, permanently?

Some seven years later we were brought back together under a very different set of circumstances, which I shall reveal in the coming chapters.

We once again met up for coffee, just as we had done before. I was very nervous but told myself that whatever I was feeling, she would surely be feeling too. It turned out that she was much more nervous than I was and even mentioned that she hoped I could 'forgive' her. I explained that it was no longer about forgiveness since so many years had gone by and we had both been busy bringing up our families and growing older and wiser. My friend then said something which she had never said before.

'I just could never understand why you wanted to go searching into your past, looking for relatives when you have your own two children and husband right here in front of you.'

'I suppose it's one of those situations where unless you have experienced it for yourself then it is impossible to know what it's like,' was all I could muster as a response.

When I relayed this to my husband I told him what I wished I had said. I wanted to tell her... 'Imagine that I am going to remove all your relatives, your parents, aunts, uncles, cousins, everyone. Then I am going to take away all your photographs of those relatives. You will be left with only your husband and children and nothing from before they came into your life. I will proceed to inform you that there is one photograph of your mother in existence and maybe, just maybe you might be fortunate enough to have it, but you are going to have to work very hard to have it. Now how do you feel? Now say those words to me.'

Chapter Twenty

I had brought my children along with me throughout my journey in a positive and careful way so that they could properly understand it and grow up never having to question who they are. I wanted to make certain that at no point in their lives would they ever have a need to ask me 'why I never told them'. It felt very important to me to acknowledge that all of my research was not just for myself but was for them also. My mother was their grandmother. It was also their family history; therefore it was their right to know and by passing my knowledge on to them from an early age, it meant they would not have the gaping holes in their lives as they grew up, as I had, and that one day they would eventually be able to tell their own children exactly where their origins lay. Moreover, my folder containing all the evidence of my hard work would always be in existence, would be a beautiful reminder of all the distant relatives which bound us together and the hidden parts to those lives which I had been able to unearth.

When I had first explained to my daughter that the people who had brought me up were not our real blood relatives, she was eight years old. She got off her chair and sat on my knee, hooked her arms around my neck and began to cry.

'Hey,' I said, 'please don't be sad. Mummy doesn't feel sad about it. I feel that I'm a very lucky person because I have my own precious wee family with me now to love and to cherish.'

To which she tearfully said, 'I just feel sad that you never had your own Mummy.'

This contrasted greatly to my son's reaction when I told him the same thing. I had decided to wait until he too had reached eight years old. They were both lying in my bed with me one morning, happily asking me to tell them funny stories of when they were babies and little toddlers. I whispered in my daughter's ear that it was now time to let her brother know the truth about my background and we looked at each other in silent understanding.

'I want to tell you something,' I said to him. 'It's something I want you to know about Mummy.'

My daughter then piped up. 'Come on now, sit up and listen carefully', she said. 'This is really important.'

My daughter has always had an old head on young shoulders.

Once I had finished my little talk he turned to me with a very serious expression on his face. I thought to myself, here we go, and I said, 'It's alright, you can ask Mummy anything you want to.'

'See slugs?' he said. 'See the frilly edge on this pillow? That's kind of like the slime they leave behind them when they move.'

From the mouths of babes I thought to myself!

Not a day goes by where I do not marvel at how special and very precious my children are. I tell them this and how proud I am to be their mum. Sometimes they say back to me, 'But, eh you're more special, because of what happened to you.'

My two children are exceptional people who have the biggest hearts of anyone I know. There is no other person in my life who I love like I love my children. They are the heart of my world. This I tell them every day.

I truly do consider myself to be a very lucky person to have all that I have. I feel able to say with integrity that I have made a good go at being successful in all that I have done. I have a great deal to be grateful for in my life and I constantly remind myself of this, especially when I can feel that my mood is low.

As I sat one afternoon writing a particular part of my story onto my computer, my two little ones engrossed in their world of play behind me, my darling eight-year-old son said a beautiful thing to me.

'Mummy, can I tell you something?'

'Of course you can, sweetie.'

'Well, one day I had a dream. I wasn't asleep, I was awake so it was a kind of day dream. We were all walking up the hill through the woods. We were holding hands and having good fun. Then I spotted a light shining down, through the trees ahead of us, you know what I mean?'

'Like the rays of the sun,' I confirmed.

'Yes, and I thought, what's that? As we got closer I saw the outline of a person and when we got nearer, it turned out to be your mum, standing in the light. She was looking at you and smiling.'

I could feel the hairs on the back of my neck stand up. Those words were a gift. They gave me a warm, fuzzy feeling inside. I put my little boy on my knee, hugging him and kissing his soft pudgy cheek.

'Thank you, my sweet, sweet boy. What a gorgeous story.'

If I were to take what I have learned thus far and pass on a message to anyone who happens to read my story and who finds themselves at the beginning of their own unique search for their true identity, this is what I would say...

Only when you feel you are ready, take a hold of your strength. Be firm in what you hope for and dream of. Then place your foot on the first rung of the ladder. Take it steady, try to have patience. Keep close to those who sincerely care and do not be afraid to lean when necessary, because you are not a burden. Then watch and you will surely see. As you bravely climb, the world which you have known will start to change. As time passes and your quest for answers grows, you will find that you have changed too. This has very much been my own experience.

To say that I will ever come to the end of my journey would be impossible. I have encountered several moments of despair when I have thought that I had come to a natural end. In those times it seemed that, evidently, there were no more options for me to try. I felt crippled, distraught at the thought of being forced to give up. The idea of having to stop my search was simply too depressing and what I have found to happen is that, when I least expect it, a new door would spring open, presenting me with another avenue to explore. Those who truly know me, know that I would never pass up an opportunity. There seems to be an unknown force inside driving me on. A tenacity which keeps me moving forward. The prospect of unearthing a photograph of my mother, discovering more relatives or of uncovering more of my past helps me breathe new air in the mornings and keeps me in motion each day. It helps me to turn my gaze away from what hurts and to focus on what does not.

The magnitude of stumbling upon a new piece of the jigsaw, no matter how tenuous or trivial it may be, forever remains completely and utterly magnificent.

Since setting off in earnest on this quest for the truth, I have been astonished, shocked and often dismayed by the unexpected surprises thrown in my path. Through it all, I have achieved goals which some people have told me I absolutely deserve and yet there are those who have said I should give it up.

I am sad to relate that I have gone through a long period of time when I have laid my story down as I have been unable to write, having no energy or focus for it. I found myself in an emotionally dark place. Yet through the passing of time and with the help, patience and kindness of those closest to me, I am now able to live a life out of that dark space. I know now what I need to do in hard times. I no longer sit on my hands thinking 'poor me'. I know how to get into action. I am now ready to take up my story once more.

The festive season was upon us and I decided I needed to make a New Year resolution. So I made a small list of four targets, all of which I planned to achieve during the course of the coming year.

Number one: I would see the headstone in place at my mother's grave. Number two: the portrait of me with my mother would be completed. Number three: I hoped to be successful in finding my grandmother's family through Birthlink. Number four: I was determined to put in the effort to finish writing my story.

Numbers one, two and three are complete and are written here in my story. Number four has taken longer to complete than I could ever have foreseen.

It was not long after my new year resolution when I received an email from Michelle at the stonemasons informing me that my mother's headstone was finished and had been placed at the lair. All the years of frustration and impatience at having to wait for permission to be granted from my sister before being able to go ahead with something which was so morally important to me were over at last. I had been unused to asking for anyone's approval before charging ahead with whatever steps I needed to take when it came to my mother. Whenever I had made up my mind that I was going to do something, I had never let anything or anyone stand in my way, even when I had been advised to be cautious or to slow down, I simply could not do so. And so it was very difficult to be told that this particular decision was not initially mine to make.

Nevertheless, I had now seen it through and it felt momentous. I had finally carried out the promise I had made to my mother all those years ago when I had first visited her grave on that miserable winter's day.

My husband came along as my chauffeur, to offer his support—and also because he wanted to see it for himself.

It had been around five years since that dismal December day when I had first visited my mum's grave. When I had pressed my hands into the sodden, freezing grass, gripped by grief and longing to feel even the tiniest glint of her essence beneath me. When I had given my word that I would put this right for her.

When my husband and I arrived at the cemetery, it took a little while for me to find the lair: such a long time had gone by since I had been there. However, after a short drive heading up over the hill and down to the very far end of the large ancient cemetery I spotted it, all the way down near the farthest row. Even from that distance away, I could tell it was beautiful. It positively glowed like a beacon, guiding me directly to it.

The stone was positioned at the edge of the cemetery so that when we parked the car just behind it, a huge expanse of the cemetery lay in my line of vision. Row upon row of floral memorials of lives remembered. Beyond that, the vast expanse of the city of Glasgow stretched before me, the hub of my life, my origins. Then when I came around to look square on at the headstone, there were fields and trees spread far beyond it and a road which meandered into the open countryside and way into the distance. My mother's headstone stood out, brand new and shiny. Modern in among the grey of the aging surrounding headstones. I remembered the very first time I had been there, how I had imagined myself running in the direction away from the city, from all that was familiar into the unknown, hoping that by escaping all the sorrow I felt in that place my heart would perhaps lighten. I could disappear and in so doing disentangle my heart, my mind, my feelings. However, that was back when the day was dark. When I had stood there in the driving rain feeling utterly alone and desolate.

This day was an entirely different experience. I felt peaceful and calm. I felt my mother and I were somehow inseparable, as though we had never actually been apart.

The empty, muddy space had now been replaced with a resplendent, bold memorial. The smooth, black and shiny rectangular column sparkled in the early spring sunshine. My mother's birth name, Hay, was written there in large letters at the very top of the triangle. To me it had a strong defiant edge. My mother's existence was now as visible and accessible as much as her image was invisible and inaccessible to me. The message behind this was fundamental. I had brought her true identity with permanence all the way back to her. No one who had shared her world had ever given her this. Though I held no memory, this memorial was her tribute in honour of her life.

If her own mother, my grandmother, had known of what I had done, would she have been proud? I believe it is everyone's right to know who they are, where they are from and where their true origins lie. No one should presume to withhold any information which pertains to a child's circumstances. It is not their information to keep; it belongs to the child.

As we quietly stood beside each other in our separate contemplative worlds, my husband turned to me and said, his voice low and heavy with emotion, 'You better be feeling good right now. You should be. This is a decent, honest and beautiful thing you have done. You are a good person.'

I was hearing his words but I was not really listening. I was in a private space. This was not about the headstone, or the research I had done, or the relatives I had found. This was more than all of those things.

It was my moment and her moment. Bound. Together. The very fabric of our souls were intertwined. Forged so much stronger than the links in a chain. The way we were connected, our very essence, was right there, within the muddied ground beneath the stone, murky and indecipherable. In that moment, we were the same. We were one.

As I stood there, I suddenly saw the headstone as a stark testament to my drive and determination to do what I knew in my heart was the right and proper thing to do and my commitment to seeing it through. My emotions, distant and ambiguous, lurked inaccessibly deep inside my heart. I think that what I was feeling was a kind of calm serenity. I laid my hands over her name, closed my eyes and I tried to imagine what we would say to each other right then if face to face, her hands in mine. I was astutely aware that again, although I could not conjure up an image of her face, I could feel her touch and her warmth. It enveloped me and settled inside my heart. I wanted to stay there and never have to walk away. All at once I felt a massive love emanating from my mother. It was so close and so tangible. It felt safe, as if I had come home.

I knew in that moment that I loved my mother, that I always had and I always would. After all, this was my mum. I was grateful.

The beautiful drawing which my children had done for the stone reminded me of a kind of analogy that had come to my mind as I was walking to my work one sunny morning. As I looked at all the beautiful bright spring flowers growing along the edge of the pathway I had suddenly found myself thinking of my mother. In that moment I imagined her as being like a seed, planted in the ground and growing into a stunning flower, perhaps a yellow tulip like the flower my children had drawn. I imagined, in the years which followed, that one flower became two, then three and eventually became multiple flowers. Their seeds were dispersed into the air, taking root all over the land and then more flowers were born from them. This is how I imagined my family to be.

My mother began as that seed sown into the earth. She grew and blossomed and she knew life. That beautiful flower grew weak and could no longer blossom. Too soon the flower lost its radiance. It was taken out of the ground and discarded, almost forgotten, were it not for her own seeds, which continued to grow strong and to thrive, unstoppable. In spite of the many obstructions placed in their way— thorny shrubs or dense coarse grass or being frequently mowed down—these were minor obstacles, for the seeds just kept on surviving, returning over and over again, to full bloom.

I am a seed that was carried off in the wind far from the flower. I may never share the same space, but I have my origins in that flower.

This memorial was now in place for evermore and would not only be a place for myself to visit, any time I longed to be close to my mother, but my hope was that it would be there for anyone who wished to be close to her. All the people who I had met over the years during my search for a photo of my mother. The many people who had been privileged to know her. I took comfort from the hope that she might be remembered in her happiest times.

It was there for all of my six sisters Rhona, Sandra, Avril, Hazel, Joanna and Edith and my one brother Bruce, so that perhaps it may extend them the same solace it has given me.

Who knows, it might even be appreciated by a more distant generation, just as I had appreciated seeing the ancestral gravestone of my family in Newton Mearns.

A while after the stone was put in place I decided to have the picture of the rainbow and tulip tattooed onto the inside of my wrist, just exactly as it was designed by my children. It means I will always have my mother with me, wherever life takes me. My daughter evidently liked this idea as she herself had a yellow tulip tattooed on the inside of her ankle, our symbol of my mother, her grandmother, which she and her brother had created.

The next important email I received came in the summer of that same year. It came from Annabelle in Dorsert, the portrait artist I had appointed to do the painting of my mother. She was writing to let me know that she had finished my painting and was now ready to have it sent on to me. Surprisingly, I felt very cavalier on receiving what should have been rather exciting news. I am unsure why I felt that way and can only put it down to the fact that so much had happened and perhaps, unbeknown to me, by this stage I was experiencing some level of emotional exhaustion. Nevertheless, when I finally took delivery of it, I did feel a level of pride. It was all that I hoped it would be and much, much more.

In the centre was me, painted from the photographs which Annabelle had taken in her studio when we visited all those months ago. I was sitting at the desk with light from the small lamp casting a soft orange glow onto one side of my face and down onto the desk where my folder sat, opened up, with my mother's birth certificate, pictures taken of the address where my mother was born as well as some other significant documents. Arranged on the desk around the folder was the letter my mother had written for

Rhona and Sandra all those years ago when they were children, a copy of which Rhona had very kindly passed to me. There was also the very first letter that Rhona had written to me. The actual writing on the various documents could clearly be read on the painting. My mother's birth name and my grandmother's name in delicate detail were there with all the appropriate dates and photographs. The words on my mother's and Rhona's letters were exquisitely legible. Annabelle had informed me that in to gain such clarity in the writing, she had to use a paint brush with only one strand of hair attached.

In the picture my gaze was directed towards my laptop. I had one hand positioned on the keyboard as though typing and the other resting on my certificates. I looked relaxed and focused, as though I was gathering all the information and cataloguing it into my computer, which was completely apt as it was very much something which I had done with every piece of information I had gained.

Then, just behind me, very subtly painted, was the ghostly image of my mother, virtually transparent so that she could only be observed in a certain light or from standing at a distinct angle. I had wanted those who saw my painting to question whether there actually was another person in the painting with me and this effect had most certainly been very cleverly achieved. Annabelle had produced my mother's image by the mere use of the descriptions which only I could give her, from what I had gained from the various people I had met, who had known her. Every person had portrayed my mother in the same way: tall, slim and glamorous. They had all described her with dark shoulder length hair, in waves from the rollers she would use and with the red lipstick and makeup she would never have been seen without. Annabelle had been careful to paint her in the clothes that would have been worn during the seventies when I had been born and when she had died. My mother's profile was facing in the same direction as my own, towards my computer screen, as though she was watching with interest all the threads of her life which I was compiling onto my computer. Her own facial expression was relaxed, with the smallest of curls on her lips.

For me, looking at her as she was in that painting, it was as if she was showing her approval for all that I had done. That at last, through me, beyond her grave, she was discovering her own origins and background from the research I had done.

My mother had her hand resting on my shoulder, and again the effect was extremely subtle and could only be seen close up. This I particularly loved, as it could be construed that throughout all the years of endless searching for a photograph or some essence of my mother, that in actual fact, for my whole life she had been just there, behind me, her hand on my shoulder to steady me, forever keeping me grounded. I only ever needed to glance over my shoulder to see her. This concept is now permanently depicted in my portrait and gives me great comfort.

Once I had received the painting, I wondered where the

most appropriate place to hang it would be. This decision was more difficult, given that my husband never found it easy to tell his family of my research and I knew that he had, in all probability, never actually had any discussions with them about it. Also, I considered it to be more than a little self-indulgent to have what would appear to the majority of people who see it, who do not know my story, quite simply a self-portrait with no significant meaning, hanging on my wall. So to have it in an obvious place might well cause some degree of embarrassment and awkwardness for both of us. I had initially come up with the idea of placing it on the wall ascending the staircase so that it was not completely unseen. Nevertheless, my husband surprised me by announcing that he thought it should be hung downstairs and actually put it up himself. It now hangs on the wall in the room where my family eat, where homework is done and where we all spend a great deal of our time together, every single day. My story is no longer a secret and is shared with anyone who wants to hear it. The painting serves as a constant reminder that my mother lived, that she had a life and the portrait, I feel, celebrates this.

In the painting, my mother and I have been brought back together, side by side sharing the same space, for the first time since those very first days of my life as a new born baby.

I emailed Annabelle with enormous gratitude and told her that this was one of the most beautiful things which anyone had ever done for me. She had given me the one thing which, despite the great lengths I had gone to in my search, no one had ever been able to do. Annabelle gave me a tangible image of my mother.

The months that followed my insightful New Year resolution were to prove to be the most unexpected and eventful, in so many different ways, since embarking on this epic journey.

Chapter Twenty-One

During the time when I was anticipating the arrival of the portrait, I received a number of communications from Jennifer at the Edinburgh agency Birthlink, who had taken on the search for my grandmother. The news from the agency began with the arrival by post of my grandmother's wedding certificate. What a day that was. Receiving the certificate completely stunned me and for the briefest of moments, I could hardly speak. The certificate confirmed what my heart had always told me, that she had indeed made a new life for herself after giving up my mother. My grandmother had moved to Wiltshire, England where she had eventually met someone and gone on to be married in 1940, at the age of twenty-two, her husband being of the same age. This verified my suspicion that she had moved away from Scotland, which also confirmed why I found it impossible to trace her within the Register of births, deaths and marriages in Edinburgh. With euphoria coursing through me, I turned to my daughter, and exclaimed, 'See this! I knew it. I was right all this time. I simply knew in my heart that my grandmother, that young girl aged just sixteen must have had a life after giving up my mother for

adoption.' At last I had the proof in my hands. 'Oh my goodness, what if she is still alive? I might actually be able to meet
my own grandmother.'

Saying those words out loud stirred a reluctant sadness.
To meet this lady would surely awaken some exceptionally
complex emotions not only in my grandmother, but also
within any potential children she and her husband might
well have gone on to have. I could not imagine explaining
to this lady, at this late stage of her life, that the baby girl
she had given up for adoption had gone on to have eight
children. That her daughter, like herself, had given away not
just her firstborn child, but all eight of her children and had
ultimately gone on to take her own life. Yet, acknowledging
these massive truths did not diminish my selfish longing to
see my own grandmother.

Around a week later I received a telephone call from
Jennifer at Birthlink. She said that she was pleased to
announce that in their search they had now uncovered a
possible child born to my grandmother and her husband
whose name was Michael, but that they had yet to clarify
that the dates and surnames all matched up. She said, however, that she felt confident that it all tied in and would be
in touch again very soon.

As I had experienced at other times in my journey, I
found it strange that my sense of anticipation did not soar
at receiving this news as it had always done in these situations. Instead I found myself feeling unaccustomedly phlegmatic. Looking back, I can now see that living in a state of

continual emotional highs and lows was using up a great amount of energy. My social worker Jill had often referred to this and had raised her concern frequently over my emotional health. I had a determination and tenacity which seemed to keep me strong and drive me on, but which of course was not endless.

It was just a few weeks later when there came another certificate through the post. This time, it did indeed turn out to be the birth certificate of my uncle. As was suggested by Jennifer at Birthlink, his name was Michael and he would have been my mother's brother. My thoughts fleetingly returned to the absence of a photograph of my mother as the reality began to creep in that, like myself, these people were her closest family members. His details showed that he was born in 1944, four years after my grandmother's marriage—which would make him ten years younger than my mother—and that he was born in Wiltshire.

By now my brain had switched on to the possibility that I was going to have a new family in my life and my heart was leaping with joy. The inevitable questions congregated in my brain, familiar and frustrating in equal measure. Daily life was a challenge as I tried to cope with my thirst to know more of this new family. My mounting impatience for answers grew ever harder to manage.

The next telephone call to come from Jennifer was with the news that Birthlink had found Michael's sister, my aunt, who would have been my mother's sister. Something inside my brain flipped over and again I felt a complete calm.

Almost like contentment, which once more surprised me. My mind and soul were hurtling through some extreme feelings and emotions. If I were to be truly honest with myself, I was struggling to manage the emotional highs and lows associated with my research and I was turning to unhealthy coping strategies as a means of dealing with these.

Jennifer told me that my aunt's name was Brenda and that she had already spoken with her over the telephone.

'She sounds lovely and seems very grounded. I have a really good feeling about this, I think it is going to go well and that you will be safe with them.'

Jennifer went on to say that Brenda was very interested in speaking with me and passed me her telephone number so that I could give her a call. She confirmed that Brenda would be expecting to hear from me any evening that was convenient. She told me that Brenda seemed very easy-going and was extremely chatty.

Brenda gave Jennifer the sad news that her mother, my grandmother whom I had for so many years searched for and longed to know, had in actual fact, passed away a mere three years earlier, in 2010. It turned out that my social worker, Jill, was right. Things do indeed happen for a reason. Although I had begun this research into my family history around seven years ago when my grandmother would have still been alive, it had taken a long time for me to discover the existence of Birthlink and therefore the opportunity for my grandmother and me to meet was missed. It was never destined to happen. My grandmother was never meant to hear of the heartache and suffering surrounding her daughter's life.

Moreover, my instinctual belief was confirmed when Jennifer told me that Brenda and her brother, Michael, had spent their whole lives never knowing that their mother had given birth to a daughter in Scotland before she had moved to England.

In spite of the unhappy news that my grandmother was deceased, my mind was in direct conflict with my heart. My brain was accelerating in forward propulsion with the idea of having a whole new family in England. This news marked the most significant point of my journey so far as it had the potential to bring with it some degree of closure. A finality to all of my searching, at least that is what I thought to be true at that time.

I said to Jennifer, 'At last, I've done it. I never gave up. Although this does not mean I have the final piece of the jigsaw, only my own mother could ever give me that, at least I can for now rest my search.'

When I put down the telephone I sensed a shift inside me. A kind of resolve. It felt like the eternal billowing sands of discontentment were settling.

With great excitement and more than a little trepidation I telephoned Brenda. I found her to be very amiable and a nice person who was easy to talk to. We spent a long time in that very first telephone conversation swapping pieces of our lives. Brenda was warm and welcoming and I liked her immediately. We described how we shared a common purpose, to raise our children to be open and honest with their feelings and to never hold secrets, so that they would always know that they could come to us and be able to talk freely about everything.

'I think you and I are going to get along very well,' I said.

Brenda replied, 'You and I already have a connection with one another.'

Brenda spoke with a very strong English accent. She informed me that she lived in Bathford in a bungalow and that her mother and father had lived in the bungalow directly behind Brenda. She said that when her parents were living there, they had put a gateway in the fence which separated the two properties for ease of access. Brenda informed me that she had four grown-up children, two girls and two boys, and that both girls each had two children.

She told me that her brother Michael lived in Chippenham, which was where the family had originally moved to from Scotland and was where she and Michael had been brought up. Michael, I was told, was also eager to speak with me. Brenda said that Michael had two grown-up children who each had gone on to have two children of their own.

My aunt and uncle were in their sixties, my cousins were in their thirties and forties—which was near to my own age—and their children were in the same age range as my own two children. I could barely speak as every time I opened my mouth, the words I spoke were almost inaudible through my stifled giggles. I felt so happy. Everything just sounded so perfect.

Brenda told me how incredulous she felt at receiving the news that her mother had been pregnant at age sixteen and had given up her child. That her mother could have kept such an enormous secret for her whole life completely stunned Brenda.

'My mum never uttered a single word about ever having a child when she had lived in Scotland although she often spoke of her life growing up in Glasgow. I don't even think my dad knew. Yet when mum was near the end of her life, I got the impression that she wanted to tell me something, but whenever I asked her, she would always reply that it was nothing. The amazing thing is that she didn't even say anything when I gave my first child Elizabeth as her middle name. She must have been feeling something towards the child she left in Scotland and whom she had also named Elizabeth, after her own mother. I had no idea that I was giving my daughter a middle name which was so significant to my mum.'

Brenda went on to explain that now that she knew the truth, it actually made a lot of sense to her because of certain situations which arose through the years when her mother's reaction confused her.

'I had always felt there was something there. For my whole life I had suspected something wasn't quite right. Not in a million years would I have guessed this. Michael and I have both agreed that we would have loved to have met your mum and feel that we have been denied the opportunity to know her. Whenever Michael and I asked mum if there was any family still living in Scotland she always answered no.'

Brenda went on to say, 'My own daughter was pregnant when she was just sixteen years old and I thought Mum would go ballistic. However, she was surprisingly very understanding and very supportive, even when it was decided that my daughter would have an abortion. I found her attitude to it all very out of character for my mum as she was always so moralistic and proper, especially living with my dad who was very Victorian in his outlook. Now I can see why she reacted to it in the way that she did.'

For me it felt rather strange to learn that this family who, up to this point, were completely unknown to me, had always known about the link to Newton Mearns and the bakery. They knew about my great-grandfather, Michael and Brenda's own grandfather, who was a Lieutenant in the Royal Air Force and whose military records I had managed to acquire. When I asked Brenda whether she had ever met him she said she never met her grandparents. She told me that her grandmother, Elizabeth Ritchie McEwen, had died in England when she was forty-nine years old and that her mother had never spoken of Brenda's grandfather, except to say that she 'could not stand him'. Her grandfather, William Scott Hay, had met someone else after Elizabeth had died and he himself had died in Scotland when he was sixty-four years old.

If it was all so very bizarre for me, I could not even imagine how it must be feeling for my English family to have me bombard them with news of a hidden Scottish family.

My grandmother had moved to England with her family and she had gone on to create a whole new life for herself. Her world would have been typical of the normal, average, everyday family. It sounded as though she had spoken freely and indeed proudly of her Scottish origins. To all concerned, she would have encapsulated the perfect family woman, the matriarch. Yet the truth was that by keeping my mother a secret, Muriel Ritchie Hay and her own parents, William Scott Hay and Elizabeth Ritchie McEwen, would actually have been living a lie.

Brenda went on to say that there were some albums which they would show me, full of photographs of all the family, including the people I had researched from Newton Mearns. She promised that they would provide copies of any pictures I wished to have. The prospect of putting faces to the names of my ancestors, whose lives were so intricately woven into my mother's and ultimately my own life, was mind-blowing. These people whose role had made such a significant impact on how our lives were to unfold did not feel like strangers to me but rather it seemed quite inexplicably like the link had never been broken. I think this might be because I already held information on them through my research.

Brenda and I spoke of how it perhaps was a blessing that her mother had passed away when she had. It meant she would not ever have to bear the burden of her family learning of her secret, so late on in their lives.

It was perhaps understandable, after hearing of their

photograph albums and some of their memories, that I felt a degree of inadequacy in having to explain that I could not offer to show them a photograph of my mother and that I was unable to share any memories of her with them. I did state, however, that I had a great deal of information gathered from a range of sources throughout my years of research and I would be very happy to go through it all with them. It reinforced my sadness to have to inform them of my mother's death and of how she had died. Again, Brenda and I agreed that it was probably best that we had found each other after my grandmother's death, as it would surely have been immensely difficult for her if she had learned of the hardship and great difficulties which the baby she had given up for adoption had gone on to endure. The decision to give her baby away was more than likely never hers to make. At the time of her pregnancy, it was most likely that she would have believed and indeed been told that she was doing the right thing in order that my mother could have had a better chance of a more prosperous life without her. Unfortunately, the reality was precisely the reverse of this.

Unlike my mother who had died in such tragic circum-stances as a young woman in her early forties, my grand-mother had continued to live a very full life and to survive well into her ninety-first year. She and her husband had even celebrated their sixtieth wedding anniversary. She had been a mother, grandmother and great-grandmother.

I knew would be a source of pain for my new found family to think of my mother, dying all alone, in a shell for a home, every one of her children lost to her and in her mere forty-second year. Nevertheless, I was also acutely aware that they could not possibly feel what I felt towards her death, just as I could not feel the way they would have done towards my grandmother's death.

Discovering a large extended family, who were so obviously deeply involved and intertwined in each other's lives and so far removed from my siblings and my own experience, was a really difficult thing for me to get my head around. However, somehow I was going to have to learn to accept that what has already happened can never unhappen. Then again, being helpless to change past events has certainly never stopped me from allowing myself to have my own secret dreams of having the fairy-tale ending and I decided a long time ago that holding on to my dreams was something that has always helped me to survive. I know that many people would say that clinging to something that could never happen was not living in the real world, but I had needed to believe that things were going to turn out well. My life growing up in foster care had been cold and completely devoid of affection and caring. To discover a new family presented me with the potential to feel loved and wanted beyond the little family I had created for myself.

The most perfect day happened for me when I took the journey down to England with my husband and children to meet with my new English family for the very first time. Everything about that day was wonderful. It was almost as if it had been staged for a television production.

The journey to Chippenham by car took us around eight hours. My one overriding memory of the trip down was at the point when we were just about to disembark from the motorway and arrive in Chippenham. Seeing the full moon and clear sky illuminating the countryside and beyond that the river of lights from the traffic flooding out from London as people headed west for the weekend served to heighten my sense of anticipation.

After a night's, albeit disrupted, sleep in the Premier Inn, we were to meet with Michael in the hotel's reception in the morning. As soon as I set foot into the reception I could immediately tell that the man standing next to the desk was my uncle. I instantly saw a family resemblance. We followed him to his address where we would meet his wife Beryl and had arranged to meet his son Paul, with his daughter Courtney and my aunt Brenda. We were then to head over to Brenda's house in Bathford in the afternoon to meet with her eldest daughter Jean and her sons, Matthew and James, also with her other daughter Lisa and her daughter Jasmine and son Jake. We also met one of Brenda's sons, Richard. As you can probably gather from this long list of relatives, it all felt rather a lot to process, but this did not detract from how great it felt to meet everyone.

Everyone was exceptionally warm and so very welcoming I could not have planned for anything better. I received lots of tight hugs. We heard beautiful family stories of summer holidays on the beach, Christmas parties and lunch at granny's on a Sunday, where the children always looked forward to having lemonade. I must confess that listening to their happy memories of normal family events did tap into my feelings of jealousy. At some points, I found my mind drifting off so that I kind of sat on the periphery and just observed the scene. The way everyone interacted with one another, their body language and their facial expressions. The way each fitted so comfortably with the other like a jigsaw, complete, strong and protective. Really, what I was watching was the natural way people behave when among those they have loved, felt absolutely safe with and have completely belonged to all their lives. They had never known any other lifestyle and I knew that I represented an alternative, less ordinary element, to their world. An element which they had not and could not, ever have imagined would come careering into their lives with a secret that could break up all that they had known as normal.

One of the first things which struck me on meeting my new relatives was their readiness to show their validation for all my hard work. This was displayed by their huge interest in my folder and its contents, the birth, death and marriage certificates I had obtained from Register House in Edinburgh of the various family members; all the different bits of information I had pieced together that were pertinent to those important people, who were bound to each other, the photographs of where they were born and all their differing occupations. And, of course, my most recent conquests, like my mother's headstone and the portrait. Another invaluable source of validation came in the form of an unmistakably strong family resemblance to my uncle and his family. This was evident when I saw photographs of my grandmother. There was a clear likeness running from my grandmother, through my uncle, his own daughter who is my cousin Karen and to myself. Earlier in the day when I had met my aunt's daughter, my cousin Lisa, her first words to me were, 'Wow, you look just like my cousin Karen.'

When Lisa had arrived at Michael's house, she gave me such a massive hug. Out of everyone, she was the most outwardly demonstrative when it came to her feelings and emotions. She brought with her the old family photograph albums and we sat at the table with Beryl, Michael, Lisa and Brenda all explaining who was in the black-and-white pictures. It was immense. Looking into the faces of my relatives, seeing them enjoying the various celebrations, laughing and posing together for the camera. One of the pictures was of my grandmother and her husband with Michael when he was around nine years old and Brenda in my grandmother's arms as a small baby. When I looked at this photograph I could not stop myself from thinking about how fake it felt for me to see my grandmother smiling so naturally with her family around her, knowing that she should have had my mother with them and that she too should have been there, happily posing for the camera.

The subject of my mother's death was inevitably something which came up very early on in the course of that initial meeting with my aunt's family and later on with my uncle's family. We met up with my aunt's side of the family during the daytime and it was Lisa who was the first to raise the subject of my mother's death. It was then that she told me she hoped to one day have some time with just the two of us so that we could have a really in-depth talk about things. Speaking of the circumstances of my mother's death always stirred a strong sense of rejection from deep within me, not only for myself but also for my mother. That day, however, there seemed to be a heightened rawness to it when telling this new family, as I was distinctly aware that the feelings of abandonment would not be something they would have ever experienced. What was heartening, though, was that I sensed that they saw it in me and I could feel that they cared.

We then said our farewells to my aunt and her family and went back to the hotel to have dinner and freshen up.

Later on, in the evening, we met up with my uncle's side of the family who came to the hotel bar to meet us. Michael and Beryl came to find us in the restaurant and showed us to where his daughter Karen, her husband Rolf and their children Lucy and Daniel were sitting. Once again, I found everyone to be so lovely and easy to get along with. I felt completely and immediately accepted, which was a surprise to me given the circumstances in which we had found each other.

Karen told me, 'I said to my dad, you must be so excited to learn of a new sister who you never knew you had. Then when I saw the look on his face I said to him, she's dead isn't she?'

I had known that our meeting would be fringed with sadness.

Michael said, 'We are coming to this from very different sides. You have spent all those years working very hard towards reaching this point and here we are having spent all our lives without ever knowing anything of this. It is impossible for us to know how this must feel for you and likewise for you to know how it is for us but now that you have brought us together we can be sure to put things right.'

When I had spoken with my aunt over the telephone before we travelled to England, I had told her, 'I am acutely aware that when I meet you all you will have so many fantastic stories of family life together, but I will be unable to bring this with me. The story I bring is steeped in sadness and tragedy. But I will also have the story of all my searching and can promise you that everything I have learned has been worth it, no matter how extreme the highs and lows have been, because my determination to thoroughly investigate every lead has, ultimately, brought me to you.'

Moreover, when I placed a photograph of my grandmother next to the portrait which I had of my mother and me, the likeness between us all was remarkable. This, in turn, provided all the validation that I needed, that I had got it right in the painting. Just as the many people I had met along the way had told me, I did look like my mother. The feeling this gave me was of total confirmation that I really did belong to a family. Finally, I could now say that I had a family which I was undeniably a part of. It was a beautiful thing. I looked like my mother and even though there was no photograph to be found of her, seeing the likeness in this new family was definitely the next best thing to being able to see her face.

It was lovely to sit next to my cousin, Karen and see that resemblance between us.

'Look,' I said to my daughter. 'Look at how alike we are.'

She took a photograph of the two of us and I love showing it off to my friends.

The sense of family surged through my heart and made me feel so happily content in a way that I could never have imagined. It was impossible to take in everything and to speak to everybody in just that one day which we initially had together, but I felt so very definite that I was in a place where I belonged.

During the afternoon at Brenda's house, some of us had decided to take a walk in the beautiful village of Bathford since the weather was so sunny and warm. When we were out, my aunt and I lingered back from the rest so that we could grab a little time to have a chat, just the two of us. While we talked, she linked her arm in mine and said, 'It is lovely to have another niece.'

In my telephone calls to Brenda before our trip to meet each other, we had spoken about the immediate connection which we had both felt between us and this was very much reinforced on the day we met.

When it was time to say goodbye, everyone told me that they wished we could stay for longer. We had arranged to leave early the next morning and so only had one day together on that first occasion. However, I promised to have a return visit and to stay for longer in the very near future and my cousin Karen insisted that when we return we must stay with them. It was like unlocking a secret gateway into a world which I had felt forbidden to enter until now.

Before we all hugged each other and said our goodbyes, my uncle turned to me and said, 'Now that we have made this connection we must never break it. We have lived out our whole lives to this point never knowing of each other and now we must never let this die.'

I could hardly believe that things could be so perfect. I truly held these beautiful people in huge regard, even though it was only the first time we had met. It was as though these people had been primed for our visit and someone had told them all the right things to say. There was nothing about that day that I wished I could change as that whole day was something I had yearned to have, for my entire lifetime.

My little boy said to me when he was tucked up in bed in the hotel that very night, 'Today feels like we've had two adventures because we met one half of the family in the afternoon and the other half in the evening and both times were really different but just brilliant. I really like our new family.'

He had hit it off so well with his second cousin, Jake, who was around the same age as himself and watching them run off to play together, you would never have guessed that they had only just met each other that day. The same was true of his older cousin, Daniel, whom he met in the evening: both boys looked so relaxed and natural together.

In the car on the way back up to Scotland, my daughter said to me, 'Mum, I feel like I've always known these people, they don't feel like strangers to me. It's like I've always known that they were there and I've just been waiting for the right time to meet them.'

My daughter had also found it very easy to get along with her older cousin, Lucy, in the evening, which was lovely as both girls seemed to share the same traits in their personalities. They were both laid back, gentle and very sensitive girls who saw a lot of good in people but whose feelings were very easily hurt. I myself found that although I was exceptionally wary and was holding onto a degree of nervous tension, this being something of a fault in my own personality, the atmosphere between us all, during the whole of that day, pulsed with excitement and anticipation.

I felt a calm, almost relieved exhaustion by the time that we were on our way home and settled into a quietly comfortable reflective mood for the duration of the journey. I very much thought that this exceptionally good first meeting boded well for us to hopefully develop strong and lasting relationships in the future.

We have since then kept in regular contact with each other through telephone conversations and texting and the ease which I felt with them when I had first visited has never diminished.

Several months later we did indeed return to England and

spent a longer time getting to know one another and swapping stories. It was a little daunting for me to travel all the way back down to England to stay for a few days with my cousin, Karen, and her family, but also exceptionally exciting for me to, at long last, actually properly meet my family. It proved to be something of the same for my new family in England to have me visit with them as they had never even known of their extended family here in Scotland.

It was surreal travelling to England to stay with my family. Had I decided to give up my search, as some people had urged me to do several times along the way, mostly when things were proving to be particularly tough for me emotionally, then I would never have succeeded in finding my English connection. We would all have lived out our lives in complete ignorance of one another. How sad that would have been.

My two children and I visited my family without my husband this time as he was tied up with work. So this time we organised that we would travel down by train, which turned out to take around six and a half hours. I had a real sense that I was no longer in limbo or rootless. Here I was heading towards my true, benign family who, with genuine generosity, were accepting us into their lives. Yet my insecurity and my wariness still permeated every positive thought. On the way there I turned to my children and said, 'I know these people we are going to be staying with are our relatives, but they are also complete strangers.'

However, when I relayed this to my cousin after we had

been with them for a few days, Karen said to me, 'Yes, this may be true but you don't feel like strangers to us.'

It was just the most wonderful experience, to be in among my new family. My uncle Michael and his wife Beryl were both standing on the platform at the train station ready to meet us and drive us to Karen's house. My children settled in with their second cousins perfectly and we were made to feel like members of the family straight away. On the first evening while we all were sitting around their living room I was feeling a little shy, when suddenly my son went into the bedroom and reappeared with a deck of cards. He proceeded to break the ice between us by performing some magic tricks, getting his sister involved and soon I felt relaxed enough to let go of my nerves. The whole time we were there was beautiful and I simply did not want our visit to end. I have never been made to feel so special and unquestionably wanted in such a warm way. For the first time in my life, I felt that I had really come home. These people had accepted us unconditionally and had totally brought us into the fold of their strong family bond.

My family told me about a rift which had occurred between my aunt and uncle's two sides of the family during the difficult time of our grandmother's death but that on hearing of a new Scottish link, coming out of the blue as we had, that they had decided to put aside their differences and heal the rift between them. My cousins told me that discovering us had caused them to think about the importance of family and of how their disagreement had been trivial in the grand scheme of things. This was special to know when I considered that, notwithstanding my own husband and children, I had entered their world having no experience of the strong family bond which they so evidently had. Although I was not consciously involved in the healing of this rift, it was nevertheless very heartening to hear that we had played a significant part in it. Moreover, it was rather ironic, given that my family in Scotland had been so broken for so many years, to discover that finding I had a family in England could potentially be construed as a catalyst for healing.

On one afternoon while we all sat in my aunt's living room, my daughter and I sat quietly listening as my new family reminisced about their youth, retelling funny stories and laughing at the quirky things our grandmother and other family members had done. Suddenly my cousin, Lisa, stood up and announced a toast to me and my children saying, 'You are one of us now and though you have missed out on so much, we see you very much as our new family and just as important.'

She then held her cup in the air and said, 'To Elaine and her daughter and her son, welcome to our family.'

She then went on to say, 'Oh, my goodness, Elaine; here we are talking away about our family memories and of our granny and you can't even contribute. I'm so sorry, Elaine.'

It was right then that the tears began flowing and I was powerless to stop them. My poor daughter was on my knee in an instant, letting her own tears fall and later saying to her cousin, Lucy, how this had all been quite overwhelming for us. I had, up to that point in our visit, managed to reign in my emotions. Whenever I looked through their photograph albums, at the face of my grandmother whom I, for so long, had yearned to find but never truly thought that I ever would, I could scarcely believe I was really there in among them all and seeing their old pictures. Moreover, Karen and Rolf had shown me real video footage of my grandmother, my aunts, uncles, cousins, all interacting and carrying on their normal family lives very much together and very much unaware that they had a family living in Scotland. One of the videos was of Lucy's birthday party, where all their relatives, including my grandmother, were sitting around enjoying the celebrations. I kept feeling my emotions threatening to overflow and having to force them back. At the points in the video when my grandmother spoke, I wanted them to slow it down so that I could hear her voice or pause it so that I could study her closer. My cousin very kindly made sure that she copied all the photographs I wished for and so I was able to have one of my grandmother enlarged. It was a picture which was taken when she was young and not yet engaged but had met her future husband. She was very striking.

I felt proud to have this picture and I very much wished to place it on my living room wall, opposite to one of my husband's mother; however, this proved to be more of a difficulty for my husband.

'I just think it's better to have a nicer picture there,' he said.

However, my daughter saw my hurt feelings and regarded his flippant remark as simply unnecessary. Although he did not come right out and say it, I wondered if it was because he would feel embarrassed and awkward having to explain the picture to his family and friends. Though I have held on to this beautiful precious photograph, I have still not put it up on the wall in my living room. Perhaps my husband felt protective towards me and was thinking he was being careful of my feelings rather than causing any hurt.

On the very first night of our visit with my cousins in England, when we had gone to bed, I whispered to my daughter, 'I can't believe that I am going off to sleep in my actual, real, blood cousin's house. This is so bizarre.'

I had to keep pausing during our visit with them so that I could properly absorb where I was and remind myself that these lovely, warm people were my relatives. It felt so natural. I was unexpectedly relaxed and exceptionally comfortable in their company. It really was almost as though we had never spent any time apart. They were so generous, genuine and exceptionally decent people and I felt privileged to be part of their family.

My uncle Michael and his wife Beryl drove us around the whole time we were there. They would arrive at the house each morning and stay until after ten o'clock every night. They were so accommodating and inviting, always saying that they would take us anywhere we wanted to go and making sure we filled our days with beautiful trips to the surrounding tourist attractions. We took a trip to the standing stones at Avebury and the quaint village of Lacock where a part of the movie *Harry Potter* and period dramas such as *Cranford* and *Pride and Prejudice* had been filmed. The part of Wiltshire where my family lived was spectacular and very affluent.

On one of the days we were there, Karen took all the children swimming, while Michael drove me to Corsham to visit my aunt Brenda and cousin Lisa. The countryside was so beautiful and extremely rich, with huge country houses in acres of land. We visited one of the large stately homes known as Corsham Court which was very impressive in its grand opulence. We had a lot of fun together and the sun shone on us the whole time. At times I would find myself having to touch Lisa to reassure me this was really happening.

'You are my actual real blood cousin. I canny believe it,' I would say.

When Lisa and Brenda drove me back to Chippenham to Karen's house, the children were all there ready to relay the good time they had spent together. Once again, I was reminded that although these people were strangers to me, they were also members of my family and it only felt natural that my new cousin should be free take them out without me.

Every morning just when we were ready to leave the house my uncle would say, 'Where's your coats? It could rain you know, or turn cold!'

To which I would reply, 'We haven't brought any coats with us and anyway we're hardy souls, we're Scottish.'

'No, you're not. My mum was Scottish and she was always freezing!' he always replied.

My uncle Michael was a tall, slim gent with an extremely gentle and generous nature. He told us that he was a retired painter and decorator and he enjoyed nothing more than pointing out the various houses and buildings he had spent time working on before he had retired.

'See that house over there?' he would say in his strong westerly English accent. 'That's one of mine, that is.'

What was also lovely about our visit with our English cousins was that all the children possessed their own unique musical talents and even spoke about forming a band. Karen's daughter would sing, her son would be on the drums, my daughter would be on the keyboard and my son would play the guitar. They had a go at playing together while we were there and I was super impressed.

At the end of our visit to England, once we had said our goodbyes to Karen and her family and thanked them for giving us such a wonderful time, Michael and Beryl drove us back to the train station. I really liked Michael and Beryl so much and felt very sad to leave them. I just managed to hold back my tears until I was on the train making our way back to Scotland then I freely let them fall.

It was the most uplifting, fulfilling and immensely validating experience to discover Brenda and Michael and everyone in England and to be able to say that these exceptionally genuine, warm and kind people were my family.

When I relayed the whole trip to my social worker, Jill,

who is the one person who has lived every single aspect of this whole journey with me, she said, 'You have been very lucky. To have found a family who are so receptive is so fortunate because it does not always transpire that way.'

I have always known from the very beginning and have been frequently cautioned by Jill, that seeking out family members is a gamble and can go either way. It is not unheard of for people who had been found to say they do not wish to have anything to do with those who are searching for them. Jill has always attempted to prepare me for every kind of scenario and therefore it was not a surprise for me to hear her say I have been a lucky person to really find what I have been looking for. I considered her words to hold a deeper meaning, especially when I remembered about all the heartache I had uncovered when finding my siblings. There were no tragic events to hear from my new family, but instead it was I who was to convey to them what had happened to our family.

Jill had quite literally known me for as long as I had been carrying out all my research, through every twist and turn, in all the highs and lows. She told me that she was very happy things had worked out so well.

'I'm so pleased for you. You deserve it,' she said.

I felt like a kite that had been floating through the air for so long, emotionally independent, unattached to anyone and unconnected to any past, but had now dared to cast down its string. Then, quite unbelievably, someone had at last glanced up and caught hold, anchoring me and silently promising that they would never let me go.

When we were back at home, I met up with a good friend and told her all about our wonderful trip. My friend said to me, 'You have travelled the full length of the rainbow and found the pot of gold at the other side. You really do have quite a story to tell.'

I took a trip into Edinburgh to meet up with Jennifer from Birthlink one more time and to show her my photographs and extend my heartfelt gratitude for finding my family for me. Jennifer had warned me at the beginning when I first contacted their office that given the fact that I had, up to that point, been so thorough in my own research, the chance of successfully finding family members was a very slim one. However, at that time Jennifer had not been fully aware of the level of my determination. This was something which she commended when I saw her again and I could tell that she had been exceptionally proud to have played such a huge role in my success.

Chapter Twenty-Two

As a child I grew up very much knowing I was not a member of the family. I had not been told I was fostered or that I had a social worker. The differences being made and the treatment I was receiving from the people I was calling Mum and Dad compared to their own children were obvious and stark. Until the age of fifteen, when I was brave enough to broach the subject, I had believed that I was adopted. The secrecy inside the family home was opaque in the extreme and it was very much my norm. I was not told about anything, such as when or where my foster parents were going on holiday. I was very used to walking in from school and finding them not at home and having no idea where they were or when they would be home. Things were kept a secret from me every day. Everything bad that was happening was behind closed doors, unwitnessed and untold, until now. Feelings and emotions were also never talked about. As a child I was never comforted, praised or given any kind of encouragement. My foster parents hid their own feelings and emotions also, except for their anger which was always lurking and very quick to surface at any given, random moment. I was taught how to be secretive from a very early age while in foster care and because of this I became ill-equipped to deal with my feelings and emotions.

My foster parents denied me my one most fundamental and profound right—to know who I was. Moreover, by removing my right to discuss or to question who I was within the home, they took away my voice and my control to relate who I was to the outside world. I was silenced.

The confusion I felt as a child carried on into my teenage years and eventually on into my adult life. Whenever I made the decision to tell someone about my background it felt as though I was breaking an untold promise of eternal silence. I was completely at a loss about whether I was permitted to speak of having been in care and of how much I could say or hold back. I was fearful of the repercussions of disclosing anything of my past. I carried on treating it as though it were my shameful, dirty secret and I worried that people would no longer wish to know me once they discovered the truth about me. I was careful when I did tell someone, because I felt confused about how much was safe to reveal. When I think of this now, I can see how utterly absurd it is.

Furthermore, I sensed that for some time there was a level of secrecy and awkwardness surrounding my past being conveyed by the man I married and by his family who, of course, were intrinsically just as important, if not more so, than the foster parents who had raised me. The difficulty and discomfort I felt in even broaching the subject of my past essentially tapped into the exact same messages of shame, low self-worth and insignificance which I had as a child. However, on reflection I could see that the subject of my past could have been something which they did not know how to approach with me and perhaps they were a little fearful of causing me any pain by talking or asking about it.

I plucked massive courage from somewhere within me to face up to these almost debilitating feelings. Seriously confronting the past and all the pain that was there meant stepping through the door of Social Services, counselling services and doctor's surgeries time and time again and learning how let go of fear and to trust a person enough to open up and bare my soul. My husband and his family eventually expressed their pride and support, and gradually I became better at facing and outwardly portraying my true past. This openness and transparency also meant that my husband became happier with me placing photographs of my natural family, whom I had travelled through a blizzard of obstacles and waded through a flood of emotions to find, around my home. It was so special to see them sitting proudly side by side with the pictures of my present family.

In the past I was expected to hide, to shield under a blanket of secrecy the facts of who I really was. The question was, was it right to allow anyone to deny me of my true self by squirreling away all that I had found out about my natural background, just so as to escape the uneasiness and embarrassment it may pose for others? In the very act of writing my story I am shedding that secrecy.

The support and encouragement my husband's family afforded me came some time during the later years of my journey. My husband's mother eventually told me she would like to meet my English relatives. This very much surprised me because it had never crossed my mind to introduce my new family to my husband's family.

When I had become rather ill and unfortunately was in a dark place, my doctor got me to disclose some of the most difficult areas of my past. She said to me, 'Isn't all this secrecy the biggest problem here?'

So I once again gathered all my courage and made the decision to tell my employers and a few of my colleagues. It was one of the best decisions I could have made because they were exceptionally non-judgemental and so very supportive. I was terribly afraid that I would somehow lose my self-respect. As I sat in front of them, revealing my past and my struggles, I cried because it was more than I could bear. They had had absolutely no idea about any of it and told me that they could never have guessed. My colleagues have reacted in the very opposite way I had feared they surely would. Since that day they have never treated me any differently and have expressed that they are more than happy to help in any way that they can. The people in my place of work have given me a lot of their time and invaluable words of support and encouragement. They have done all they can to continue to ensure that I feel part of the team and frequently enquire as to how things are with me. There are no words that could properly convey the gratitude I hold in my heart.

When my child comes to me at Christmas time and says, 'My friends talk about their families and getting together over Christmas. I just wish...' I tell her to be honest with her feelings and to always speak out about them. I tell her she is the most important person in her own life and that she is entitled to feel and express her emotions. I tell her she is special and so very loved.

So, this is my plan. Everything begins from scratch. The change starts with me. I am the present. My children are the future. I become the grandmother, they become the parents. And so on and so forth.

I have made sure that my children who have always been extremely receptive are aware that my origins ultimately are also their origins and, as I have stated, I have shared with them all the different aspects of my research I have unearthed.

As I mentioned when I promised to write the truth, there are always consequences, good or bad, to our actions and something I have taken out of this whole experience is that the importance of consistent trust and respect and living without secrets, no matter what form they take, is imperative for maintaining strong and lasting relationships.

Just as there is a consequence for every action, for each consequence there is an emotion and it is not the emotions themselves I must be aware of but how I react to them. My reactions were becoming damaging to my health and threatening to my life and the stability of my family. The outcome of this as I have mentioned was that I underwent some therapy which is enabling me to unpick and to recognise these emotions for what they are and to be equipped to deal with them in a positive and healthy way. It is a life-changing process which is specifically designed to put in place structures and mechanisms which will help me to combat negative, potentially destructive feelings and emotions when they are at their very earliest stages and to ultimately avoid reaching a crisis point. Although I was fearful of undergoing this therapy in the beginning, I am getting on with it because I know that this is a positive thing to do, off the back of the most difficult things I have experienced. I am doing it in the knowledge that when next I am facing painful memories and thinking unhealthy thoughts, I will be able to look at them and handle them in a much healthier way.

At one of my earliest appointments I was asked what I hoped to take away from this.

'All I know is that I never want to go backwards again. I never want to be stuck. I want to learn how to deal with my past and how to move forward.'

At that first, most nerve-racking session, what I took away with me was something which anyone who is living with the slightest ounce of self-loathing, should hear. The therapist removed a twenty-pound note from her purse. She held it up and asked, 'What do you see?'

'Twenty pounds,' I answered.

She then proceeded to crumple it, spit on it, throw it onto the floor and stamp on it. She then flattened it out, smoothed it over and asked, 'Now what do you see?'

'Twenty pounds.'

'What do you think this says about you?'

I could provide no answer.

'It says that you are not what happened to you. You are who you are, regardless of it.'

I liked this scenario. It felt comforting.

My husband and I continue to work very hard towards a secure and healthy life together, keeping our focus firmly on the future and filling our children's lives with openness, honesty and respectfulness. My recovery is well on course and I try my best to keep a tight rein on perspective whenever I feel my mood slip.

'I love you, Mum, and I am so proud of you.' These were the most amazingly beautiful words, which came from my daughter.

When she was a little toddler I used to sit on the edge of her bed watching her while she slept. She was pure perfection. As I watched her, I would think to myself: I wonder what it is like to be a child and to know that you are loved? Now, as a mother, I very much knew how it felt to give my love.

When my daughter was almost fourteen years old we were sitting chatting. I told her that someone had told me that same day that they considered me to be a strong and very resilient person to have come through all that I had done. Though I did not feel that way, simply to hear it empowered me to keep some belief in myself that the strength to survive must already be inside me.

'It just shows that even someone as small and unimportant as I am can survive it.'

My daughter looked at me and said, 'Mummy, you are not unimportant, you are very special indeed.'

These words I hold onto very tightly now and will keep with me for all of my days. I only need to look upon the faces of my two miracle children to know that I have everything and more to live for.

Later that same year, her English teacher set the class the task of preparing a solo talk on someone who they find inspirational, to be presented in front of the whole class. This is what my daughter wrote and read out:

A person who inspires me is Elaine, my mum. She was born in Nineteen Seventy two in Glasgow. She had six older sisters and one older brother but unfortunately their parents couldn't look after them so all eight children went into care. My mum went into permanent foster care where she grew up with three older brothers and one older sister. One of my mum's half-blood sisters was the only child out of all eight to be adopted. My mum had a tough time growing up and she didn't know anything about her natural family and wasn't allowed to ask any questions about her mother. Her mother had died when my mum was only five years old but she was not told of this until she was fifteen. Eight years ago my mum started to research her natural family. Her research took her back to Eighteen Forty three to the poor east end of Glasgow. She found three of her half-sisters living in Glasgow and she also found one full sister living in Brisbane in Australia and that is where my one and only full cousin lives. She also found six cousins living in Chippenham and Bath in England and we went to visit them and their families twice last year. She is very determined and she never gave up. My mum is inspirational because she kept my brother and I on the journey with her the whole time. She talked to us about any achievements and disappointments. I think she is inspirational because she had a hard childhood and she wanted my brother and I to have the complete opposite childhood than she had.

She is inspirational because we had neighbours who were deaf and who couldn't communicate with the rest of the community. So my mum went to college for two years to learn British Sign Language so that she could talk to them and she taught my brother and I so that we could play with their children. And as a result of learning this skill she now works with deaf children in the local school for the deaf. Unfortunately, my mum became very ill last year. But this also makes her very inspirational because she has had to work very hard to make herself better again and throughout everything that she went through she never stopped being a great mum to my brother and I.

My son said to me during one particularly emotional moment. 'When you cry I always know when to stop hugging you. I put my head on your chest and I can hear your heart speed up. I know you've stopped because I feel it go back to normal.'

The word 'perspective' is one which I say out loud almost every day. I keep the perspective in my mind that I am healthy, lucky, loved and safe. When I was young I felt none of these things. My choices were made for me, my mistakes were always punished, my helplessness and vulnerability were daily reinforced and being reminded that I am alone was my one constant. I took all these feelings into my adult life and instead of opening my eyes, looking around me and placing my trust and belief into what I had achieved for myself and had done so by myself, I did not know how to stop from looking backwards. I left that world behind me, but the core beliefs remained and because of this, it damaged my confidence and my self-esteem. However, these things, I now know, can be repaired just like any injury that is inflicted upon a person. That person just has to receive the right kind of care and attention and for them to know and never to doubt, that they deserve to receive love.

All of the exceptional people I have been fortunate enough to meet, who have stayed by me, pushing me forward and allowing me to lean on them whenever I was really struggling, I will hold in my heart and never ever forget. I have not at any time become complacent about how lucky I am to have them, although in my darkest moments I did question whether I deserved to have them. My need for constant reassurance has not changed and my tenuous trust is something on which I continue to work very hard.

My own precious little family I love, cherish and adore.

My social worker and my doctor are two people who I

hold in exceptionally high esteem and I trust them explicitly. On my darkest day when at my lowest ebb, were it not for the actions of both of these people, I would not have survived. They saved my life.

My closest friends who have never sat in judgement over me nor shunned me but who offer their endless friendship and support, I love and feel exceptional gratitude towards.

As I write this, my husband and I are in our twentieth year of marriage and our love for each other continues to grow.

I have not given up hope of some day having a photograph of my mother and I continue my plans to explore every avenue which may present itself in the future. I have been given the advice to go down my mother's adoption route as it could be presumed that if anyone would have a photograph of her, it would surely be the people who she spent time with while growing up. Despite having had no success from her adoptive brother he has managed to tell me the names and occupations of some aunts and uncles. So perhaps it will not be long before I am headed off in this new direction.

In the writing of my story I mentioned a little about what life was like for me in foster care. I have talked about the strength and courage it has taken to do my research and of the peaks and troughs that have been a large part of my journey. I have touched on throughout my story the emotional endurance of being a person who has been through the care system and survived. This journey of emotional growth, self-awareness and discovery has given me a sense of spirit, of wholeness and of being no longer broken or damaged. I have learned that I have a voice and people have listened. I have shed the secrecy by removing the stigma of being fostered and this I have done for myself.

All of this has led me to a point where I have been able to report to the police what happened to me as a child. Moreover, by finding all of my siblings I have discovered that out of the eight children my mum had, one was adopted and the other seven fostered. Out of the seven who were fostered, five of us have suffered at the hands of our foster family. The very people who put themselves forward as carers have harmed us. This extends to social workers who were negligent in their job and to the so-called care system which failed in its duty of care.

It has been as a result of the support and caring of my social worker, my doctor, my counsellor and my husband, that I was able to give my statement to the police. I gave the statement in the presence of my counsellor, inside the offices of *Open Secret,* within their *In Care Survivors Services, Scotland.* It took sixteen hours over the space of one month. I checked with my two teenage children, without giving any specifics about what I was reporting, that in doing this it was not going to cause either of them any adverse effects to their own lives. My daughter's reaction was, 'Mum this is something you have to do, you were just a child.'

My son then said, 'Will you have to go into the police station? Because if you do, I'll come with you.'

I was setting an example to my two utter amazing children.

The instant sense of relief and unburdening was palpable. I knew that I had handed over my dark secret past and that there was nothing more I could do. It was no longer in my hands. I would from this point onwards be able to say out loud, 'This is what happened and this is what I have done about it.'

In foster care I experienced abuse. Verbal, physical, emotional and sexual. The last sexual assault was when I was twelve. The last verbal and physical assault was when I was twenty-six and the last time I was emotionally abused was in my thirties. By handing over my truth to the authorities I can say that I am no longer afraid of those people. I feel so happy that everything is now out in the open. For far too many years I held on to the abuse as being my dark, dirty secret. What happened to me has never been my secret, it has always been their secret. I am at last able to look in the mirror and feel happy in my own skin and with who I am.

As regards my foster mum, I now strip her of any title which entails the word Mum. Speaking personally and only for myself, that woman represents nothing of what that word actually means. Its very definition cannot be, in any sense, associated with her. Her motives, to me, are clear. The way she blithely continues her lies and secrecy even in the face of a police investigation demonstrates to me her true malign intentions for taking me into her home. It is evidence of the lengths she is prepared to go to in order not to carry out the position she herself chose, in my life. I have not known and will never know a mother. This is my true reality.

In carrying out their investigations the police have led my oldest friend back into my life. Also, two of my foster siblings have been decent and honest enough to speak the truth; they did not turn their backs nor shy away from it.

I have reached who I am today because I sought help from the correct sources and found the right people to guide me towards the emotional, spiritual and personal freedom that I have now.

Chapter Twenty-Three

I always have kept a kind of journal or have had notebooks in which I have written the thoughts and feelings each day has brought up. I would write about what happened and reflect on it. All through my childhood and into my adult life the ability to drift into a fantasy world has been easy for me. I believe my brain adapted and became so good at leaving reality and entering the freedom and comfort of an imaginary existence because it provided everything I needed: escape, love, attention, acknowledgement, validation, safety, security and faith. In effect, when I was a child this ability helped me to cope when reality became more than my young mind could cope with. My life was morphed from the loving, nurturing environment of the children's home into the complete opposite in foster care. My brain was forced to adapt in order for me to survive.

For a very long time, I believed that there was no safe outlet for the morass of emotional mayhem in my mind. Before I began talking to Jill and entering therapy, so often I would try, with difficulty, to express openly the feelings I had left over from being a child in care and all that went along with that. Often what I would find happening was that my words would be misconstrued because of my unwillingness to be fully truthful. I would feel that I was coming across as a messed-up, damaged person and this made me keep secret the pain from my childhood. I truly believed that no matter what happened, whether it be good or bad, there would always be that ingrained, deeply familiar, impenetrable pain right at the core of me.

Yet I have begun to experience a sense of comfort and inner contentment for the very first time in my adult life. Though I have not removed the sadness, I think I have accepted it and with acceptance has come a brand-new way of thinking. I have had the courage to change, with the support and guidance of some new friends, with the love of my new English family and of course with the massive love I have for and receive from my own little family. If a person were to give me a magic wand I would absolutely wish to change some things. My mother, for example, would not be dead. Nevertheless, I have learned that I have choices. I have the ability to choose to do the right things. I can say, hand on heart, that my perception of life has been greatly enriched.

Just before Easter, my lovely new cousin, Karen, telephoned to tell me that she, her husband and two grown children would be visiting with us in the summertime. I was immediately overjoyed and somewhat anxious. I have never had anyone come to stay in my home, let alone my real, actual, blood cousins. As well as staying with the family they never knew they had, this would be their first ever trip to

Scotland, which felt like added pressure to make sure they had the most perfect holiday. My husband and I revamped what was known as the playroom, considering our teenage children have not actually played for some years now. We took our time, completely changing everything in the room, the furniture, the paint on the walls, carpet and so on, transforming it into a kind of den. We put in a sofa bed as this would be where Karen and Rolf would sleep when they come.

Another thing I turned my attention to was my sisters in Glasgow. We had never been able to establish any real relationship. People are confusing, and our lives were so far apart in the extreme so it was hard for us to find any firm common ground to build on. The other factor in this was that I was putting so much time and effort into my recovery and, as I have stated, things were changing for me.

I firstly decided I should inquire with Karen if she would like to have the opportunity to meet with Rhona and the others in Glasgow while she was in Scotland with us. Karen agreed that she would indeed like to meet up with them. So next I picked up the telephone to Rhona, whom I had not had any proper contact with for over two years. Rhona expressed her surprise to hear from me after such a long absence and I felt compelled to be honest about my ill health and that I was now very much in recovery. I then told her the lovely news regarding Karen's impending visit. Rhona seemed very enthusiastic and eager to meet our cousin and her family when they would be here in August.

What Rhona said next completely threw me. Rhona told me, in the most cavalier way, that our sister and brother, Hazel and Bruce, had been back in touch after over twenty years of nothing. I could not believe what I was hearing and asked her when they had been back in touch. Rhona then told me it had been around three months ago. It stunned me how differently our minds worked. Here was I straight onto the telephone to tell her all about Karen coming to visit, to allow her the opportunity to meet, and there was she, holding onto this vital piece of information about our brother and sister and only passing it on to me because I was contacting her. When I asked her why she had not told me at the time, her response was, 'I didn't think you wanted to be in touch anymore.'

I was incredulous and completely perplexed.

Rhona gave me Hazel's telephone number and I wasted no time. After a brief introduction, Hazel's first words to me were, 'You wouldn't happen to have a photo of our mum would you?'

Once again I felt a weight of sadness rise to my chest and thicken in my throat. I told Hazel briefly of my endeavours to find a photograph of our mother, how I had been so close so many times but that I had not been successful so far.

Hazel and I spoke about where our lives had taken us. It turned out that Hazel and Bruce still lived very close to one another and that they were in England, having moved away from Scotland over twenty years ago. Hazel told me that Bruce suffers very poor health and that she had custody of his two children and was raising them both on Bruce's behalf, having given up nursing to do so. I told her that I felt she must have a big heart to have sacrificed so much, on behalf of her brother for the two children. To this Hazel simply replied, 'What are the alternatives?'

We made a plan for me to travel to England so that we could meet one another and hopefully Bruce too if he was able to; however, his health was so poor that there was a large question mark over whether he would be there.

So in early April, the very start of the Easter break, I drove down to England with my children to meet my remaining two siblings for the first time. It was such a big thing to happen for me, as Bruce and Hazel were the only two siblings I had not traced and although I had thought often about searching for them, so much had happened which required such a great deal of energy that I had told myself that I would wait for a time when I felt settled and ready to pick up the search. I was full of all the usual questions such as, 'Will we look like each other?', and 'Will we hit it off?', and I hoped so much that Bruce would be well enough to be there. It truly amazed me that this was actually happening at this time in my life, when a lot had changed and the turmoil inside my head had eased. I was excited and so happy to be completing my search for my siblings after so long.

Just as we had done when we had travelled to England to meet my cousins and other family members for the first time, my two children and I stayed overnight in a Premier Inn. We planned to meet the following day before returning home after our meeting. Seeing my sister at long last was both wonderful and painful. My two children and Bruce's two all sat in awkward silence initially while Hazel and I spoke together. Hazel eventually sent the four of them upstairs to play pool so that she and I could talk properly. Listening to what had happened in her life broke my heart. Like myself, she and Bruce no longer had anything to do with their foster carers. They had moved to England and remained very close to one another. I could see that we did not look alike, Hazel looking very like Avril. Hazel seemed like a very down-to-earth person. I got the impression that there was no hidden agenda with her, that what you see is what you get. She called Bruce's children her son and daughter and they called her Mum. Bruce's daughter was very affectionate with Hazel and it was obvious that they were very close. At that moment, I felt that Hazel was the very best of us all. I liked her immediately. Although I did speak briefly to Bruce over the telephone, coming away having not met him was very difficult to accept when considering he lived so close by to Hazel. I wanted so badly to ask him to please allow me to drive over to where he was, just so that I could see my only brother in the flesh. However, he was just too ill to see me. He sounded very nice and amiable. Our conversation was short and filled with the awkwardness and the eagerness you would expect between long lost siblings. He told me he was very sorry not to be able to meet me and hoped that we would do so very soon.

While I was there I took some photographs and I asked Hazel if she could kindly give me a photograph of Bruce, at which she opened a very large, very deep plastic box full of photographs and passed a few of herself and Bruce for me to keep. We were in each other's company for around two hours that afternoon. After our farewells my children and I were back on the road towards home.

The journey home took some six hours and by the time I was in bed that night I was both physically and emotionally depleted but grateful to have, at last, made contact with every one of my siblings. However, now that I had met all seven of them, I was full of sadness to learn that three had gone on to put their own children into care.

Once home, I opened my folder and placed my new photographs next to the ones of my other siblings, satisfied that once again I could put in place another piece of the puzzle and that I had completed another hugely important part of my journey.

Since the time when I had spoken to Rhona to let her know of our cousin's visit, she and I had not had any contact. There had in fact been very little contact between us for a long time. Except to say, that there was a day in which we were texting back and forth about the fact that any proper, real contact between us was always initiated by myself and that any time we ever spoke was when I picked up the telephone or any time we ever saw each other was when I travelled through to Glasgow. This was despite past conversations in which I would suggest that Rhona could come on the train to visit me for lunch or coffee, and that I would meet her at the station and afterwards I would drop her back for her train home. Despite Rhona agreeing, nothing would ever come of it.

I received a message from Karen that they had booked the flights and that they were all very excited about coming to Scotland. I then messaged the exact dates when they would be here to Rhona.

Exactly one week before our cousin was due to arrive I sent a text confirming that she would be here the following week and asking Rhona which day would be best for her to meet up. Rhona messaged me back saying that the Wednesday would be best for her and Sandra to meet. So we agreed to meet at two o'clock at the Millenium Hotel in Glasgow's George Square, which happens to be where I met Rhona for the very first time all those years before.

On the lead up to my cousin and her family visiting with us, my anxiety levels peaked quite considerably. I worried about everything from picking them up from the airport to whether they would be comfortable in our new sofa bed. I wanted everything to be perfect and worried that things might be awkward between us and that we would not be able to properly relax in each other's company. Of course, I am so very happy to say that we got on superbly well and that the week we spent together was beautiful. We happily filled every day. We had fun and adventure and I felt so immensely proud to be able to introduce my real, blood related cousin to anyone who happened to be nearby.

The bond we had begun to weave between us when we had visited with them in England was strengthened tenfold while they were here and I felt so very close to my cousin. I could be myself around them all and it was amazing for me to watch them move around my home with ease and comfort, helping themselves to food in the kitchen, anytime. Throughout their stay I would turn to Karen and hug her and she would simply say, 'I know!'

We only had three full days together. On the Tuesday we had a fabulous day in Edinburgh at the castle and the festival. We took in a show which was brilliant and which was enjoyed very much by all of us. We made sure we took a lot of photographs everywhere we went and I proudly put them onto my Facebook page to show off my family to all my friends.

The next day was Wednesday and that morning I sent a message to Rhona, confirming that we were looking forward to seeing them at two o'clock at the Millennium Hotel. What happened next completely took me aback. Rhona's return message said, 'You have left it too late. You have obviously found the family you have always wanted. Never contact me again.'

Frozen into silence with the shock of it, I passed my mobile phone to Karen who was standing next to me. Karen was dumbfounded. After showing the message to my husband, my children and my cousin's husband and children, it was agreed that I should not send a reply. Since the Monday when my cousin had arrived in Scotland we had been noticing Facebook messages passing between two of my sisters in Glasgow and my sister in England. The messages ranged from, 'I know who my true family are and who are not' to 'A certain person on Facebook thinks she's better than everyone else because she's got money.'

However, each time I or my family and cousin saw these messages we refused to believe they were aimed at me. How wrong this belief was. The messages continued over the time while my cousin and her family were visiting and on the last day of my cousin's visit, my new niece approached me and said, 'I don't know if you want to see it but there's another post on Facebook...?'

I simply handed my own mobile to her and asked her to block them. I did not wish to see any more nasty messages aimed at me. My cousin said that she took from my sister's actions that they did not want to meet her after all. I wondered if it had been easy for my sisters to behave this way because they had always had each other to lean on. They felt almost pack-like to me, with Rhona at the helm and the others following her example. This felt especially so because I had grown up without my siblings in my life.

Despite this happening, my cousin, her husband and me all agreed not to let my sisters ruin our time together and we duly travelled into Glasgow together as we had planned to do and I took them on a beautiful trip into the past. We visited our grandmother's place of birth, my mother's place of birth and the old tenement block where our grandmother had lived while she was pregnant with my mother. I kept finding myself saying, 'And this is where your grandmother…', to which my cousin would interrupt, 'Our grandmother!'

And I would reply, 'I know. You're right. It just doesn't feel natural to say this given that I never had her in my life.'

We also travelled to Newton Mearns to visit the ancestral grave of our great, great, great grandfather, James Scott, the baker. After a delicious and relaxing lunch in Newton Mearns we did a lot of reflecting over my half-sisters' actions and of all the places we had visited so far.

We rounded off our wonderful adventure with a trip to visit my mother's grave. For the first time I was able to have someone I was blood related to stand at her headstone with me. It had now been three years since I had put it in place. It was an immensely emotional and deeply precious moment in my life. All three of us stood holding one another as we admired the beautiful headstone. My cousin's husband shed a tear and held us tightly. I thought of my mother watching us from where she was and I hoped she knew she was loved.

We had made the very most of our day together with no time restrictions, since we were no longer meeting my half-sisters. While we had been in Glasgow, my husband had taken the four children go-karting. It was so lovely to listen to them tell us of the great fun they had together. My heart was soaring with pride.

On the Thursday we spent the day visiting Stirling. We saw the castle and my cousins took some photographs of some highland cows! Afterwards we went swimming and then topped the day off with pizzas and curries. Having us all around my dinner table was so magical. We had some happy photographs together, the kids had even taken some funny snaps while they were together.

On our last day together I was exceptionally sad, knowing they were leaving. I could not stop hugging my cousin. She reiterated more than once, 'Remember this is just the beginning.'

My family's first ever visit with us could not have gone any better. Everyone had enjoyed each other's company and there was no awkwardness whatsoever. We were very relaxed and comfortable together and for this I was exceptionally grateful.

The night before my family were due to leave Scotland to return home, I had a brainwave. We had spent the week together pondering why nobody had any photographs of my mother, that surely there must be at least one out there somewhere and how Rhona could possibly have lost the photos she had received from my mother's adoptive brother and his wife. In the morning I turned to my family and said, 'Why don't I put a post on Facebook, putting in all the details I know about my mother and asking if anyone remembers her and has a photograph?'

Everyone agreed this was a good idea. We all sat around the table to piece together the appropriate wording, making sure we included schools, street names, dates and other pertinent information. We then added some photographs I had received from Isobel of me from the children's home as well as a more recent photograph on the post, in the hope of tugging heart strings. I handed my phone to my cousin's daughter to type everything I had written down because she was so much faster at typing onto a mobile telephone, being young as she was. Once we had all read it and were satisfied with how it looked, my cousin's daughter passed the mobile phone back to me to press 'post'. I knew that when I did so, everyone was going to know that I had been in care. It was a scary thought, throwing it out there; however, the idea that it might mean I got a photograph was of much more importance than people knowing about me.

My Facebook message read:

Can you imagine living your whole life never knowing what your own mother looked like?

I have spent the best part of ten years painstakingly research-ing my family background in the hope of discovering a pho-tograph of my natural mother. I have reached a point where I have no one else I know to ask about her.

I am appealing to anyone who might have gone to school with her, worked with her or otherwise known her. I live with hope in my heart of seeing my mother.

She was born ELIZABETH HAY in Glasgow in 1934 to Muriel Ritchie Hay. My mother was adopted as a baby to a couple named CULLEN and her name then changed to *IRENE CULEN. The family lived in Reidhouse Street, then moved to 10 Croftbank Street Springburn. Irene attended Wellfield Primary School, Albert School and Keppochhill School between 1940-1947 and between 1947-1949 she attended Colston Junior Secondary. At aged 23 (in Springburn Register Office 1957) Irene married a man named SMITH. She was working as a hotel waitress. Her brother-in-law and his wife, James Smith and M Smith (8 Oatfield Street, Glasgow) were the witnesses. Her husband's parents were William and Helen. She lived in Croftbank Street as a child and as an adult.*

My mother wrote a letter (no date) to my eldest sisters when they were little girls, stating her address as Ayr Street, Springburn. My mother had five children.

My mother separated from and met my dad Gordon Mann. According to Gordon they were together for nine years. They had three children, me being the youngest. My mother was living in Fairbairn Street when I was born. All eight of us were put into care.

My mother died in Edgefauld Road, Springburn, Glasgow March 1977 aged 42.

I am hoping that someone, somewhere may have a photograph of her. Please, please, please share this post.

Immediately people began to share it and by the end of that first day when my English family had returned home to England, the share count had reached one hundred.

I have travelled to England a twice more since my family came to Scotland, once on my own and once with my daughter. Being with them on my own gave my cousin and I some time alone to get to know one another even more. We share a lot together and our bond grew stronger for it. It felt so important and so special to be able to travel to see my family on my own and I knew that by doing this, my self-confidence and sense of belonging was also strengthening.

I had very much wished to take the opportunity while visiting without my husband and children to see my grandmother's grave. So my aunt and uncle arranged for the three of us to go together. How utterly amazing it felt to see my grandmother's name, to be able to stand there and to put my hands upon it, just as I had done at my mother's grave. Being there with my mother's brother and sister made it all the more special and unique. I said to myself, 'I bet never in a million years could my grandmother guess that I, the daughter of her own child whom she had given away and kept a secret, would be standing at her grave'. But then someone turned that around by saying, 'I bet she could never have known she'd have a granddaughter who cared enough to do all this hard work to find her.'

Meanwhile my Facebook post continued to be shared and climbed to as much as two thousand two hundred times at the last count. As the share count climbed higher people began to send messages. They started off coming from people who knew me but who had never known my story and who wished me well. Then began the messages from perfect strangers from all around the globe, taking time out from their own busy lives to pass me pieces of advice, suggestions and kind wishes. It was suggested by someone that I share my post on a Glasgow Facebook page and I was sent a link so that I only needed to press 'join'. The page was called Barmulloch Memories. This suggestion inspired me to join lots more groups, a lot being Glasgow-based, such as I Belong to Glasgow, Dear Auld Glasgow Toon and Lost Glasgow Group. I also joined pages such as Colston Secondary School and Albert School, these being two of the schools my mother had attended. I was making sure that my message was being seen as far and as wide as possible.

One month after my family's visit to Scotland, after I had put the post onto Facebook, a lady from Dunoon sent me a private message. She told me her name was Fiona and that she happened upon my post on Barmulloch Memories. Fiona told me that her mother had been born in the same year as my mother and had also attended Colston Junior Secondary in the same year as my mother. Fiona's message was initially to tell me this and to let me know that she would speak to her mother to ask if she could remember my mother. When I read this message I did not allow myself to become too hopeful as, after all, I had been very close to finding a photograph so many times in the past.

Instead I simply stored it away in my heart and tried to be patient. I did not tell a single soul about it lest I put myself in the heart-wrenching position of having to tell them of yet another disappointment. This I had learned from past experience.

The unbelievable day came when the message I had been waiting for, dared myself to hope for, hardly able to believe was possible, appeared on my phone. It was a Sunday and my husband and son were both playing golf as was usual for a Sunday. My daughter and I were lazing on the settee watching a film. I nonchalantly picked up my mobile when it buzzed its alert to a message and read, 'Elaine, my mother remembers your mother and confirms she has a picture of her.'

I turned to my daughter and said, 'Oh my goodness, oh my bloody goodness, I'm getting a picture of my mum. Someone… this lady's mum… remembers my mum. She and her best friend from the school my mum went to, both remember my mum and they've got a school photo of her. Fuck! I can't believe it's happening.'

I am not normally a swearer, but on this occasion I said to my daughter, 'It's okay to swear right now. You can swear if you need to! Oh my goodness, I'm actually going to see my mum's face for the first time in my life. I can't believe this is really going to happen. God actually said yes!'

My daughter burst into floods of tears and hugged me tightly. She held me for too long. I needed to move. I could not be still. My body and mind had been cast into a world of extreme happiness. This was one of the most momentous moments of my life. My heart was being elevated in my chest and I felt like I could fly.

This selfless lady from Dunoon told me that her mother and her mother's friend remembered my mother as being rather refined and remembered her having very shiny hair. She remembered being asked by the teacher to take my mother under her wing as my mother had come later to Colston and that this had caused some friction between the two close friends. However, very quickly my mother made friends of her own and left them to it.

Reading this message was like receiving my own personalised drug. A feeling of complete elation shot through my entire body and mind and left me feeling too high to focus on anything else. I wanted to dance and shout. I wanted to pick up the telephone and tell someone but I did not know who I should tell first. My husband. My social worker. My cousin.

The realisation that I was at last going to get the one thing which had eluded me for my entire life and which I had fought so hard for, screamed inside my head. I could not cry as my daughter had. I was experiencing a happiness on an entirely new level.

The photograph was firstly sent to my mobile telephone. The lady who had received the photograph from her mother said she wanted me to see my mother immediately and not have to wait for it to arrive in the post. So she took photographs of it using her own mobile phone and emailed it to me. When I looked for the first time in my life at my mother's face I did not know what to feel. A plethora of emotions flashed through my mind at such a pace so that I could not get a handle on what I was really feeling.

I was at my work at the time and although I showed the photograph to my colleagues with great enthusiasm and pure joy, I was not sensing the real emotion of it. I needed to be away from people and in a quiet place so that I could properly study my mother's features. When the photograph arrived by post I could hardly put it down. My mother was such a pretty child, with a gentle and kind face. There were forty-one children and one teacher in the photograph and they were in five rows. The front row were sitting on the ground with their legs crossed. The second row looked like they were sitting on a bench with their hands clasped in their laps. My mother was standing in the third row, fourth from the left. It was all girls in this row and they were standing up straight with their arms by their sides. My mother was the only child in the photograph to be holding the hands of the two girls on either side of her, which could be seen by the way her arms were linked to the girls. When I sent the photograph to my English cousin Karen, her immediate response was, 'She's holding the girl's hands, each side of her.'

This gave me a real sense that my mother was a bold child who was not afraid to break a rule and who had a huge capacity for love. My mother was a special girl. Having a photograph of her, seeing her in this way, deeply enhanced the love and care I felt for her.

I held onto the photograph for some time before deciding I was ready to put it into a frame. By hanging my mother's picture next to one of myself, I was staying true to our reality of being apart and yet we were now side by side in this tangible way, forever. This, for me, was beyond special. My daughter and I came up with the idea of beginning a family picture wall in the room we had recently redecorated. My mother's photograph alongside my own now sits centre place and around them our ever-growing family memories are being placed.

Though for forty-four years of my life I had thought of my mother every day, I could see nothing. No solid image to look at. My mother's photograph was a true gift. It was like putting the final piece of the jigsaw into place. I no longer had an empty void in my life: my mother had at last filled it.

Chapter Twenty-Four

Gordon died on a Monday in the freezing month of January. I woke up to the sound of my phone bleeping its alert to an email from Joanna in Australia. Her words were immersed in her heartache and pain at the loss of Gordon. Joanna's emails to me over recent years had been filled with her avidly expressing her love for Gordon and her email that day positively oozed this. I felt irked at the way she could apparently hold any amount of love for someone whom I perceived as being callous and self-centred. In her email she said she hoped I was 'sitting down' as she had some bad news for me, that our father had passed away. She wrote how she 'just loved him so much' and wished she was not living so far away that she could not attend his funeral. Rather presumptuously, she asked that I 'please let her know how it goes'.

Joanna had never shown any interest in what my feelings might be towards Gordon. I had a sense that she would rather ignore the fact that I did not want him in my life and instead she would talk ceaselessly about how happy she felt at having him in her life. I recalled receiving the invitation to her wedding all those years ago when she had expressed 'how wonderful it will be when we are all together'. I remembered being forthright in my choice not to attend the wedding because of this. Looking back, I feel very glad that I did not go against my instincts just to please Joanna. I simply did not wish to have any part in her happy family charade. It seemed to me that my sister had some delusional expectations of me, that because she had these feelings for Gordon that I too should feel the same way. However, my experience of Gordon had never been positive.

On the handful of occasions when I had met Gordon, I had always come home with my heart in shreds. The terrible, hard-hearted truth about how he had lived his life and the events surrounding me being put into care were coldly thrust upon me. I was utterly baffled at how he could appear so emotionally detached when he was passing on such difficult information to his own daughter. I had no sense that he felt any degree of care for my feelings. He very much hid behind his illness, unashamedly remaining steadfast in using it as his excuse for his behaviour. Whenever he spoke to me it was not his disease of alcoholism that I hated hearing about, after all he had over three decades of sobriety under his belt. It was his personality. His arrogance and how self-absorbed he seemed. It seemed to me that he was trapped in a world of self and was so inward looking that he was unable to see past his own feelings to see and to have any regard for how his words might be affecting me.

I asked that Joanna pass my telephone number to the cousin who had telephoned her to inform her of Gordon's death so that I could speak to him. On receiving his call, it was instantly clear to me that this man was virtually impossible to talk to. He positively ranted at me about how highly he thought of Gordon, telling me Gordon was a 'hero'. He was intense when telling me of how Gordon had travelled to England to confront a brother about some seemingly terrible thing his brother had done. However, when I had asked what the awful thing was that the brother had done, this man was unable to tell me anything about it. I was utterly bewildered. The bizarre thing was that I could recall Gordon ranting to me, years before in one of our few meetings, something similar about a brother. I remembered how he had very openly displayed the anger and resentment he held against his brother and how he had bragged about charging down to England on a mission of vengeance. I have no memory of Gordon telling me what this gripe was about. The cousin went on to tell me that Gordon was a 'good man' who 'never touched alcohol' and did a lot for people in this capacity.

His voice got louder as he continued to spout his adulation for Gordon. I found myself feeling increasingly frustrated at not being given a chance to speak and having to raise my own voice to interrupt, so that he would stop long enough for me to respond. When I did reply, letting him know of the Gordon I had met, he shouted down the telephone, firmly defending Gordon. I decided that this man clearly had his mind firmly set. I felt that, just like Joanna, my own experience of Gordon was very different. When he mentioned about me attending the funeral and I expressed my doubt and indecision, he again raised his voice to say, 'He was your dad.'

When I telephoned Gordon's partner, who I remembered as being warm and very gentle, she told me that Gordon had confessed 'I was never a dad to them'. She told me that Gordon had spoken a lot about me. Yet when I asked her what he said about me, considering he never had me in his life, she could give no answer and I could feel her delicately evading the question by saying he was a 'good man'. She informed me that Gordon had suffered for many months before he died. She said it had been a very slow decline and that she had done her best for him in all those months but that it had been very hard for her. When Gordon died his partner said the doctor had comforted her by saying she should not feel any shame for having a sense of relief by his death. It had taken a lot for her to look after Gordon as she had in his slowly declining health. She ended the call by saying she hoped she would see me at Gordon's funeral. When she said this her tone eluded no expectations or pressure on me to go. I thought back to the very last time I saw Gordon so many years ago and again, I remembered his partner's kindness and warmth and just as I was back then, I was grateful to her for that. I thanked her and I said goodbye.

I gave very careful thought to whether I would attend Gordon's funeral. I imagined walking into a church and sitting somewhere near the back, surveying the rows of strangers sitting in the front. His family. My family. All grieving their loss. I thought about how they would not know my face and would therefore be unaware that I was Gordon's daughter. I asked myself the question: why would I put myself through such torture? I came to my decision much in the same way as I did all those years ago when Joanna had invited me to her wedding, stating how wonderful it was going to be to have Gordon and myself with her. It would be false. I did not grieve for Gordon. I shed no tears. I felt nothing for him in his death. After my last encounter with Gordon, once I had dealt with what I had thought of as his final crushing blows, I decided at that time that I would not see him again. I knew back then that I would not attend his funeral when the time came.

I instead settled on the decision to visit my mother's grave on the day of Gordon's funeral. I reflected on the fact that when I had asked, Gordon had blatantly told me so long ago that he had not attended my mother's funeral. I also remembered that when I had asked my mother's adoptive brother and his wife, they had told me that Gordon was absent, that it had been my mother's husband, whom she had never divorced, who had come to inform them of her death. I felt a very strong sense of loyalty towards my mother and against Gordon.

I emailed Joanna the next day to let her know of my decision. Joanna did not acknowledge what I had told her. Her emails continued to confuse and unsettle me. She would appear to be in her own world as her messages would often be long-winded and very random in their content, unrelated to what was actually going on. She was overbearing regarding her feelings for Gordon and in truth I was glad when this time had passed. I felt a massive sense of release from the onerous task of having to explain to anyone who happened to ask me why I had no contact with my 'natural father'. I could now simply say 'both my parents are deceased'.

Being at my mother's grave on the day of Gordon's funeral felt so very right and as it should be. I knew I was where I belonged. Both my heart and my mind were in sync with my mother that day. I gave my mother yellow tulips and I told her how special she was, especially to me.

Four months later I received a shock. My sister Edith contacted me. I was about to turn forty-six years old and there had been no contact from this sister since I was eighteen. I had resigned myself to the belief that I would never see her again. Edith's message to me was about Gordon's will. She initially informed me that he had left us money and she was letting me know who the solicitors were so that I could contact them to let them know whether I wanted to claim my share. I was completely dumbfounded, firstly that Gordon had left us money and secondly that Edith was the one to let me know. I replied to this effect and I told her that I would love to have a chat with her if she was up for it. However, Edith kept her first few messages solely focused on the solicitor and the will. She seemed to be ignoring my offer to connect. Once again I felt very confused. I simply could not comprehend why Edith would contact me and then not even want to talk. Was she not even a little curious as to my life now? Was she not eager to tell me about her own life? I had so much to share with her about all the research I had done on our natural background, our half-siblings, our new family in England, not to mention the photograph of our mother. I messaged her again listing these things to her and inviting her to contact me should she wish to talk. However, her reply ignored this and was solely about the will. I felt so confused and sad that she was seemingly so uninterested. All I could do was to tell her that if she did not wish to remain in touch with me then I 'respected' this.

On checking my emails I duly came across one from the solicitor. The email was very harsh and I was initially shocked by the way the solicitor did not try to cushion her words. I could feel myself recoil as I read it. Here are the initial paragraphs:

As you may be aware, your father appointed me as his Executor in terms of a Will he made in April 2017.

In terms of your late father's Will, he did not leave any part of the residue of his estate to you. Under Scots Law, Children of a deceased who are not left anything in terms of a parent's Will, can choose to accept the terms of the Will, as reflecting their deceased parent's wishes, or they can choose to make a claim for what are known as Legal Rights in their deceased parent's estate.

After reading the email through a few more times I then had my husband and daughter read it. When they had finished reading it my husband turned to me and said, 'You take that money. It's legally yours. Put it away and when there comes a time when there is something positive and good that you need money for, you use that money for it.'

I felt very strongly that my husband was right. I acknowledged that Gordon had given us nothing of himself at any point in our lives. No nurturing, no love, nothing material and no grounding. By using this dark money for something nice and worthwhile I would be turning it right around. For me it would be as good as saying a big fat 'fuck you' to his face.

Even in his death this man could still hurt and completely enrage me. I thought about him making his will and how intentional and calculated his actions were. For what felt like the umpteenth time in my life, I felt small and insignificant. It was brutal to be reminded of those horrible feelings of being unworthy, unwanted and uncared for. I cried with the debilitating pain of it, the ache that came from a vulnerable, fragile, primal place deep inside of me. I released the revived intense anger that I held back purely and solely for him. I swore out loud and wanted to punch and to kick and to wreck. Just as I had done after the very last time I had seen him, I cried for a few days. One morning when I woke up crying about what Gordon had done I told myself that I was a nobody, I was nothing. This was how Gordon had made me feel. Later that same day I told myself to let that

day be the very last time I said those words to myself. I am
not a nobody, I am a somebody. When the crying stopped I
knew that Gordon's final cold, selfish act would not set me
back ever again. I would never, ever cry again in relation to
him. I knew I had it in me to work to remove him from
my thoughts because I had done it before. Gordon was not
worth the energy.

I quickly discovered that taking Gordon out of the equa-
tion was going to take a little time as the emails continued
from Joanna in Australia. She asked me why I had not ever
wanted to have Gordon in my life. I wondered why she
had waited until his death before asking me this question.
I told her what Gordon had shared with me so brutally all
those years ago when I was eighteen. My email was unre-
stricted in its honesty of Gordon's physical, emotional and
verbal abuse of our mother. Sadly, Joanna replied by saying
that Gordon had kept this side of himself hidden from her.
Joanna said she felt betrayed by Gordon as he had portrayed
a very different version of events. Gordon had told Joanna
that he had tried to help our mother but that our mother
was 'too far gone in her depression'.

It became suddenly clear to me that Gordon must have
worked very hard to keep the truth back from Joanna for all
of those years purely in order to keep her in his life. Perhaps
this was why he had been so reluctant to give me Joanna's
contact details. He wanted to keep us apart to protect his
relationship with Joanna. I remembered how he had told
me he 'loved me' and that if ever I needed anything I just

needed to phone my 'old dad'. I remembered how he had told me that he often felt he wanted to phone me. Yet his words were never, ever backed up with any actions. I surmised that by giving me the true version of events back then he had seen how it had put me off him, so by keeping the truth back from Joanna he was able to keep her in his life.

I was reminded of Gordon's selfish neediness and that in reality this man was incapable of putting anyone before himself.

A few days later I received another message from Edith asking whether I had heard back from the solicitors in response to my email regarding going ahead to claim my legal right. She herself had received no email confirming receipt. I decided I would telephone them there and then. I spoke to the executor of Gordon's will. The solicitor told me that Gordon had been too ill to go to her offices so she had gone to his house. She told me that Gordon gave her the impression of being rather self-centred and very much came across as 'petty'. The solicitor told me that he was purely thinking only of his own feelings and showed no concern for the feelings of the people he mentioned. When I enquired whether I was entitled to know who was included in Gordon's will, I was told he had specifically chosen four people. Gordon told the solicitor he wanted 'only the people who were in his life' in his latter years to be included. Those four people were my sister Joanna, his partner, and his niece and nephew, the nephew being the cousin who had informed us of his death and who had spoken so highly of him over the phone to me. By leaving two of us out of his will and one in I could clearly see that Gordon was still trying to keep us sisters apart.

I was instantly glad that I had not gone to his funeral, as to have gone against my gut feelings and attended, only to discover he had done this, would have tormented me very badly.

Like me, Edith had met Gordon and had decided not to have him in her life. My own reasons for this were valid and the correct choice for me. Gordon had told the solicitor that he felt, 'He did not deserve to be abandoned by us.'

Gordon had stuck a knife into my heart when I was a tiny vulnerable baby and in the handful of times I had met him in my adult life, he had continued to twist that knife, doing so once again even in his death. Doing this felt like a final twist of the knife and though he did hurt me, I know that he will never be able to do so again.

Nevertheless, had it indeed been his intention to keep Edith and me separated by keeping us out of his will, then his plan failed miserably because the very act of doing so simply led us back to each other. Edith and I have now spoken over the telephone, for the first time in twenty-eight years, and it was positively awesome. She sounded wonderfully well and grounded and I was so very happy to speak with her. Edith told me that she still lived with her foster mum who she was very close to. She said that when her foster mum read the solicitor's email she had told Edith much the same thing as my husband had told me: 'You take that money. He gave you nothing, so you take what you are entitled to.'

I made another telephone call to Gordon's partner. I wanted to tell her that although things were very complicated between Gordon and me, I had always felt a warmth and kindness from her and I thanked her for it. She again told me that Gordon was a 'good man' and that caring for him right to the end had been a 'labour of love'. She said again that Gordon loved us all and went on to ask if I had seen the will. When she asked the question I could sense a level of awkwardness from her. I told her I had indeed seen Gordon's will and knew that he had left nothing to me or to Edith. She went on to tell me of the right I had to claim and asked if I was going to do so. I told her I would be claiming and that I had informed the solicitor of this. She proceeded to say, 'Good, he wanted you to have it.'

In my heart I felt a knot tighten, for if he had wanted me to have money from his will he would have specified this when making it. I did not say this to his partner; I simply said goodbye. She finished the call by telling me to keep in touch and that she 'loved' me.

I had known all along that Gordon was not a good person. The making of his will would have been his last chance to do the right thing, but he did not have it within him. It would have been nice to have been proved wrong.

My sister Edith and I went on to have the most fantastic reunion. Leading up to the day we had planned to meet each other I said a silent prayer. I was praying that out of the seven siblings I had found and met over the years, please, please could I have just one in my life. Please let me have at least one of my siblings to have even the smallest meaningful relationship with. I did not feel that I was asking for miracles, I just wanted so very much to have a sister in my life. Someone without ulterior motives or who meant me harm or upset. However, I need not have worried as meeting up with my full blood sister after all those years was everything and more than I could have wished it to be. We spoke happily and relaxed for three hours. We were at ease with each other, sharing our experience of foster care and what our lives were like now. My sister was brought up loved and nurtured. She had told me over the phone she remains to that day living with her foster mother, her foster father having passed away some five years ago. She explained that she had felt socially awkward in her teens and found she did not care for pubs or nightclubs. My sister had never married nor had children but came across as a very nurturing person, speaking fondly of her nieces and nephews whom she loved, and she was actively involved in their lives. Edith was interested in some of the research I had done and attentively looked at the photographs of our English family, of our mother's headstone and of my own two children and husband.

There was a dark element hanging over our lovely reunion, sadly. Edith told me that, unlike herself, her twin had had a difficult upbringing. She said that her foster parents had treated Joanna so badly that Edith even suggested to me that Joanna would have grounds for going to the 'police'. Edith told me an example of the treatment Joanna had received at the hands of her foster father, the same foster father who she had loved and still to that day was grieving for. Although I had heard from Joanna a little of how bad things had been for her and how she had stopped all contact from her foster parents, I was still very shocked to hear Edith speak of it to me and in such a seemingly detached way. As Edith spoke about Joanna, she did not know and I did not tell her that I was completely identifying with Joanna. Although what I heard about Joanna registered with me, in that moment with Edith I did not let it show. It was in the small hours of the following morning that I woke deeply distressed and I sobbed into my pillow and for a lot of that day. I told my social worker Jill about how happy I had felt to meet Edith and how extremely sad I felt for Joanna. I have decided that I do very much want to go on to have Edith in my life but that I had no desire to meet her foster mother. After all, I had met her all those years ago when my twin sisters had their twenty-first birthday party and I had my suspicions then that their foster parents were favouring Edith at the expense of Joanna. My suspicions very sadly have turned out to be correct. I emailed Joanna in Australia after meeting Edith as I did not want her to hear about it later and to feel left out or that I was hiding our reunion from her.

Edith and I talked about the will and she told me that Gordon had told Joanna and herself nothing of his drinking days or of the circumstances of our mother's death. She told me they were in their twenties when they had met Gordon, just before Joanna's wedding and some six years after I had first met him. Edith said that although Gordon did not tell them the truth back then, she simply did not like the man and unlike Joanne did not care to have him in her life. I could by now understand why Joanna had wanted Gordon in her life, because by holding back the truth, Gordon was providing the kind of father figure that she did not have in her foster father. Edith told me, 'Joanna replaced our foster dad with Gordon.'

Edith went on to tell me that her foster mother was not taking it at all well that we had reconnected. She said her foster mother was upset and worried that I was going to introduce Edith to my family, her full blood relatives, and that she was going to lose Edith. When I considered that Edith would be turning fifty the following year, I found it completely outrageous that her foster mother was so emotionally attached in this extreme way.

Edith and I hugged each other warmly and took photographs of our first meeting. Edith walked me all the way back to the train station and waved on the platform until I was inside the train and out of sight. We both agreed that we had felt a connection between us that day and I felt some excitement at the prospect of seeing my sister again. We both said that there was so much more to tell each other but that it would have to wait for our next meeting, as we had already covered so much in the three hours we had been with each other. I felt so very joyous when I returned home. The emotion of our meeting did, as I have stated, hit me the next day but I was able to handle it by talking with a few close friends and most importantly by seeing Jill, who has always been there to help me in the biggest and most difficult moments of my life.

Edith and I continue to see each other whenever we want to and I very much love having a sister in my life.

Chapter Twenty-Five

One day when I was not thinking about anything in particular, I received a private message from a lady called Janette who had read my Facebook post looking for a photograph of my mother. She told me that she knew one of the girls in the group photograph taken in Blairvadach Children's Home. She said that her sister Eleanor had worked there and often she would tag along when Eleanor was on duty and that she had played with one of the taller girls in the photograph who was called Catherine. Janette very kindly put Catherine and me in touch with one another. It felt surreal when we began to message each other: I was speaking to someone from such a fundamental time in my life. Catherine told me she had no memory of me from her time at Blairvadach, even though we were both in the group called Jura, which I felt a little sad about. I wondered whether this was because she was one of the oldest and I was the youngest in Jura and so our daily routines would have been very different. In spite of having no recollection of me, Catherine went on to surprise me by stating that she did have photographs of me and she sent two of them to my phone. I immediately saw that both photographs were taken on the same day as one of the photographs I had received from Isobel all those years ago when I had discovered the online forum, after our family outing to Blairvadach way back when my children were still little.

Catherine and I arranged to meet each other at John Lewis in Glasgow on a Saturday. My daughter came with me. I was very excited to see whether Catherine had any more photographs of me as she had told me over the telephone that Eleanor had given her a lot of photographs from when she had worked at Blairvadach. Catherine was warm and very talkative, and we had a very interesting chat in the café about life at the children's home. Catherine brought with her all of the photographs from her time in Blairvadach. As she talked happily of her fond memories, I felt a degree of jealousy as I could not tell her anything from my time there and again felt a familiar sense of isolation and loneliness because she did not remember me. I suppose I was hoping that Catherine was going to fill in a lot of blanks for me. Catherine told me that Janette's sister Eleanor had been very fond of her and that she was Eleanor's favourite. She told me that she 'loved' Eleanor. When we said our farewells that day, I had in my possession three more photographs of myself as a little toddler.

A few days later as I browsed through Facebook, I typed in Blairvadach and pressed search, feeling curious as to whether anything would come up, as it had done on my computer all those years ago. Two pages for Blairvadach Children's Home popped onto the screen. I eagerly looked through the posts, paying particular attention to the actual people who had put the posts up. I began to message random people, asking whether they were there when I was and if they remembered me. I received a message from a lady called Moira who told me she had worked at the home before my time there. Moira informed me that a group of ladies from the children's home had been having regular reunions and that I would be very welcome to come along. She went on to tell me that she knew a lady called Mary who remembered me as a baby. Moira passed me Mary's telephone number.

I could hardly believe that I was actually going to talk to someone who remembered me from the earliest time of my life. I remembered how I had almost begged Isobel to have a chat with me when she had kindly given me the photographs from Blairvadach and how she had not been interested in talking with me. Mary was an exceptionally softly spoken lady. She confirmed that she remembered me as a baby and even recalled holding me as the tiny newborn arriving straight from Rottenrow Maternity Hospital. Mary told me that she had photographs of me and that she would happily send them to me. She said she would love to see me at the next reunion. That sealed it for me, I was absolutely going to be there. When I asked Mary what I was like as a baby she told me that I was, 'a very quiet, contented and happy baby'.

I telephoned Catherine so make her aware of the reunion so that she could come along with all her photographs, which she was very enthusiastic about doing. Catherine told me that Eleanor now lived in Italy but that she would telephone her to see if she would be interested in having a trip to Scotland so that she could attend the reunion too. Catherine told me that Eleanor remembered me as a toddler at Blairvadach and that Eleanor had said she had more photographs of me. Eleanor wanted to have a chat with me over the telephone before the reunion. Unbelievably, Eleanor actually did telephone me all the way from Italy. She told me that she remembered me as a toddler and that I was 'very shy and quiet'.

Eleanor said she planned to take the trip to Scotland in time for the reunion and that she would bring any photographs she could find with her.

On the day of the reunion I was full of anticipation. My daughter again was with me. Walking into that room felt like being in a dream. There were a lot of ladies all chatting together, looking relaxed and comfortable in each other's presence. At first, I almost felt like I was intruding. However, Moira was quick to welcome us. I was very glad when Catherine arrived, however; I could very much see that she had more to offer because, unlike me, she had a lot of memories to share. I then met Mary. The image I had conjured in my mind from talking with her over the telephone was confirmed by the meeting with her. She was exceptionally gentle and kind.

Mary had indeed sent on the photographs of me as a toddler. They were of a time when my hair was still wispy with soft curls. It was beautiful to be able to associate this with my own daughter at the same tender age. I was cute.

Sitting in among all those ladies—I think there were around sixteen present who had all worked in the children's home—was like having lots of mothers around me. I could feel their sense of care and concern for me. They were all so interested in my life both after I had left the home and my new life.

These reunions turned out to be a six-monthly affair and I made sure to attend every one. I went on to receive more photographs of myself, in black and white, as a baby. One of them was of me in the bath.

I listened to unique and real special stories from these wonderfully exceptional women. One of their stories was of the sailors who had been stationed in the Faslane Clyde Submarine Base, which was close to the children's home. The ladies would take bedsheets with messages of 'welcome home' up onto the roof of the children's home and display them with enthusiasm as the submarines sailed down the river en route to Faslane. There were photographs of the naval officers who had come along to the home to spend the day with the children, bringing picnic hampers and games with them.

The ladies I met in these reunions told me that they loved the children they cared for. They told me that they would carry the babies, two at a time, down the stairs to the waiting prams for our daily walks in the fresh air and how they hurried for the best prams. These stories I clung to. They helped me to build a picture of what my life would have been like in those crucial years of early development. It was so very reassuring to learn that I was loved and nurtured with such care and compassion.

A few months later, on an evening when I was with a few friends, my phone alerted me to a new message. It read, 'Hello. I wonder if your name was Elaine Mann? I may have been your house mistress at Blairvadach.'

Her name was Sue and she went on to write that she had known me as a toddler in 1974, when I would have been two years old, and that she had photographs from that time. I was so happily surprised to hear from another lady who knew me as a toddler. Sue sent four photographs to my phone. One with Sue sitting outside on a wall, Catherine who I had recently met standing on the wall behind Sue, another girl standing beside Sue with one arm tightly around her neck and the other holding my arm, myself as a very small toddler standing between Sue's legs and a little boy sitting on the wall beside Sue, Sue having her arm protectively holding him. Then there was one of me on my own standing in a cute little pose with my arms up in the air and a big smile. One of the photographs was of the ladies in a social setting. Then in a photograph of just the two of us Sue is crouched down with me sitting on one of her legs. I am wearing a dress which Sue told me she had given to me and there is a toy in front of me, which Sue said she also gave to me. Later when I studied this photograph in more depth, I could recall that same toy sitting at the bottom of a toy cupboard in the foster home. I had no memories of it as being my toy, of hearing anyone tell me it belonged to me or indeed of ever playing with it. This photograph I truly loved the very most out of all the photographs I had gained from the ladies in Blairvadach. Sue is hugging me so tightly with her arms completely enveloping me and the loveliest smile on her face which she is pressing against my own. From the picture I could see that she loved me.

I mentioned to Sue that there was a forthcoming reunion and although she said she would not make it, she did say that she would love to meet up with me. We arranged to meet at a garden centre café which lay in between where we lived.

We gave each other a warm hug immediately we met. Sue told me that she had indeed very much loved me and that whenever she was on duty I would follow her around saying her name with a strong lisp which I had as a child. She said she wanted to hear me speak to see if I still had the lisp, but I no longer had. Sue told me, 'In the evening we would give you all a bath and then you would come and huddle with me and the other ladies on the sofa with your warm milk and biscuit to watch a little television before bed.'

I loved hearing this story, especially since it was very much the routine I had my own two children in when they were little.

'You were a very happy little toddler, so quiet and shy.'

Sue went on to tell me that when she no longer worked at the home, she would continue to come and visit me because she loved me so much and found it hard to keep away. On the day Sue gave me the dress and the toy it was my third birthday and she told me that her wish was to come back to adopt me. However, by then the wheels were already set in motion for me to go into permanent foster care.

'How different my life would have been,' was all I could say to that.

I felt the sense of love Sue had towards me still as I sat in that café. She gave me one more photograph that day. I think I would have been aged two in the picture and I looked so happy and healthy. We asked someone to take a photograph of us on that day as Sue frequently hugged me. It was such a special day for me to meet Sue. To know that I was loved, to hear Sue tell me this was like healing a place inside me that had been raw for my whole life to that point.

The very next day Sue sent me this message:

I just want to say what a pleasure it was to meet up with you yesterday. I had so often wondered what had happened to my favourite girl. I'm sorry you had all those bad years but am so in admiration of you for getting the life and family you wanted and deserved. Stay strong. Thinking of you often. Love from Sue.

Some time after meeting Sue, when I was casually look-ing at all my photographs as a baby and toddler, I paid par-ticular attention to one of me sitting on a bed with two teddies, one of them a giant, white teddy bear, next to me. Then I remembered the day when I was leaving my foster home to go and live with my then boyfriend, now husband. The big white teddy bear that my foster mother had put on top of my boxes of possessions and which I had only ever remembered as belonging to one of my foster brothers. I remembered how I had asked her why she had put it on my boxes of stuff and how she had nonchalantly replied, 'It was with you when you came here.'

Sue had not been the person to give me this particular picture as it had come from Catherine, through Eleanor, but I decided, since I had been particularly fond of Sue as a toddler, to send it to her and ask if she knew how I happened to have the teddy. I wrote, 'I am just wondering who would have given me the teddies I am seen with in the photo, particularly the big white one?'

'It was me!' Sue replied.

I could hardly believe it and felt instantly heartbroken. I telephoned Sue to ask her more about it. She told me that the teddy bear had in fact been her own which she had brought with her to the home. Sue said that she had decided to leave it with me when she had left Blairvadach. As Sue relayed this to me over the telephone I struggled to hold in my tears. I explained to Sue that if my foster mother had not allowed her son to claim it as his own and instead had told the truth that it belonged to me from my time at the children's home I would have completely cherished it with all my heart. It would have been at least one comforting possession to own and to hold onto from that special and unique part of my life.

I felt robbed.

I was enraged that yet again my foster mother had been so cold and so callous. To have withheld this beautiful item from me and not to be honest or caring enough to make sure I held onto it as my own was unforgiveable. I regretted so much having left it that day when I had left that place. I felt bereft that it had not felt like mine. I cried to my social worker, Jill about this and she confirmed what I already knew. That person had never ever had my best interests in her mind when she made the decision to become my foster mother. The only positive thing I could take from this happening was that I had now solved the mystery of the big white teddy bear left on top of my pile of boxes.

Chapter Twenty-Six

Finally gaining a photograph of my mother was one of the most momentous moments of my life. Even so, as I gazed into her face, I had trouble feeling any real sense of connection to the child looking back at me. I felt very strongly that seeing the face of the woman, seeing my mother as an adult, would help me to connect to her in a bigger sense and at a deeper level. I would be looking at the woman who gave birth to me, the grown up. The person who had struggled so much in her adult life who had endured great pain, who had suffered. As her daughter, I longed to see my mother.

Once more, I browsed through Facebook and I happened to come across a post from the *Evening Times*. It suddenly occurred me to write to them, enquiring if they could put in their newspaper a message of my search for a photograph adding in my mother's details. A reporter replied to my request stating that he could do an actual article of my search. A day later I received a call from the reporter, to give me a brief interview over the telephone. I gave him as much information as I could and included my telephone number so that anyone who read the article and knew my mother could contact me direct. The reporter asked if it would be alright for him to use my Facebook profile picture to put into the article, which was of myself and my teenage son, to which I agreed. The article was headed, 'Help me find a picture of the mother I never knew.'

Less than two months later, I received a message on my phone, this time from a reporter from the *Sunday Mail*, asking whether they could help in my search for a photograph by doing an article in their newspaper. Being the kind of person never ever to turn down an opportunity of help with my search, I agreed. This time the article was a little longer, with a little more detail about my search and about who I was. The reporter sent their photographer to my house in to take a photograph of me holding the photograph of my mother as a child which I had already obtained. It was all so very surreal but it also gave me fresh hope and anticipation of finding an adult photograph of my mother.

Around one month later, while I was busy preparing dinner, my mobile began to ring. When I answered it a male voice told me that his name was George and that he remembered my mother. I could hardly believe my ears. George told me that his brother had seen my article in the *Evening Times* and had contacted him to ask whether he had seen it. George apologised, saying he had no photographs of my mother but that he did remember her very vividly and that he would have been twelve years old when he last saw her. I eagerly asked George if he would please meet with me, which he kindly agreed to do. I was ecstatic.

I met George—on a Thursday—again in the city of Glasgow. He greeted me warmly at the train station and we went to a café nearby.

George was very kind and gentle. He told me that his own father and Gordon had both drank heavily together and that Gordon had often stayed at their house drinking. George was surprised to hear that Gordon had gone on to live for so long because of the way he remembered his drinking habits. He told me that when the drinking became too bad to live with in his house, his mother would take his brother and himself onto a bus and the three of them would go to stay with my mother 'to get away'. He said that because Gordon was drinking with his father in his home, he was never there when he stayed at my mother's house. He also told me that he was not aware that my mother had ever had any children. By that time I would have been in the children's home.

George said the reason he remembered my mother so clearly was because of her appearance and her behaviour.

'I remember your mother as being strikingly thin. She looked fragile and vulnerable, like she needed protection. My mother would make food and we would bring it with us. One day when my brother and I, with my mother, walked into your mum's house with a pie my mum had made, your mother said, "I'm glad you brought that, Ella, because I haven't eaten for a week." I can remember hearing your mother telling my mother that she was "hearing voices". These are things which my twelve-year-old self just wouldn't be used to hearing. She seemed to me as being scared and timid.'

It was quite unbelievable for me to sit in this stranger's company knowing that he had actually stayed in my mother's home, that he had been in her presence, close enough to reach out and touch her. To know that he had seen my own mother when I had not was a hard truth to swallow. George continued by saying, 'I'm sorry, this must all be very hard to listen to.'

I replied, 'Please don't hold back anything from me so as to protect my feelings. I need to know it all no matter how difficult it is to hear. I am feeling a lot of emotion right now but not so much that I need to cry.' It had always been my experience that the sadness and tears came later.

George told me that the longest time he had stayed with my mother was seven days. He said that his own father had died because of his drinking and again he expressed his surprise at Gordon living for so long and to hear that he had been sober for three decades.

When we said our goodbyes, George walked me back across to the train station and even gave me a warm hug, apologising that he did not have any happy or more positive memories of my mother to share with me.

When I was on the train journey home I felt so elated to have once again been in the company of someone who had known my mother. I could not keep my mouth shut and I told the two strangers who happened to be sitting at the same table about what had just happened, whether they wanted to hear it or not. I just could not keep quiet. I had found out more about my mother and even though it was not happy news it was still extremely important for me to have been given this part of my mother's life. It made me love her even more. It gave me the clarification that she was so very ill and that she could never have looked after a child. It was also confirmation for me that Gordon had been completely neglectful of my dear mother, to the absolute extreme. I will forever be grateful to George for answering my newspaper article.

The next astonishing message to come onto my phone was from a lady who worked in Kaye Adams BBC Radio Scotland programme. She asked whether I would be interested in coming into their studios to be interviewed by Kaye Adams about my research and my search for an adult photograph of my mother. The lady told me that if this was something which could possibly assist me in my search then they would love to help in this way and gave a number for me to phone. This message completely stunned me and before I did a thing, I gave my phone to my husband so that he could read the message.

'Have you phoned the number?' he asked.

'No.'

'Why not? Go on. Give them a phone.'

Just like that, after giving a brief outline of my story to a lady working for the programme, a day and time was arranged for me to go to into the BBC studios in Glasgow to be interviewed by Kaye Adams. I was completely astounded.

As I was led into her studio, through the door, the light

above it lit up in red to alert everyone that her programme was currently 'live'. It was without doubt right up there with the most unbelievable experiences in my journey. I felt like pinching myself to remind me that this was actually happening and was not just a dream. Kaye Adams was standing at the other side of two large desks covered with computers, microphones and other radio paraphernalia. She was talking into her microphone, doing her job, a professional working on her own radio programme. As I was silently gestured to sit down and to put on my own set of headphones Kaye smiled her hello to me. There was a microphone in front of me and it was adjusted so that it was at the correct height and I was again gestured to lean in to it when my time came to speak. I could hear the Kaye Adams programme clearly through the headphones as she interviewed a man about some challenges he had in his life and Kaye glanced at me fleetingly, her expression filled with sympathy, as the man relayed his experience.

When that interview had finished and a few advertisements had been aired, Kaye then turned her attention to me. She firstly introduced me and said a little about why I was on her programme. Kaye Adams then proceeded to ask me questions about my experience in the care system. I answered her questions as candidly as I could. When I told her that I had not been told that I was fostered until I had asked the question at the age of fifteen, Kaye told me that she was 'flabbergasted'.

She then cut to a break for a few more advertisements.

In those few moments I thought about my reason for being there and I knew I was on a mission. So when she came back to me I focused everything I said towards finding a photograph of my mother. Kaye began by saying she had received an email from a lady who was listening to the programme and was saying she was 'in tears as she listened to what I had to say'. I continued the interview by telling Kaye about the lengths I had gone to in my research and the places it had taken me, of all the people I had met who had known my mother and who had no photographs.

'You became detective,' Kaye remarked.

She went onto ask me what it had been like having never seen my mother for all those years, to which I replied, 'It is the most painful feeling to be able to think of my mother purely because of all the things those people who had known her had told me about her, but see nothing.'

Kaye then asked me why, having now gained a photograph of my mother as a child, was I still searching for a photograph of her as an adult? What would it mean to see my mother as an adult?

'I love the photograph I have of my mother as a child. It is precious to me and I will forever treasure it. However, to be able to see the woman, the adult who had given birth to me and who had so struggled and suffered. To be able to see that face, especially given that I am a mother myself, I believe it will give me a true and proper sense of a connection to her. I know I never had her in my life but I love her even so. I feel care for her.'

Kaye Adams then thanked me for coming on to her programme and I said goodbye. I felt like giving her a hug, or
asking for a selfie, but the programme continued as I stood
and left that room. Kaye very much a professional. As I was
walking out of the studio I turned back to Kaye and I made
as though I was taking an imaginary photograph of her, to
which she silently laughed.

Unlike the newspaper article, I received no response from
being on the Kaye Adams BBC Radio Scotland programme,
but I had certainly had an experience to remember.

I continued to believe that there was more I could be
doing to find a photograph of my mother. My mind turned
to all the addresses where she had lived. Before going on the
Kaye Adams programme I had made a list of these addresses
and the dates when she had lived there in order to read out
on her programme just in case someone might be listening
who had lived in the same streets at the same time as my
mother. It then suddenly occurred to me to actually go to
Springburn, where all of those addresses were situated, and
to put up a notice for people to see. My daughter had a
friend whose mother happened to have lived in Springburn
and while she was over one day at my house, I asked her
if she would come with me as she would be familiar with
the area and therefore could be someone who would be a
good guide. This friend told me that she felt privileged to be
asked to come along with me to help.

I typed up a notice with the heading 'PLEASE HELP
ME FIND PHOTOGRAPHS OF THE MUM I NEVER

KNEW'. In my notice I wrote her adoptive name and her married name. I listed all seven addresses I had managed to obtain from her adoption certificate, the birth certificates of all my siblings including my own, the Social Work records, the address where George had stayed with my mother aged twelve and the address which was on her death certificate. I listed the three primary schools and the secondary school she had attended. I made sure to include the appropriate dates pertinent to every detail I had written and I finished by listing the people I had learned had known her at school and those who had known her as an adult. At the bottom of my notice I put my name and telephone number.

My friend, Lisa, came with me as she had promised. As we drove through the streets of Springburn, putting up my notice wherever I could, I took photographs of all the street signs where my mother had lived. It turned out that Springburn was a deprived area of Glasgow and my friend confirmed that this was indeed true from her own experience of living there. As I stood in the streets where my mother would have walked I took time to take in my surroundings and to allow myself to acknowledge the feelings that were coming up for me. Knowing that I was where my dear mother once was meant something deeply special to me. In those moments, I was very much loving my mother, completely. I had a sense of something warm washing over me. I had an awareness of being protected like a glow around me, that my mother's spirit was right there beside me. I felt safe.

I handed my notice into a local shop, a hairdressers and I put it on the information board of a block of flats. I then went to a nearby home for the elderly and I put my notice on their information board.

As my friend and I were looking for one of the streets where my mother had lived, an elderly lady came out from a residence, assisted by her daughter. I approached them to ask if they would kindly point us in the right direction. These two lovely ladies were very interested to hear about my reason for putting up my notice and after a lengthy chat they suggested that I go along to a local group that was held every Wednesday for the elderly. They suggested that I give the lady who runs the group a call before I go and very kindly gave me the name of the group.

I duly telephoned this lady who again was extremely interested in my story and invited me along on the following Wednesday.

My experience of this group was not a positive one. I stepped into a large hall with tables around a vacant dance floor. It was very busy, with lots of old people having a meal. I was initially led away from the hall and into a corridor to wait for the meal to be over and to meet the group's organiser. I felt very exposed. Once this kind lady had introduced herself to me she led me back into the hall. I quite simply did not know where to put myself. I was embarrassed and felt I was intruding on their regular afternoon recreation. The organiser took a microphone and stood at the top of the empty dance floor. She urged for silence and then proceeded to announce my presence and my reason for being there. I had imagined that I would then speak to everyone from the microphone; however, the organiser told everyone that I would come around the tables to show everyone my notice and ask whether anyone might know anything or remember my mother. She described my quest to them as, 'A very human story'.

It was torture going around each table, interrupting their chat. I felt feeble, like I was a nuisance. When I reached the table of the elderly woman who I had met on the street in Springburn she was the only person up to that point who seemed happy to see me and I was instantly relieved to see her. She allowed me to take a photograph with her. This lovely lady wished me well, her sincerity and her kindness emanating from her. Her daughter was at a separate table and she surprised me by saying that she had seen my original post on Facebook. She and I remain Facebook friends to this day and she often comments on the messages I post.

Neither my trip to Springburn nor the group have brought up any new information—nor indeed have produced an adult photograph of my mother.

Whether this is something that is meant to happen for me or not, I will continue to refuse to let go of my hope. I have come further than I could ever have imagined possible. So much has happened. Giving up are words that are just not within my vocabulary.

My foster father died at some point during my research and not a single second did I waste on thinking about him.

However, an aunt and cousin from my time in foster care have been back in touch with me. A lot of years had gone by since I had seen them. For all my life I had very much had the belief that anyone associated with my foster parents hated me. I thought that they would see me as being selfish for walking away from the people who had taken me in. At first I was scared of having contact with my cousin and my aunt as I thought of them as being dangerously close to my foster parents. However, we took it slowly and I was able to let go of some of my wariness and eventually we did meet. I firstly met up with my cousin. She told me that she had always wondered why I had stopped communication with them and where I was. She told me that on the day of my foster father's funeral she had asked my foster mother, 'Why is Elaine not here?'

My cousin told me that she was answered with, 'Elaine has issues with alcohol and mental health'.

At this point in my life there had been no communication between my foster mother and me for over a decade and I wondered where my foster mother took this kind of information from, not to mention how blatantly cold and unfeeling she was to actually come out with such a judgement. My cousin went on to tell me that a foster brother was getting married and that on receiving the invitation she was considering whether she would go, questioning why she had even been asked, given that there was no relationship between them. I knew my foster mother was at the helm, being sure to dish out invites to all the right people, still clinging to the happy family charade. Still living the lie. Doing her damnedest to present herself as the caring matriarch. I felt fresh rage on hearing of the wedding. I imagined everyone toasting the groom, wishing the couple happiness and good health. No matter how hard I tried, I could not stop the old feelings of fear and of pain from rising to my brain as I remembered the daily agony of living with that family. I thought of the struggles I had gone through in my adult life as a direct result of being in foster care, of the help I had needed to seek out to stay healthy, to find my own sense of inner happiness, and I could not rest.

It was this that was the catalyst to my decision to go to the police. As I have stated in a previous chapter, with the support I had completely surrounding me, I at last handed my truth over to the authorities. I was letting go of my fear.

When I met my aunt, she told me that she had been 'bereft' when I had 'disappeared'. She said she had asked my foster parents on numerous occasions where I was and had been told nothing. Yet I was living in the same address I had been for the last two decades. All my foster parents would have needed to say was that I was still at the same address. Yet they had chosen not to.

Meeting with my aunt, I am so glad to be able to say, has very much proven to me that my belief that I was not wanted by anyone associated with my foster parents, was wrong. Though she is not my aunt by blood, I choose to continue to call her my aunt. This aunt was and still is utterly wonderful to me. She has even told me that she and her husband had listened to me on the radio and that she had cried as they had both always believed that I was adopted. She went on to say that she and her husband, my foster father's brother, have always, 'Loved the bones of me'.

My aunt was in need of my reassurance that my memories of being with them were good ones and I was very eager to tell her what I remembered from spending time at their home as a child.

'I remember being in the bath and my uncle walking in. He was gentle and kindly said, "Oh, it's Elaine", giving me a warm smile. I remember you drying me on your knee and your sweet-smelling pink powder puff.'

I told my aunt that these things I remember so vividly because they were alien to me, that this had never been even remotely close to my experience of my foster mother.

My aunt remains ever eager to stay in touch and to meet up with me. I have visited her and my uncle with my two teenage children. She has told me that she feels sorry that she did not know what was going on for me when I was a child. When I asked her what she remembers of me as a child she told me, 'I remember you were always very quiet and seemed a sad child. I always put that down to the lack of love you were getting.'

Although my heart screams at me to grab the love my aunt obviously has for me, I simply feel blessed to have learned that, without knowing it, I did actually have people in my life when I lived in foster care who genuinely cared.

The lady who gave me the photograph of my mother then

sent me another message, over a year after I had received the photograph. She happened to be looking at an old school photograph which someone had put onto a Facebook page. As she had been scanning the faces of the girls, wondering whether her own mother might be in the photograph, she came across another photograph of my own mother. This time the photograph was taken around 1946 and was at Wellfield Primary School, where my mother had indeed attended. Fiona sent the photograph to me.

I did not need to scan the faces. I immediately homed in on my mother's face. It was like looking back at a photograph of myself as a child. My mother's hair even had the same side parting as I did and she had a light-coloured bow in it. The photograph was again in black and white, but it was very clear. I could really make out her features. We have the same eyes and lines around our mouth. My mother was pretty. I was utterly stunned that Fiona had managed to find two photographs of my mother and this second picture I put straight into a frame and placed it on our living room mantlepiece. I felt so proud to show her picture off to anyone who happened to come into our house and could hardly stop looking at it.

Little had I known that ten years ago when I set off in earnest to seek out a photograph of my mother, that all these years into my journey I would have two. I keep hope strong in my heart that I will see her photograph as an adult one day.

Throughout my whole life people have stepped into my

world and saved me. The ladies from Blairvadach children's home, the old lady who lived next door to my foster home, my friends, my husband, my amazing social worker, my doctor, my counsellor and, of course, my children. It has been the love and care from all of these people which has sustained me and carried me, as I have grown in the learning of my origins, my family and ultimately my true identity.

Developing the ability to believe in myself has played a large part in my journey. Finding out that when my own ability to believe was weakened that there were always a small number of people who never let go of their ability to believe in me. Being believed when handing my truth over to the authorities was particularly huge in my healing.

In all the years I have known Jill she has constantly told me, 'I still believe there is a book in you.'

Then there is the fact that I will always believe that there is an adult photograph of my mother somewhere out there and that one day I am going see it. That is what I believe.

My Wish

I wish dear Mum you'd chosen life for just a little longer,
and stayed with me through good and bad, together we'd be stronger.
To get to know you like a friend, to have a glimpse of you.
To know I'd love you oh so much, perhaps you'd love me too.

You left my life too early dear, forgot to say goodbye,
but made your choice to leave us all, to leave us all and die.
There wasn't a reminder left or memory to hold.
But I will keep on searching, all my life, if truth be told.

I know that you were hurting Mum, that something broke inside.
But no one tried to help you heal and that I can't abide.
For you were oh so special dear, especially to me.
I promise I'd give anything, for you to wake and see.

For children I can call my own, I'm blessed, for they are whole,
a gift which shines unsteadily, a flicker on my soul.
For should I miss and grieve for you, I'm sorry I'm unsure
But you are gone, my heart is torn, is there, for this, a cure?

I hope someday that I can have a little peace of mind.
The smallest glint of comfort would be wonderful to find.
Part of me is missing Mum that's truly fundamental.
Still I am here and living well. I'm not inconsequential.

With special thanks to...

My husband, my girl and my boy. Without you my darlings this story would never have happened. You have been on this journey with me and have always shown great patience and endless love. There are so many ways to say thank you to you, my gorgeous family, but none of them will ever be enough.

Jill. This book is dedicated to you. My gratitude for your consistent guidance, support and encouragement runs deep. You are and will always be someone special to me and my family. You are a true credit to your profession.

DrF. My thanks and respect for you comes straight from my heart. You have literally saved my life and have been there in many other moments of need. You also are a real credit to your profession.

Margaret. I thank you for so kindly offering and taking the time to proof read my story and for the great many times you have listened to me, supported and encouraged me. You are someone who I have enormous admiration for and a person I aspire to be more like.

My neighbours. Fiona for being like the big sister I never had. Linda for being the kind of person I think everyone should have in their lives and to Yvonne, both of you have taught me about how to be the kind of mother I wanted to be.

My dearest friends who have been there right from the start of my journey, Evonne and Suzanne. I am more grateful to you than you will ever know.

The friends I have made in my journey of self discovery and change. Jen, Yvonne, Gwen and so many more, you know who you are. You guys truly know me and for this I am deeply grateful.

My colleagues, Mae, Cathie, Gillian, Lynne, Jan, Susan H, Sam, Sarah and more. My heartfelt thanks to you all for standing by me, ever ready with words of comfort and support.

Open Secret's In Care Survivors Service. Cath, Janine and my friends in the Monday group. Particular thanks to you for the very special support you have and still do give to me.

My friends on Facebook. All your words of encouragement and support I have read. I have taken great strength from each and every one. I thank you all.

The Kaye Adams Radio Scotland programme for inviting me into your studio to be interviewed by Kaye. Thank you for a real day to remember.

Vivienne Nicoll at the Evening Times and Jenny Morrison at the Sunday Mail for putting articles about my story into your papers.

Future Pathways for so very generously funding my book. Massive thanks to you.

Duncan and his team at Lumphanan Press. Thank you for all the help you have given me.